The Radical Pedagogies of Socrates and Freire

Routledge Studies in Rhetoric and Communication

1. **Rhetorics, Literacies, and Narratives of Sustainability**
   Edited by Peter N. Goggin

2. **Queer Temporalities in Gay Male Representation**
   Tragedy, Normativity, and Futurity
   Dustin Bradley Goltz

3. **The Rhetoric of Intellectual Property**
   Copyright Law and the Regulation of Digital Culture
   Jessica Reyman

4. **Media Representations of Gender and Torture Post-9/11**
   Marita Gronnvoll

5. **Rhetoric, Remembrance, and Visual Form**
   Sighting Memory
   Edited by Anne Teresa Demo and Bradford Vivian

6. **Reading, Writing, and the Rhetorics of Whitenes**
   Ian Marshall and Wendy Ryden

7. **Radical Pedagogies of Socrates and Freire**
   Ancient Rhetoric/Radical Praxis
   S.G. Brown

The Radical Pedagogies of Socrates and Freire
Ancient Rhetoric/Radical Praxis

S.G. Brown

Routledge
Taylor & Francis Group
New York London

First published 2012
by Routledge
711 Third Avenue, New York, NY 10017

Simultaneously published in the UK
by Routledge
2 Park Square, Milton Park, Abingdon, Oxon OX14 4RN

First issued in paperback 2017

*Routledge is an imprint of the Taylor & Francis Group,
an informa business*

© 2012 Taylor & Francis

The right of S.G. Brown to be identified as author of this work has been asserted in accordance with sections 77 and 78 of the Copyright, Designs and Patents Act 1988.

Typeset in Sabon by IBT Global.

All rights reserved. No part of this book may be reprinted or reproduced or utilised in any form or by any electronic, mechanical, or other means, now known or hereafter invented, including photocopying and recording, or in any information storage or retrieval system, without permission in writing from the publishers.

Trademark Notice: Product or corporate names may be trademarks or registered trademarks, and are used only for identification and explanation without intent to infringe.

Library of Congress Cataloging-in-Publication Data
Brown, S. G.
　The radical pedagogies of Socrates & Freire : ancient rhetoric/radical praxis / by S. G. Brown.
　　p. cm. — (Routledge studies in rhetoric and communication ; 7)
　Includes bibliographical references and index.
　1. Rhetoric, Ancient. 2. Critical pedagogy. 3. Socrates—Criticism and interpretation. 4. Freire, Paulo, 1921–1997—Criticism and interpretation. 5. Radicalism in literature. I. Title.
　PA3265.B67 2011
　370.1—dc23
　2011018282

ISBN 13: 978-1-138-09782-7 (pbk)
ISBN 13: 978-0-415-89792-1 (hbk)

To all those *teachers* who
by breaking down the walls
between classroom and community
free the self
into the public domain,
The Word into the World,
and knowledge bound in books
into a reality
forever changed by this communion.

Contents

	Acknowledgments	ix
	Introduction: Socrates and Freire—The Origins of a Genealogy	1
1	The Radical Critique of Radical Pedagogy: The Trial of Plato and Freire	6
2	The World, the Word, and the Wound: A Genealogy of Origins	20
3	A Radical Genealogy: Mapping Goals and Assumptions	44
4	The Dawn of Analysis: The Method of His Madness	61
5	The Signifying Hood: The Dialectics of Recantation	90
6	The Error of His Ways: Getting It Wrong to Get It Write	121
7	Plato and the Tyranny of the Transcendent: A Radical Re-Reading	139
8	Love in a Time of War: The Ethos of Eros	163
9	Radical Pedagogy Reconfigured: Toward a Neo-Humanist Pragmatism	187
	Conclusion: Ancient Rhetoric/Radical Praxis— The Personal, the Political, and the Rhetorical	209
	Works Cited	213
	Index	217

Acknowledgments

A book, any book, is largely a labor of love enacted by an individual but enabled by the helping hands of many others. *The Radical Pedagogies of Socrates and Freire* is no exception. This book had a long gestation period, insofar as its genesis is rooted in my M.A. thesis on Plato's *Phaedrus* (1993) and my dissertation on Freire (1997). The thought of reading one through the lens of the other, however, did not occur until quite recently.

Like the two teachers whose work it celebrates, this book drew inspiration from teacher/scholars whose work inspired my own. At the University of California, Santa Barbara, they include Douwe Sturman and Frederick Turner III. At the University of Hawai'i, Hilo, William Carse. At the University of South Florida, Gary A. Olson and Philip Sipiora, who heightened my appreciation and interest in the works of Paulo Freire and Plato, as embodied in *Pedagogy of the Oppressed* and *Phaedrus,* respectively. I owe a special debt of gratitude to Professor Olson, for directing my dissertation, which drew deeply on the work of Paulo Freire. At the University of Nevada, Las Vegas (UNLV), I want to express my gratitude for the enabling encouragement of my colleagues and department chairs, and of Chris Hudgins, Doug Unger, Richard Harp, Tim Erwin, and John Unrue, in particular, all of whom offered guiding words along the way.

At UNLV, I also owe a special debt of gratitude to the students in my graduate seminars, who sparked lively conversations on the works of Plato and Freire: exchanges which were important in the development of this comparative study and which enabled me to experiment and hone my own ideas in "conversation" with theirs. Two, in particular, deserve special mention: Homer Simms and Cara Minardi, whose dissertation, "Re-Membering Ancient Women: Hypatia of Alexandria and Her Communities," influenced my thinking regarding Plato's mother, Perictione. At UNLV, I also want to give special thanks for the skilled guidance of research librarian, Priscilla Finley.

This brings me to that broader community of colleagues whose work and careers have, in important ways, influenced and intersected my own. This book, in many ways, is the offspring of a critical "conversation" with these important works, by which it was influenced and without which it could not have been written: Susan Jarratt's *Re-Reading the Sophists;* Cheryl Glenn's *Rhetoric Retold;* Jasper Neel's *Plato, Derrida, and Writing;* William Covino's *The Art of Wondering;* Joe Hardin's *Opening Spaces;* Henry Giroux's *Theory and Resistance in Education;* Cornel West's *Prophetic Pragmatism;* Peter Brooks' *Reading for Plot;* and Byron Hawk's *A Counter-History of Composition.* Material from Paulo Freire's *Pedagogy of the Oppressed* (1989) is printed with permission from the Continuum International Publishing Group (NY).

Finally, I must thank those dear colleagues who were there at the start, in the high-spirited heydays of the Rhet/Comp program at USF, who first gave me that taste for the intellectual life, lived and played in solidarity with like-minded souls and kindred spirits: Sid Dobrin, Christian Weisser, Julie Drew, Judith Edminster, Raul Sanchez, Todd Taylor, Andrea Greenbaum, and two who deserve mention for their special friendship: David Marcus and Stephanie Moss. Finally, I am grateful to have found in Elizabeth Levine (Routledge), an editor whose guidance was as critical to this book's evolution as her interest and faith in it.

Introduction
Socrates and Freire:
The Origins of a Genealogy

> The question of what educators teach is inseparable from what it means
> to invest in public life and to locate oneself in public discourse.
> —Giroux (xxvi)

Education, to be meaningful, must be real, must be useful, and must serve not merely the interests of the individual, but those of the common good. Further, the medium for the eternal return of the Word to the World by which education fulfills its democratic wish is radical pedagogy. Surprisingly, this radical praxis is rooted in an ancient rhetorical tradition, and in the radical critique of power of Plato's Socrates in particular, of which Paulo Freire's radical praxis is a genealogical descendent, operating across 2,500 years of critical inquiry. Finally, the radical pedagogies of Socrates and Freire provide a theoretical and pedagogical warrant for a neo-humanist pragmatism that moves beyond the constraints of "teaching resistance" to engage the problematic realities that so poignantly inform our own post "flash-crash" historical moment.

These, then, are a few of the assumptions guiding the polemic in this book. No one to my knowledge has ever brought these two dissident scholar-teachers, Socrates and Freire, into "dialogue," has ever examined the teachings of one through the lens of the other's pedagogy. Yet, when the flint and stone of their separate teachings are brought into contact, sparks fly—revealing affinities that are surprising, significant, and generative with respect to their profound implications for contemporary education: for what we teach, how we teach, and why we teach it. These similarities across two-and-a-half millennia not only invite comparative analysis, but insist upon and reward it.

The dynamics of this pedagogical alliteration are reflected in the questions it awakens. Is Socrates' ancient "elenchus" genuinely radical? Might it be usefully "read" through the lens of contemporary social epistemic pedagogy, and Freirean praxis in particular? Where specifically do we discover common ground between these two radical pedagogies, and what are the theoretical and practical implications for contemporary social epistemic praxis of their pedagogical alliteration? More fundamentally, is it possible to map the genealogy of their respective assumptions, goals, methods, and "program content?" Finally, might the radical pedagogies of Plato's

2 The Radical Pedagogies of Socrates and Freire

Socrates and Paulo Freire provide the impetus for a neo-humanist pragmatism, moving beyond liberatory pedagogy and "teaching resistance" into a new space, suited to the poignant exigencies of post "flash-crash" America, under the signs of "dialogic learning," "problem-posing analysis," and "civic engagement?" Is it practical, or even desirable, to wed the radical pedagogies of Socrates and Friere to the pioneering pragmatism of Peirce, James, and Dewey, the cold-war pragmatism of Kenneth Burke, and the post-modern "prophetic" pragmatism of Cornel West—toward a reconfigured radical praxis enabled by the radical critique of radical pedagogy? How might such a dialogic pragmatism be informed not only by an ancient rhetorical tradition and by American pragmatism, but by "post-humanist" pedagogies of complexity, such as Byron Hawk's pedagogy of "vitalism," in which the rhetorical is informed not only by the technical, but by the creative? In the course of this polemic, I hope to address these and other enabling questions.

As soon as we place the embattled careers and radical pedagogies of Plato's Socrates and Paulo Freire in "dialogue," points of contact begin to proliferate. Each radical pedagogy was the brain-child of a dissident scholar persecuted, exiled, and/or executed by a state whose excesses of power each brought under radical interrogation as part of an educative inquiry. Each radical praxis assumed the centrality of analysis, not as an academic end in itself, but as a vehicle of socio-political reform. Each praxis was an intervention against the excesses of power, circulating through the power of persuasion, as manifested, respectively, in the justice and education systems. Each, consequently, brought the signifying practices of domination under radical interrogation. As an enabling, liberatory critique of power, each was oriented toward the good, the just, and the possible, operating in the interest not of powerful elites, but of the common good, the socially just, and the humanly possible—as a check against the excesses of a ruling class, whether sophist or colonialist.

Even though Socrates' critical elenchus had oligarchic underpinnings, its effects (desired and real) were beneficial to common Athenians inasmuch as it mitigated the corruption of the justice system by exposing it, and ended, at least temporarily, the abuses of power enshrined in sophistic domination. Each radical praxis posited the literate self as a catalyst of the common good, acting in dialectic solidarity with the Other to mitigate the abuses of power. Thus, Socratic inquiry, like Freirean praxis, configured the intellectual as always and already a public intellectual. Each used discourse in an educative setting to curb the abuses of discourse in the body politic, inaugurating what was tantamount to a war of discourses between analysis and persuasion, curbing the excesses of the latter with the actions that arose from the interrogations of the former. Each pedagogy underscores the centrality of an honorific Rhetoric, in which logos drives ethos and the analytical serves the ethical—in contradistinction to a debased rhetoric that serves the interest of Power through the power of persuasion.

Each radical educator was, consequently, a "gadfly" of critique relative to the state, forced to suffer the consequences of exile or execution for his counter-hegemonic educative practices. The pedagogy of each was oriented toward the material, toward the real-world problematics of domination, whose excesses each systematically exposed. The teachings of each were similarly disseminated in writing, giving to the resistant word an afterlife, fulfilling Socrates' prophetic fears relative to writing in the *Phaedrus*, even as his words prefigured by two-and-a-half thousand years the efficacy of a "prophetic pragmatism." The eternal return to the World of the pragmatic Word, enacted in the radical pedagogies of Socrates and Freire, underscores the extent to which an edifying critical inquiry acts as a "check and balance" on the excesses of power—is always and already a democratic enterprise.

The socio-political problematics of Freire's time (and our own) are fundamentally no different from the problematics of power confronting Plato's Socrates. As Cheryl Glenn asserts in *Rhetoric Retold*, "rhetoric always inscribes the relation of language and power at a particular moment" (1), unveiling the degree to which power circulates through the power of persuasion. This relation between power and persuasion defines the focus of social-epistemic inquiry today as it did the focus of Socrates' elenchus in fourth century BC Athens.

This book situates inquiry at this intersection of classical rhetoric and liberatory pedagogy, at the confluence of the personal, the social, the political, the ethical, and the rhetorical. Theoretically, it is informed not only by the synergy of ancient and contemporary radical pedagogies, but by the pioneering pragmatism of Peirce, James, and Dewey, the cold-war pragmatism of Kenneth Burke, and the post-modern pragmatism of Cornel West. Its theoretical "ragout" is also deeply informed by the post-Freudian theories of Jacques Derrida, Lev Vygotsky, Peter Brooks, and Otto Rank. Additionally, it draws on contemporary theorists of radical pedagogy, including Joe Hardin, Jessica Enoch, Byron Hawk, and Kate Ronald and Hephzibah Roskelly to inform its polemic.

My hope is this book will enter into conversation with others that similarly offer fresh re-readings of ancient rhetoric (Derrida's *Dissemination*, Jarratt's *Rereading the Sophists;* Glenn's *Rhetoric Retold;* Neel's *Plato, Derrida, and Writing;* Covino's *The Art of Wondering;* and Hawk's *A Counter-History of Composition*), while at the same time giving a fresh twist to that conversation by revealing the ancient roots of critical pedagogy, by bringing Plato's Socrates and Paulo Freire into "conversation." In the process, I hope to reinvigorate an older conversation about Freire that has called into question his relevance to contemporary American education.

My premise is that the radical pedagogies of Socrates and Friere "speak" to each other in surprising, significant, and transformative ways—with profound implications for contemporary educators: for the assumptions we make, the methods we use, the outcomes we desire, and the contents we develop. By virtue of its focus on the relationship between language and power, the subject and reality, this neo-humanist pragmatism moves in a common rhythm with new pedagogies of "vitalism" and "complexity," as theorized by Byron Hawk, whose hard-wired humanism, networked literacy, digitally distributed consciousness, and dialogically webbed inquiry has deep implications and generates fresh possibilities for radical pedagogy: for extending Freirean praxis into protean digital terrains that dramatically distribute the "consciousness" and therefore facilitate the conscientization (awareness-as-action) of Freirean praxis.

RADICAL PEDAGOGY AND THE POST-FREUDIAN TURN

Pedagogy of the Oppressed, no less than the *Phaedrus* and the *Apology*, can be usefully "read" from post-Freudian, psychoanalytic perspectives, given its similar focus on the enabling and edifying effects of "analysis" (including analysis of language) and of "talking back" to power, as evidenced in the liberatory transfer from teacher to student of the opportunity to "name the world" within the context of a dialogic inquiry into oppression and its causes and effects. To the extent the student's agency is fostered by the ability to "name the world," language is central to the edifying process, from the moment of the world's unveiling through analysis, to the moment of its alteration through the application of this analysis to it. To the extent the radical pedagogies of Socrates and Freire posit language as the locus of the meaning-making process, they can be usefully "read" through the lens of post-Freudian theory. This liberatory, Freirean "word" is akin to the Bhabhian "sign taken for wonders," even as it reinscribes Freud's "talking cure." I use post-Freudian theory to usefully inform the psychological origins of the radical pedagogies of Socrates and Freire, to commence the mapping of their genealogy, drawing on the theories of Peter Brooks in *Reading for Plot* and of Freud's heretical protégé, Otto Rank, in *Art and Artist*.

THE GENEALOGICAL MAP: SYNOPSIS OF CHAPTERS

If the "Radical Critique of Radical Pedagogy" is the focus of Chapter 1, in Chapter 2, "The World, the Word, and the Wound," I theorize the psychological origins of Socrates' elenchus and Freire's radical pedagogy from the a post-Freudian perspective. In Chapter 3, "A Radical Genealogy," I map the genealogy of their respective assumptions and goals. In Chapters 4, 5, and 6, the focus shifts to a comparative analysis of their radical methods: "The Dawn of Analysis," "The Signifying Hood," and "The Dialectics of Recantation." In Chapter 7, "Plato and the Tyranny of the Transcendent," I offer a radical re-reading of perhaps the most significant critical crux in post-modern Plato scholarship: his assumption of an a priori truth that always and already "comes before" language, that exists independent of the signifying subject. This fresh re-reading occurs within a radical re-reading of Plato's attack on writing, calling into question the assumptions and claims of Derrida's critique of Plato in *Dissemination*. In Chapter 8, "Love in a Time of War: The Ethos of Eros," I interrogate the generic integrity and ethics of Socrates' dialectic elenchus, developing the implications for social-epistemic praxis. In the final chapter, "Radical Pedagogy Reconfigured: Toward a Neo-Humanist Pragmatism," I offer my response to the radical critique of radical pedagogy presented in the first chapter, crafting a neo-humanist pragmatism that moves beyond that narrow focus of "teaching resistance" into a broader application of Freirean praxis under the signs of "dialogic learning," "problem-posing analysis," and "civic engagement." A concise conclusion assesses the implications of what has "come before," even as it prophesizes a dialogic pragmatism that "comes after."

I offer this book not only to those scholars, students, and practitioners working in the field of Rhetoric/Composition Studies, but to those pursuing dialogic edification across disciplines: in Anthropology and Sociology, Psychology and Political Science, Philosophy and Technology, History, ESL (English as a Second Language), and the Theater. I offer it to those practicing (or interested in practicing) dialogic inquiry not only in American classrooms but at sites of mutual edification across boundaries: in Brazil and the Philippines, Japan and Germany, Costa Rica, India, and Malaysia—to those in every site or field site to which the far-flung, vagabond spores of Socratic inquiry and Freirean praxis have been blown, whose ravaged yet fecund soil provides the ground for education as "the practice of freedom."

1 The Radical Critique of Radical Pedagogy
The Trial of Plato and Freire

THE CRITIQUE OF ANCIENT RHETORIC

A recent body of criticism has brought radical pedagogy under radical attack, calling into question its "feasibility," methodology, ethics, even its relevance to contemporary education, and to writing instruction in particular. This contemporary critique of radical pedagogy, to the extent it calls into question its relevance, feasibility, and indeed its viability, replicates the contemporary critique of ancient rhetoric. Therefore, any polemic intent on demonstrating the efficacy of Socratic inquiry and/or Freirean praxis, either separately or conjoined, must first demonstrate its efficacy in the face of this radical renunciation of radical pedagogy. Borrowing a trope from Plato's *Phaedrus* and *Apology*, I want to restage this "trial" of radical pedagogy, and of Plato and Freire in particular, to gain, if not their acquittal, at least a more appreciative "reading" of their radical pedagogies. Therefore, I offer this "trial" of Plato and Freire by way of "appealing' to the "verdicts" of criticism, which are fatally flawed by their reductive representations of radical pedagogy, and of Freirean praxis in particular. I will begin with the oldest defendant.

In the *Apology*, Socrates performs his critical elenchus within the context of his trial, in defense of a life dedicated to philosophic eros. He uses his defense to put his accusers, and sophistry in general, on trial. In the *Phaedrus*, Plato restages this trial of sophistry, reversing the adversarial roles: positing Socrates as the prosecutor and Lysias as the sophistic defendant, who is "tried" in absentia, as Socrates claims he was in the court of public opinion in the run-up to his trial, whose "first accusers" he must confront in absentia. I want to similarly confront the radical critique of radical pedagogy within the context of a figurative trial, with two defendants: Plato and Freire, each of whom is a voice who speaks, metonymically, for the broader discourse of radical pedagogy.

The relevance of Plato's pedagogical philosophy, mouthed through the construct of Socrates, has come under radical attack by postmodern theorists, who assert his view of knowledge and knowledge-making is incompatible with theories that posit the social construction of knowledge. Perhaps the most problematic critical crux in the entire Platonic canon is Plato's oppressive construct of an ultimate truth, filtered through Socrates: a truth that is always and already an a priori, transcendent signified—a truth that "comes before" language, that exists independent of the knowing subject. In Chapter 7, "Plato and the Tyranny of the Transcendent," I will address this criticism, opening a critical space between Plato and Plato's Socrates that calls this claim of an "a priori" logos into question. I will develop this counter-critique within the context of Plato's critique of writing, and in an effort to complicate Derrida's "reading" of Plato's assault on writing.

It is not merely Plato's assumption of an Intelligence that always and already "comes before" that has come under radical attack by postmodern theorists, but the reliance of classical rhetoric on superficial, antiquated forms whose lack of rhetorical complexity undermines their relevance to contemporary writing instruction. This claim suffers from the same reductive analysis as those who critique Freirean praxis: ironic in a criticism that recants classical rhetoric for its reductive forms. In Chapters 4, 5, and 6, I hope to unveil the rhetorical complexity of Socratic inquiry, by way of refuting this criticism.

At the extreme end of this radical critique of classical rhetoric are the assertions of Knoblauch and Brannon, who caution that "teachers of composition should be wary of blending the epistemologies of ancient and modern rhetoric" (17), adding that "the classical genres, as well as their modern successors, really *are* superficial shapes" (31), and particularly "those related to methods of argument," with their reductive emphasis on "invention," "arrangement," and "style," which have "haunted Western discourse theory, solidifying the distinction between thought and language"(34). In offering a corrective view to Knoblauch and Brannon's reductive analysis, I will argue that the emphasis on improvised argument, dialectics, critical thinking, analysis, civic rhetoric, as well as the goals, methods, and assumptions governing the relation between thought and language, teacher and student, education and politics that define Socrates' radical praxis, denote that educative model as an early precursor of social-epistemic pedagogy: a (pre)cursive precursor, if you will. The useful re-readings of classical rhetoric by Jacques Derrida, Jasper Neel, Susan Jarratt, and Cheryl Glenn have likewise exposed its inherent contradictions, its political and patriarchal biases, and its anti-democratic and misogynistic tendencies.

THE CRITIQUE OF RADICAL PEDAGOGY

Radical pedagogy, and Freire's liberatory praxis in particular, has been under radical attack for over a decade. Much of this criticism has focused almost exclusively on the "revolutionary," "resistant," "emancipatory," or "liberatory" aspects of Freire's praxis, while de-emphasizing or ignoring altogether equally significant aspects of his pedagogy: dialogic learning, problem-posing analysis, and civic engagement. Joe Hardin's *Opening Spaces* provides (at least to my knowledge) the most cogent and significant review of the criticism of radical pedagogy: one that continues to exert a deep influence on the field of composition studies. At the same time, Hardin's landmark analysis and polemic of critical pedagogy proves fertile ground for re-theorizing and re-envisioning critical praxis in a post "flash-crash" America—for "opening spaces" that are new, humanist, pragmatic, and inventive. Though different from the "space" Hardin defends, these new sites of critical pedagogy are enabled by that space, whose articulation was a necessary precondition for the genesis of these radically new pedagogical sites.

Hardin commences his review of the critique of radical pedagogy by observing that "there are clearly those who worry that critical pedagogy, and especially the teaching of resistance, is a futile or ethically suspect activity that should not be a primary concern of the composition classroom" (3). As opposed to a misplaced focus on resisting problematic realities to transform them, these critics assert that "compositionists should concern themselves exclusively with supporting students with the skills necessary to succeed in the academy and in the current economy . . ." (3). Yet, this criticism of the goals and content of radical pedagogy presumes a false, either-or binary between these two pedagogical approaches, as if one can only be taught at the exclusion of the other: as if a focus on analyzing to transform problematic realities cannot also foster a skill-set that facilitates academic and/or economic success.

Richard Miller succinctly describes perhaps the most common criticism of Freire: one that calls into question the relevance of a pedagogy of revolution in a post-colonial setting to American classrooms, "whose students do not need to be liberated because they are not oppressed, at least not in ways that Freire's subjects were oppressed" (qtd. in Hardin 100). Miller continues his summary of this critique:

> [Freire's] work was with illiterate peasants who were struggling to combat their government's oppressive policies. . . . It would be foolish to equate the challenges Freire has confronted in the field . . . with the challenges we face teaching composition in the academy: we teach those who have already found their way into the system, those who wish . . . to *gain access* to the material benefits that higher education is said to promise. (18, qtd. in Hardin 101, my emphasis)

Ironically, in attempting to underscore the irrelevance of Freirean praxis to contemporary American education, Miller unwittingly underscores its relevance, under the sign of "access." It is the denial of *access* to increasing numbers of citizens in post "flash-crash" America to the benefits of the American materialist dream, whether we are talking about *access* to affordable health care, education, jobs, or political power, that reinforces the enduring relevance of Freire's teaching to contemporary American education, insofar as it was nothing if not a *pedagogy of access*. American students, like its citizenry in general, are being systematically excluded from *access* to the traditional material benefits of the American dream, as a result of the effects of a class war accelerated by the "flash crash" of 2008, that has seen millions lose their jobs, with the result that access to higher education is being denied to countless numbers of students whose parents can no longer afford to send them to college, as well as by the increased tuitions necessitated by the financial collapse and the gutting of academic budgets by the state, by leaders who are playing politics with our children's future. Diminished *access* to higher education will only further limit *access* to the job market, further polarizing the realities of haves and have-nots: realities which the latter are being asked by the former to accept as "the new normal." This systematic and willful exclusion of the middle and lower classes from access to the American materialist dream by an increasingly politicized upper class further underscores the relevance of Freirean praxis, of its critique of power, of its enabling analysis, and finally of a critical literacy that serves, not the interest of the privileged few, but the common good.

The more Americans are denied access to the American materialist dream and its benefits, the more relevant Freirean praxis becomes, for it is nothing if not a pedagogy of access: to education, jobs, health, wealth, and power. What does it matter whether access is denied to citizens as a result of colonial domination or corporate greed; they are equally disenfranchised and dispossessed: of their jobs and entitlements, their dreams and health—of an affordable education and gainful employment—all as part of the "new normal" that caters to the interests of the few at the expense of the many. These new realities, instead of antiquating, further authenticate, Freirean praxis.

If formerly, conditions underscored the disparity between Brazil and America regarding access to the American materialist dream, today's historic, material, and political conditions reinforce the growing alliteration of diminished access across cultural, political, and geographic borders. Analysis of the problematic realities that deny access to health and wealth, education and employment, to say nothing of political power, may serve as a springboard toward civic engagement with those problematic realities, as part of a twofold process for transforming those realities. Criticisms of Freirean praxis that may have been relevant ten years ago are far less cogent today, due to the effects of class warfare, which have narrowed the reality gap between colonial Brazil and corporatist America.

Other critics, focusing less on the goals and content and more on the methodology of Freirean praxis, cite the uncritical hypocrisy of teachers who purport to educate in solidarity with the Other when they "are actually already 'junior members' of the managerial class" (101). Having questioned the relevance of Freirean praxis to American schools, these critics interrogate the ethics of imposing a teacher's radical agenda of resistance on students' assimilationist ambitions relative to the American materialist dream. Radical pedagogues, these critics assert, "do a disservice to these students by undermining their legitimate goals" (100). As Hardin observes, "critics have charged that this is an elitist attitude that privileges the world view of the teacher [and stereotypes] the student as a naïve or misled innocent." Such a critical pedagogy is predicated on the circulation of negative stereotypes of the untutored student, who "labor[s] under a veil of ideology that can only be lifted by the interposition of a 'liberatory' pedagogy" (101). The student's "false consciousness" is posited in sharp contrast to the teacher's "authentic consciousness," thus reinscribing a hierarchical power dynamic that radical pedagogy purports to critique (R. Miller 19, qtd. in Hardin 101).

Continuing this ethical assault, other critics argue that radical pedagogy substitutes one form of ideological indoctrination for another, subsuming the student's voice and world view in the teacher's, reinscribing the practices of the pedagogies it putatively critiques. Susan Miller, for example, "worries that such practice infantilizes students, assuming their cultural naiveté, and that critical pedagogy, no matter how well-intentioned, may unfairly endorse the teacher's or institutions ideological perspective" (qtd. in Hardin 3). In "Rescuing the Subject," Miller calls into question the tendency of radical pedagogy to "teach a universal moral sense . . . to normalize and covertly coerce conscience" and to "install a universal vision of 'democratic' subjectivity" (498).

Criticism of Freire's "liberatory" praxis is thus grounded in a critique of a seemingly fatal contradiction at the heart of his radical praxis—and by implication of all radical pedagogy: that it merely reinscribes a "banking model" of education-as-*inculcation,* unwittingly reinforcing the hierarchical power dynamics it purports to resist: in which an ideology of resistance is proselytized in lieu of an ideology of domination, in which the student is "inculcated" with the political world view of the practitioner. However, this argument is itself based on a flawed, if not fatal, assumption: that education is not always and already an act of "inculcation." Education always inculcates. Without inculcation, there is no education. All teaching inculcates, from the advent of Socrates' elenchus in the fourth century BC to the liberatory pedagogy of Freire. *Webster's Dictionary* defines "inculcate" as "to teach" (379). Under "teaching," *Roget's Thesaurus* includes the following verbs: "instruct, edify . . . inculcate" (564). This calls into question the assumption that "inculcation" is somehow distinct from "teaching." Teaching is always and already "inculcation."

The critical question is not whether teaching "inculcates," but whether such inculcation is ethical. Given the inescapably political nature of all pedagogy, pedagogical ethics is only determined by the ends it serves: domination or freedom. To insist that pedagogy be apolitical is to deny its inherently political nature.

Given the impractical imperatives to act beyond the classroom in order to intervene upon or transform problematic realities, radical practitioners run the risk of generating nothing more than a passive awareness. *In Self-Consuming Artifacts*, Stanley Fish underscores the dangerous risks that the impractical imperatives of "action" and "resistance" pose to radical pedagogy, if it offers nothing more than the "lure of political hope," or ends by becoming nothing more than a "dangerous new 'modification' to the subject of English studies" (101, qtd. in Hardin 5). Byron Hawk advances another criticism of a radical pedagogy that fails to deliver on its promise of liberatory change: "students can come to believe that they cannot change the world to correspond to their desire. In practice [this] has the potential to transform itself into its opposite—cynicism" (79). But even this failure and this cynicism are enabling if they do nothing more than enable the student through analysis of discourse and rhetoric to defend himself or herself from the manipulative effects of it, to make a conscious choice relative to the affective power of rhetoric. This is precisely the problem addressed by Socrates' elenchus and the ameliorative effect of the critical consciousness it developed. Yes, failure to alter material conditions may foster cynicism, but it is a radically different kind of cynicism from that engendered by an paralyzing ignorance, insofar as the subject may be impotent with respect to the world, but is no longer impotent before the Word, and therefore less likely to have his or her behavior in the world determined by a Word that serves the interests of domination.

It is a critical as opposed to an uncritical cynicism, which leverages a liberatory space and a measure of agency between the knowing subject and the state-sanctioned Word that would gain his compliance, manipulate her response, or construct and control the subject through a rhetoric of opaque deceptions. Critical analysis, even sans the actions that authenticate it, is an edifying end in itself, is always and already a form of action, insofar as it alters the relation between the Self and the Word—it arms a self that has stood unarmed before a Word and a World that serve, not its own interests, but the interests of domination. These critics problematize what they see as the tendency of "teacher or institutional concerns [to] overwhelm student autonomy in an attempt to create a liberated subject" (R. Miller, qtd. in Hardin 9). The effect of creating a "liberated subject," however, has prompted critics to dwell on this aspect of Freirean praxis, calling into question the tendency of "teacher or institutional concerns [to] overwhelm student autonomy," in the process blinding these critics to the edifying aspects of Freire's emphasis on dialogic learning, problem-posing analysis, and civic engagement.

More recently, Freire has come under radical attack at a much more fundamental level, by critics who call into question the relevance of Freirean praxis to a pedagogy that has purportedly moved beyond its antiquated notions. While some critics assert Freire's praxis reinscribes the dogmatic pedagogies it purports to resist, others contend it is either irrelevant to American classrooms by virtue of its emphasis on revolution and resistance or an antiquated discourse that is no longer discussed. This last criticism undercuts its own credibility by virtue of its hyperbolic claims. This criticism is easily dispelled by a selective search of the MLA International Bibliography or JSTOR. A key word search of these databases using "Paulo Freire" turned up 50+ recent sources (2006–2010), as evidenced by the following selective sample:

"Teaching Freire and CUNY Open Admissions," by Kristen Gallagher. *Radical Teacher: A Socialist, Feminist, and Anti-Racist Journal on the Theory and Practice of Teaching* 2010 Spring 87: 55–67.
"Critical Pedagogy, Democracy, and Capitalism: Education Without Enemies or Borders," by Nick Stevenson. *Review of Education/Pedagogy/Cultural Studies* 2010 Jan–Mar 32.1: 66–92.
"Freire's Bottom-Up Bridge to Student-Centered-ness: A Rebuttal. . . . " by Kashani A. Salouri. *Asian ESL Journal* 2009 May 5.1: 107–113.
Subject to Reading: Literacy and Belief in the Work of Lacan and Freire, by Eugene Henry Klerk. Newcastle Upon Tyne, England: Cambridge Scholars, 2009.
"Understanding Critical Pedagogy & Its Impact on the Construction of Knowledge," by Janette Zygamantas. *Pedagogica* 2009 23: 63–78.
ESL Education in Taiwan: An Approach Applying Paulo Freire's Pedagogy . . . Cultural Contexts, by John Chang. 2008 Jan DAI. 68.7: 2918.
"The Future of the Past: Reflections on the Present State of Empire and Pedagogy," by Peter McClaren in *Critical Pedagogy: Where Are We Now?* New York: Peter Lang, 2007: 289–315.
"Liberation Theology and Liberatory Pedagogies: Renaming the Dialogue," by Shari J. Steinberg. *College English* 2006 Jan 68.3: 271–290.

These recent works evidence the enduring relevance of Freire across disciplines and cultural boundaries: not only in Rhetoric/Composition Studies, but across disciplines in English as a Second Language (ESL), African Studies, Philosophy, Anthropology, and Theater Arts; not only in America, but in Taiwan, Africa, and South America; not only with major scholars (Peter McLaren) and to major theorists (Lacan), but as evidenced by discussions of his praxis in tier-one (*College English*) and tier-two journals (*Review of Education*) in Rhetoric/Composition Studies.

Similarly, a glance at the mission statements of most American universities evidences the ubiquitous relevance of Freire's emphasis on critical thinking and civic engagement. To argue that Freire (or an application of his praxis to contemporary classrooms) is irrelevant and "no longer discussed" says more I think about the limitations of the critic than Freirean praxis. These claims are the by-product of "wishful thinking" rather than evidence-based analysis, even as the criticisms of their peers are in many cases the by-product of a reductive analysis of Freire's praxis that "cherry-picks" some aspects (revolution, resistance, liberatory learning) while ignoring others (dialogic discourse, problem-posing analysis, and civic engagement with problematic realities).

The Radical Critique of Radical Pedagogy 13

To contend that Freire's problem-posing praxis is irrelevant is to assert that teaching that foregrounds civic engagement is irrelevant; is to assert that a pedagogy that emphasizes the posing of social problems to students is irrelevant; is to argue that a praxis that privileges not merely analysis of a problem, but engagement beyond the classroom to resolve it is irrelevant; is to assert that the teaching of "critical reflection" (one of the two components of Freire's praxis) is "not relevant anymore"; is to contend that applied learning is of no use in the modern classroom, despite its emphasis in university mission statements throughout the nation and around the world. To assert that Freirean practice is irrelevant is to argue that a concern for social justice has no place in the classroom. Finally, to argue the irrelevance of Freirean praxis is to argue the obsolescence of the student-centered, interactive classroom which is central to composition pedagogy (and to teaching across the liberal arts curriculum), and has been for 40 years—unless the workshop approach to writing pedagogy is also "not relevant anymore."

Finally, Hawk criticizes radical compositionists who discover in Freirean praxis a warrant for its broad application in American education. Hawk critiques this attempt to turn "pedagogical practice into a universal model, which makes it a general process imposed as law" (210). Yet, the signifiers Hawk uses, "universal," "imposed," "law," are in themselves problematic insofar as they are reductive, inaccurate, or hyperbolic. The signifier "universal" suggests a totalizing implementation of Freirean praxis that vastly overstates its adoption, or intended uses. As opposed to wanting to universalize Freirean praxis, most practitioners are looking for ways to make their own pedagogy more effective, by making it real, by making it have some connection to material reality, as opposed to a mere academic discourse. The effort to disseminate their radical pedagogy through books, journals, conference presentations, and conversations arises, I believe, more from a desire to share their pedagogy with peers, than to universalize it. The irony of Hawk's critique is that while purporting to seek a more nuanced pedagogical "complexity," it actually erases complexity by positing pedagogical binaries, as for example under the polarities of universal/local, in effect erasing complexities of praxis that exist in the continuum between the polarities of universal/local, absolute/partial, comprehensive/selective.

Here I want to speak in defense of Freirean praxis, not under the sign of a "universal model," of a "general process *imposed as law*," but simply under the sign of a broad as opposed to a narrow application. If a practice is edifying with respect to desired outcomes, such as dialogic communication, critical thinking, and/or civic engagement, why would we not seek for a broader as opposed to a narrower application? Embedded in Hawk's use of "universal" is the assumption that such a broad application is inherently problematic. Yet, if an invention improves life, do we not seek for its broad application (telephone, television, computer, iPhone, iPod, etc.). Again, it is ironic that in a polemic that touts the broad, should I say "universal," application of pedagogies of technology, Hawk should decry the same broad application of Freirean praxis, again positing an either-or binary that erases the very complexity he purports to seek in lieu of a both-and continuum that envisions the possibility of merging the two pedagogies, of conjoining a neo-humanist Freirean pragmatism and a digitally networked, post-humanist, pedagogy of inventive complexity. Again, if a pedagogy is enabling, it has human value, whether it enables the individual self to loose the shackles of writer's block into a deeper agency of self-expression (as is the case with process-expressivist pedagogy) or fosters political agency by arming the self through rhetorical analysis against rhetorical manipulation or by fostering greater access to the benefits of the American materialist dream (as is the case with Freiren praxis). Again, given these edifying effects of pedagogy, why shouldn't we seek its broader application? Lost in Hawk's critique is the nuance, the complexity between universalizing a dogma and seeking the broader application of an education that edifies—not "imposed as law," but modeled as an example—but one of many, that adds to the complexities of the pedagogical spectrum.

THE PITFALLS OF TEACHING RESISTANCE

Hardin succinctly captures these criticisms of radical Freirean praxis in *Opening Spaces*, which he uses as a springboard into a compelling warrant for teaching resistance, effectively nuanced by his own problemetizing of resistance pedagogy. Yet Hardin, like other defenders of radical pedagogy, and of Freire's praxis in particular, repeats the error of Freire's critics: emphasizing the imperative to teach resistance, while effectively putting under erasure the other critical aspects of Freirean praxis, all of which foster success within the academy and the professional marketplace, by virtue of the skills they enhance—dialogic communication, critical thinking, problem-solving analysis, and civic engagement. The emphasis of Freire's defenders on "teaching resistance to the unconscious reification of ideological values as they are encountered in texts," actually constrains Freirean praxis to a narrow application, ignoring its broader pedagogical implications and applications, which are, moreover, entirely consonant with the dominant theories and goals of education, and composition pedagogy in particular, ubiquitously enshrined in university, department, and program mission statements under the signs of "interactive/active learning," "critical/analytical thinking," and "civic engagement." This is the broader pedagogical "space" I hope to "open" for Freirean praxis under the sign of dialogic pragmatism—one that moves beyond the narrow application of "teaching resistance," despite Hardin's useful, articulate, and compelling defense of it.

This narrow defense of Freirean praxis, with its reductive emphasis on teaching "resistance," "emancipation," or "liberation" as "counter action to the acculturative and normative mission of the academy" (42), likely does as much harm as good, insofar as it misrepresents Freirean praxis and the broader relevance of it to contemporary education, thus limiting the "buy in" of teachers. It is reductive in a dual sense: not only confining Freirean praxis to "teaching resistance," but confining its analysis to a meta-academic discourse. This meta-academic analysis, while no doubt useful as a focus of radical pedagogy, is reductive and harmful if advocated as *the* focus of radical pedagogy, to the exclusion of other foundational aspects of Freire's pedagogy. It is a "boxed-in" defense, walled in by the signs of "resistance," "emancipation," "liberation," and "revolution" that misrepresents, radicalizes, and constrains Freirean praxis, eroding the "buy in" of countless teachers interested in dialogic methods, analytic content, and participatory citizenship. Is "teaching resistance" a useful component of Freirean praxis? Absolutely. Is it the "be all and end all" of Freircan praxis its defenders advocate? Hardly. In the final analysis, the arguments of critics and defenders alike are undercut by a "can't see the forest for the trees" perspective that reduces Freirean praxis to "teaching resistance." Each is complicit in the same reductive mis-reading of Freirean pedagogy, blind to its broader implications and application, which if anything are increasingly attuned to problematic American realities.

Though the liberatory ends I am proposing are the same as those advocated by the defenders of radical pedagogy, what I am calling for is an equal emphasis on the other aspects of Freirean praxis: dialogic discourse, problem-posing analysis, and civic engagement, which are obscured by the narrow emphasis on teaching "resistance." The goal of this more broadly defined radical pedagogy is not merely "the liberated consciousness of the students" (Berlin 492), but the transformation through analysis and action of problematic realties in the interest of the just, the human, and the good. The goal, as Knoblauch and Brannon observes, is "cultural and political reflectiveness . . . that enables liberatory action in the face of oppressive social conditions" (45)—including the poverty, unemployment, homelessness, and untreated illnesses induced by the increasingly polarizing effects of class warfare. The focus of radical pedagogy should be much broader than the concern with the "values and ideology promoted by the conventions and genres of academic and disciplinary discourses" (46), with the "exploitation of graduate students and part-timers" (Sledd 147, qtd. in Hardin 47). The focus of such a radical pedagogy is too narrowly concerned with the "cultural, economic, and political institutions of the academy," while the problematic realities of society are all too often treated as an afterthought. This exclusive focus on "a self-reflexive, continuing critique of the part played by the academy and its scholars and teachers in resincribing hegemonic cultural ideology" (48) reduces radical praxis to a meta-academic discourse that has no real value or application beyond the academy—reducing it in effect to a mere academic exercise. Thus, both the goals and program content of radical pedagogy are reductively configured under the signs of "resistance" and meta-academic analysis.

Though articulating a compelling defense for teaching resistance, which in many ways negates the assertions of its critics, Hardin ultimately notes the necessity and efficacy of "abandoning the discourse of emancipation," which is constrained within its own oppositional tendencies. A radical praxis which more broadly emphasizes dialogic communication, problem-posing analysis, and civic engagement would not force students to choose between their own personal/professional goals and this broader "program content" of radical pragmatism. The terms that denote student empowerment would be re-defined under the signs of "dialogic communication," "problem-posing analysis," and "civic engagement" rather than narrowly inscribed under the sign of "resistance to ideological discourse." Instead of privileging the aims of resistance over assimilation, such a radical pragmatism would serve the interests of both, insofar as the skill-set of critical civics would enable assimilation into the marketplace, enabling the prospects of mitigating problematic realities from within the system, by altering the critical DNA of the workforce—toward the development of a more civic-minded worker, of a workforce with a social conscience, of managers and junior managers in whom a spirit of civic ethos has been "inculcated," and in whom the economical and the ethical are not at odds, nor mutually exclusive—which goes to the root cause of the recent "flash crash."

An enduring concern for the ethical within the economical, if inculcated dialogically, may mitigate against the rampant, self-serving, corrosive, if not criminal, effects of corporate greed, which has consequently expelled masses of citizens from the American materialist dream, is continuing to shed workers by the thousands, and is denying access or reentry to millions, in what has devolved into an American materialist dream that is of the few, by the few, and for the few. If education does not serve the interests of the common good, it too devolves into a mere elitist academic exercise. The more access is denied to an education, to a job, to health care, and to political agency, the more relevant Freirean praxis becomes—for it is first and foremost a pedagogy of access, granting agency to those who have historically or catastrophically been denied it.

This is the common ground of the post-modern movement across disciplines, across ethnicities, across genders, across sexual preferences, across class, across cultures and sub-cultures: the struggle to entitle with agency those denied access to it—not only African-American, Native American, and Hispanic-American, but female American and gay American, poor and middle-class American. A neo-pragmatism that mitigates the problematic aspects of reality for these citizens, that works for the common good through heightened understanding of problematic realities and an enervated civics, is the new "program content" of education as "the practice of freedom."

RADICAL PEDAGOGY: A DEFINITION

As James Berlin observes in *Rhetorics, Poetics, and Cultures,* what distinguishes social epistemic praxis from its pedagogical predecessors is its concern with "three important domains of experience: what exists, what is good, and what is possible" (78). Inquiry and intervention into these realms, as Paulo Freire observes, define "the program content of education" in the social-epistemic paradigm (*Pedagogy of the Oppressed,* 86). This "program content" evidences the tripartite conjunction of the analytical, the ethical, and the political, insofar as "what exists" is unveiled in the interest of "what is good" (individually and collectively), toward the realization of "what is possible," defined in terms that are humanistic, ideal, even utopian. The social nature of inquiry is characterized not just by the reformist ends it serves, but by the assumptions from which it proceeds. Foremost among these assumptions is the assertion that the individual is always and already social, "that each person is first and foremost a member of a community. Thus, any claim to individuality can be articulated only within a social context" (Berlin 79). To the extent it serves the common good, critical literacy is always and already social—and the intellectual is first and foremost a public intellectual.

This represents a radical departure from the orthodoxy of expressivist pedagogy, whose social classroom methods (small collaborative groups) serve individual ends: the edification, empowerment, and agency of the individual writer. Ethical intervention into a problematic reality in order to transform it toward a more fully human existence in that reality is beyond the scope of the "program content" of expressivist pedagogy. Social-epistemic inquiry's concern for "what is possible" evidences its "utopian" hope for "the good democratic society and the good life for all its members" (81). In this, social-epistemic praxis reveals its deep affinity with "the program content" of Socratic inquiry, as I hope to demonstrate in this inquiry.

As an "intervention in the political process" that proceeds by unveiling "what exists" in the interest of "what is good," social-epistemic praxis and Socratic inquiry evidence the liberatory struggle of inquiry into the social regimes of domination across 2,500 years. As opposed to the expressivist paradigm, "political agency, not individual autonomy, is the guiding principle"—insofar as autonomy is always and already political and is a by-product of political agency, it cannot exist without it in an atomistic vacuum. To put it another way, the autonomy of the individual is never pursued as an end in itself, but only insofar as it is accompanied by (or is a by-product of) political agency.

At the heart of the "program content" of social-epistemic praxis is its inquiry into language, and into the signifying practices of domination in particular. In this, it also reveals its pedagogical alliteration with Socratic inquiry, which is likewise an interrogation of sophistic signifying practices within the context of a comparative polemic, which by way of contrast advocates and dramatizes the signifying practices of an honorific, enabling philosophic discourse, similarly focused on the real, the good, and the possible. As Berlin observes, "signifying practices are always at the center of conflict and contention. In the effort to name experience, different groups vie for supremacy, for ownership and control of terms and their meanings in any discourse situation" (82–83). This is not only evidenced in our own recent and current history, in the agonistic civil discourse of the partisan culture wars, but in Socrates' era as well, in the bitter, partisan war of discourses that raged between sophistry and philosophy, persuasion and analysis from the moment of Pericles' death to the verdict at Socrates' trial (427–399 BC)—with the multiple tribunals, exiles, and executions of the foremost advocates on either side: from Aspasia and Anaxagoras to Alcibiades, Critias, and Charmides; from Socrates and Plato to Antyus and Meletus (his accusers).

The incestuous intimacy of power and language is the focus of inquiry in social-epistemic praxis today as it was in Socratic inquiry two-and-a-half millennia ago. That ancient inquiry has much to offer contemporary educational praxis, given its identical preoccupation with the real, the good, and the possible. As Berlin avers, "language is always an arena of struggle to make certain meanings—certain ideological formations—prevail. . . . defining and directing the material conditions of experience as well as consciousness. . . . situat[ing] signifying practices at the center of politics" (83). Language, thus, determines not only what is real, but what is possible—depending on what ends signifying practices serve: domination or liberation; the interests of ruling elites or the common good. Inquiry into the signifying practices of domination and resistance comprise the "program content" of Socratic and social-epistemic praxis. Berlin continues:

> Signification is described as a material force that must be studied in its complex operations of enforcing and challenging power arrangements. Social-epistemic rhetoric is in accord with this perspective, pointing out that rhetoric was invented not because people wanted to express themselves more accurately and clearly, but because they wanted to make their positions prevail in the conflicts of politics. In other words, persuasion in the play for power is at the center of this rhetoric, and studying the operation of signifying practices within their economic and political frames is the work it undertakes. (83)

This focus on language, and on the signifying practices of domination in particular, comprises as well the "program content" of critical praxis.

As long as power depends on the power of persuasion, language will be complicit in regimes of domination, as evidenced in Foucault's interrogation of the relation between language and power (*Two Lectures*), in which he reveals the extent to which language is the circulatory system of power: the means by which it consolidates and perpetuates itself. To the extent persuasion (the analysis and practice of it) defines the "program content" of first-year writing, such an inquiry into the relation between power and the power of persuasion is warranted in the writing workshop, in a "program content" characterized by inquiry into the real, the good, and the possible.

Yet, if language serves the interests of domination, it also serves the interests of liberatory resistance, to the extent it subverts or redistributes power in the interest of the real, the good, and the possible. This too is the common lesson of Socratic inquiry and Freirean liberatory praxis, insofar as each recuperates power by recuperating the ability to "name the world," to "unveil" or "decode" the problematic aspects of reality as a means of altering or transforming "what exists." As Giroux observes, "the critical spirit of theory should be represented in its unmasking function.... the ultimate purpose of critique should be critical thinking in the interest of social change" (17–18). As such, "critical thought becomes the precondition for human freedom" (19). For social-epistemic praxis and Socratic inquiry, the "program content of education" as evidenced by their respective assumptions, goals, and methods, is largely concerned with "describing and analyzing the operations of signification" (93). With respect to the radical pedagogies of Socrates and Freire, to what extent might a genealogical map include not only their goals, assumptions, methods, and "program content," but their respective origins?

2 The World, the Word, and the Wound
A Genealogy of Origins

> A history can be, and should be, a tracing of origins . . . the authority of narrative comes from its capacity to speak of origins in relation to endpoints.
>
> —Brooks (276)

Every history, as Brooks asserts, is a search for origins. With respect to the psychological origins of the radical pedagogies of Socrates and Freire, to what extent can they be understood from a post-Freudian perspective—and informed by the theories of Peter Brooks and Otto Rank, in particular? Is it possible to map a genealogy of origins as a springboard into a broader genealogy of goals, assumptions, methods, and "program content"? Despite their historical estrangement, is it possible their radical pedagogies shared a common origin—and if so, what might it be? Seen through the lens of Brooks' post-Freudian theory, what common desires may have informed their edifying impulses? From a Rankian perspective, to what degree was the educative urge informed by a creative impulse—and even more significantly, to what degree might it be seen as the origin of the creative impulse? To what extent were their radical pedagogies rooted in individual and collective ideologies, and the conflict between them? Finally, in theorizing the psychological origins of these two radical pedagogies, an interesting question arises: to what degree does each radical pedagogy reinscribe the psychoanalytic process: as a return to the site of a trauma, of a "buried, yet living past," in order to mitigate its violent effects through a liberatory discourse of dialogic "analysis" that enacts the eternal return of the Word to the World—as a radical intervention at the site of the trauma: the signifying subject? Might it be useful to "read" the radical pedagogies of Socrates and Freire as a "talking cure" with political overtones?

THE DAWN OF A SCAPEGOAT: THE POLITICAL, RELIGIOUS, AND AESTHETIC ORIGINS OF A RADICAL PEDAGOGY

As evidenced from Socrates' defense in the *Apology*, his elenchus or dialectic inquiry was a life-long calling, rooted in his personal religious beliefs and his deep sense of personal destiny and piety: a calling that underscores the grim irony of the accusation of "impiety" brought against him at his trial, which is precisely the reason he launches his defense with this exhibit of autobiographical evidence. This moment of his defense is but one example of the extent to which his pedagogical Word is always and already rooted in a political Wound, at both the individual and the collective level. This wound is akin to the scene of a crime, the site of a trauma to which Socrates repeatedly returns throughout his career in an effort to construct a dialectic narrative that not only mitigates the effects of the wound, but intervenes against the state that inflicts it. The wound is first inflicted with the political exile of one mentor (Anaxagoras) and the trial of another (Aspasia). It is deepened with the exile of one former lover-student-statesman (Alcibiades) and the executions of a second and third (Critias and Charmides), the uncle and cousin, respectively, of Plato. As personal as these wounds no doubt were, they were at one remove from Socrates' own person, in contradistinction to the wounds inflicted directly on him by the state: first, through surveillance and persecution, then by trial and execution.

It comes as no surprise then that for Socrates, dialectic discourse was a blood sport, waged incessantly against sophistic power in the public arenas of the marketplace, the agora, and the courtroom. His dialectic discourse operates very much in an adversarial, prosecutorial mode, not only during the trial of the *Apology*, but during his inquisition of Lysias' sophistic text in the *Phaedrus*. It is difficult to tease apart the discourse of Plato's Socrates and Plato. Yet, in the final analysis, the problem is moot insofar as the discourse of each enacts the return to the scene of a crime or trauma perpetrated by the state against an ideal exemplar. If Socrates' dialectic interrogation of sophistic power acts as corrective against its excesses, then similarly Plato's discourse, particularly in the *Apology* and the *Phaedrus*, signifies an attempt to "actualize the [traumatic] past in symbolic form, so that it can be replayed to a more successful outcome" (Brooks 24). Plato, in effect, restages the trial of Socrates in the *Phaedrus*, re-casting Socrates and Lysias in the roles of prosecutor and defendant respectively to mitigate the traumatic effects of Socrates' trial and execution and to reverse the outcomes of that trial: by effecting Socrates' eternal acquittal on appeal to posterity and by effecting the ruin of sophistry for 2,500 years.

Socrates' radical pedagogy is rooted not just in a personal wound, but in a collective wound as well, inflicted on the Athenian citizenry through the excesses of sophistic power (which controlled the state's legal, political, and ceremonial apparatuses during much of Socrates' career), and through the manipulative effects of sophistic rhetoric through which that power circulated. As Foucault, Glenn, and others have theorized, there is always a relation between language and power. Socrates is a human metonym for the Athenian masses manipulated and subjugated by the excesses of sophistic domination, including the excesses of sophistic persuasion.

Socrates' radical pedagogy, no less than Freire's, was motivated by the subjugating effects of power on the citizenry and by the desire to counter these hegemonic effects through dialogic education. His defense is perhaps the most compelling demonstration of the symbiotic relation between analysis and action, the word and the world, insofar as he uses dialectic discourse to expose the hegemonic effects of sophistic persuasion and its corruptive influence on the legal institutions of fourth century BC Athens—and on the perceptions of the 500-member jury in particular. His defense is perhaps the most dramatic example of his tendency to practice what he preached, to embody the dialectic Word in political action, at the point of contact with a problematic reality: an Athenian justice system corrupted by sophistic power.

His defense signifies as well the individual and collective roots of his radical pedagogy, insofar as he unveils its deeply biographical origin as well as the public interest his adversarial, "gadfly" discourse serves: as a check on power and as a living, breathing monument to the power of critique. His goal is not just to remove the stain against his honor inflicted by the charges of impiety and corrupting the youth, but to liberate the Athenian citizenry from the subjugating effects of sophistic power by exposing its manipulative effects and the extent to which it has corrupted the entire justice system. His martyrdom achieves both ends. In the aftermath of his trial and execution, Meletus and Antyus, his sophistic accusers, are respectively exiled and executed, while sophistry fades from the arena of Athenian politics—effectively put under erasure for twenty-five centuries by Plato's pen.

Not to be overlooked in Socrates' defense is the significance of his date of birth, which coincided with the annual rite of the scapegoat: a ritual of collective purification in which sacrifices were offered to the gods in the interest of the common good. In this light, it is not difficult to envision his trial for impiety to the gods of Athens as a reinscription of this ancient ritual of communal purification, facilitated by his own impulse toward martyrdom. Did Socrates sense that his fate, and his trial in particular, were predestined from birth: as the fitting bookends for a dissident scholar born on the day dedicated to the cleansing ritual of the scapegoat? Did he embrace martyrdom as the logical, inevitable, and necessary end to his life, by which that life alone could be consecrated—as the ultimate, counter-hegemonic action arising from his life-long interrogation of Power and Persuasion? Possibly then, his praxis was rooted in a deep sense of pre-destination in which both his critical inquiry and the death that was its inevitable consequence were individual acts of collective liberation, fueled by self-destructive tendencies. Like the Irish martyrs of the Easter Rising of 1916, Socrates foresaw the liberatory effect his martyrdom would have on the Athenian populace relative to the abuses of sophistic power. This much is clear in his climactic address to his accusers, when he prophesizes the effects of his execution by the state.

Socrates' voluntary sacrificial execution was not only an effect of his teaching, but the inevitable effect of it, to the extent it was necessitated by his praxis: as the climactic act of redemption and critical intervention against a state whose political ideals had been corrupted by the excesses of sophistry—in the education, legal, political, and ceremonial apparatuses that consolidated and enshrined it. Thus, the psychological wellsprings of Socratic dialectic elenchus are as deeply personal as they are social and political, are inseparably yoked to his personal religious beliefs and to his religion of personal philosophical genius. Throughout his defense he gives voice to his personal religious beliefs, speaking of his personal "daemon," of his epiphany before the oracle of Delphi that revealed his pedagogical calling to him, in order to refute the trumped-up charge of impiety to the gods, which is essentially a refusal to worship false idols, embodied in the deity of the city, Peitho, the goddess of Persuasion.

The thirty-year partisan war of Athens from the time of Pericles' death to Socrates' trial (427–399 BC) was nothing if not a violent war of discourses between persuasion and analysis, sophistry and philosophy, democrat and oligarch, Meletus and Antyus et al. versus Socrates, Charmides, Critias, Alcibiades et al. His refusal to recant his philosophy and the practice of it during his trial ironically underscores the central role that recantation plays in his dialectic methodology, wherein he repeatedly assumes a position only to recant it through dialectic analysis, as so effectively dramatized in the *Phaedrus*. In his trial, Socrates refuses to recant a critique of power, which, through dialectic recantation, recants sophistic power. To recant his beliefs would be to recant his entire life—which would be tantamount to committing a public suicide. If recantation enacts his public disgrace and death, the life he gains thereby is moot—is tantamount to a living death. By sacrificing his life to his beliefs, he lives immortally, ensuring the afterlife of his beliefs and of the soul that harbored them.

Socrates' martyrdom to a corrupt state was not only the ultimate act of intervention, but the inevitable destination of his dialectic interrogation. It extended that interrogation from the here and now to the hereafter, not only consecrating his life, but giving his interrogation of sophistic power an afterlife. Speaking in the penultimate moments of his trial with the prophetic power of the oracle of Delphi, he calls down upon the heads of his accusers, and the entire corrupt state they represent, an eternal curse empowered by a vision of their damnation and his redemption, perhaps while smiling on the face of Plato as he spoke. There is a rectifying, if not retributive, impulse to the corrective discourses of Socrates and Freire, who speak truth to power with a vengeance.

In his defense, Socrates unveils the spiritual-psychoanalytical origins of his pedagogy, attributing his calling to his faith when he observes, "I shall call upon the god at Delphi as witness to the existence and nature of my wisdom, if it be such" (21a). Again, he traces the origins of his philosophical/pedagogical calling to his personal religious beliefs, noting that "when the god ordered me, as I thought and believed, to live the life of a philosopher, to examine myself and others," he obeyed (28e). Far from being impious, he asserts, "I was attached to this city by a god" (30e), yet again demonstrating that the origins of his pedagogical philosophy were as personal as they were pious. He goes even further, lifting the veil on the spiritual origins of his philosophical calling in a statement whose significance is difficult to understate:

> I have a divine or spiritual sign, which Meletus has ridiculed in his deposition. This began when I was a child. It is a voice, and whenever it speaks it turns me away from something I am about to do, but it never encourages me to do anything. (31d–e)

As with many educators, his profession is a calling, is deeply bound up with his identity, and therefore is a richly personal experience. He has, as Rank observes, a 100% vocational identity, akin to that of the artist, insofar as he is what he does. Recanting his philosophy and the practice of it would be tantamount to a renunciation of the Self: a form of self-execution that does the self eternal dishonor. Better to kill two birds with one stone: die with honor to kill your enemy and immortalize the self.

This statement in his defense not only refutes the charge of impiety by revealing the pious origins of his calling to philosophy, but shows that those origins are rooted in an ancient pagan religious tradition from which the contemporary Greek pantheistic tradition had broken and which it was struggling to suppress if not eradicate. This is evidenced in the scorn which Meletus heaps on this ancient pagan tradition in his written deposition ("which Meletus has ridiculed in his deposition"). It is evidenced in the libelous rumors his sophistic enemies spread about his pagan beliefs, accusing him of trafficking in the occult, of practicing witchcraft, of being a "student of all things in the sky and below the earth" (18c). Finally, this hostile attack on Socrates' pagan beliefs is evidenced in the charge of impiety itself.

From a historical perspective, there is nothing new in this kind of religious persecution. That it should be as prevalent in Socrates' time as in our own merely underscores the continuity of religious persecution across time and space. The rhetorical tropes deployed by the sophists to demonize or de-legitimatize Socrates' pagan beliefs prefigure those used by Christianity to suppress paganism for centuries: paganism is not an authentic religion, but mere superstition and witchcraft. The violence of its persecution by orthodox religions of state is merely a reflection of the extent to which the state's ideological religious apparatus felt threatened by paganism's alternative world view, even as it felt threatened politically by Socrates' oligarchic beliefs and his relentless dissemination of those beliefs.

What Socrates' tribunal crystallizes is not merely the conflict between two rhetorics, (sophistry and philosophy), nor merely the conflict between two religions (paganism and Greek pantheism, or between an older and a newer paganism), but the conflict between the state and the individual. What sets Socrates' pagan faith so violently at odds with the collective pantheism of Athens was its individual character. As articulated in his defense, Socrates' paganism is deeply aligned with an ancient nature-worshipping tradition, whose beliefs bear a common resemblance across continents and millennia. His "divine or spiritual sign," his personal "daemon," reinscribes the Native American trope of the "spirit helper," or personal guide, similarly acquired in youth ("when I was a child") during a personal vision quest, which leads the individual away from the community to a place of personal power in nature (the oracle at Delphi), where he was brought into deeper communion with the gods, one of which would approach the individual in the form of an animal, dream vision, or "voice"—which remained a guiding source of personal power, which could be contacted through ritual, and which often revealed the individual's calling in life from that point forward: in Socrates' case, as a philosopher "attached to the city" like a "gadfly" to a sluggish horse, to rouse it from the corrupting influence of its sophistic stupor. His religion of individual genius is at odds with the official pantheism of the state, as is his pre-ordained, god-appointed role as the conscience of the state.

His elenchus is a species of performance art, forever holding a "mirror up to nature, to show virtue her feature, scorn her own image, and the very age and body of the time his form and pressure" (*Hamlet*, 3.2. 22–24). The purpose of his defense is the same as Hamlet's mousetrap: to unveil the crimes of the state—in his case, the corruption of the justice system by sophistic rhetoric. I would further argue that, like Hamlet's grand inquisition of power at Elsinore and Freire's indictment of colonial power in Brazil, Socrates' live-action, on-its-feet, embodied critique of sophistic power is very much rooted in a "buried, yet living past," in which the exiled and executed ghosts of Anaxagorus and Alcibiades, Critias and Charmides enact the eternal return of the word to the world: as an absence made present during Socrates' trial of sophistry. The unveiling done before a jury of 500 Athenians, and a keener jury of posterity embodied in Plato, it only remains to crown the truths unveiled with action, to "suit the action to the word, the word to the action" (lns 17–18). For Socrates, as for Hamlet, that action is a vengeful martyrdom, which enacts as well as the death of his sophistic prosecutor and life-long sophistic persecutors. Ironic, that the mouth and the sword are the mediums for their mutual destruction, for the hemlock and the poison that kills philosopher and prince, prosecutor and king, that effects the mutual ruin of philosophic avenger and a state corrupted by its sophistic excesses, where rhetoric is the weapon par excellence for deception, is wielded like a cloak and dagger respectively, to conceal and avenge the crimes of the state. There is definitely a lethal, perhaps even vengeful edge to the discourses of Socrates and Freire that unveil the crimes of patriarchal power to kill it and stand in its place. The non-violent unveiling of the mechanisms and apparatuses of state violence, including state signification, does liberatory violence to them. Perhaps the only sword power is powerless against is the sword of criticism, as if dueling a headwind.

Socrates' tribunal is nothing if not a state's effort to silence a voice that poses a threat to its domination of the citizenry, operating through a counter-hegemonic discourse that calls into question its purported goodness and putative wisdom, in every public forum in which it can find a ready ear, which arms not only citizens, but generals and statesmen (Alcibiades, Critias, and Charmides) with arguments against its domination. It is evident from his trial that the wound from which his critical word arose was a multiple wound, which maimed him politically, religiously, and intellectually, as an oligarch, pagan, and philosopher. It is further evident that Socrates' radical pedagogy was his liberatory response to the wounds of power, operating through sophistic persuasion. His dialectic elenchus is not only an effort to speak truth to power, to curb its excesses, but a manifestation of the desire to mitigate the effects of state violence on the self, by constructing a narrative that evidences the eternal return of the word to the site of that violence—in what is a discursive struggle for freedom, relative to the abuses of sophistic power, and the webs of sophistic signification, played out over a lifetime of public intellectualism. If social epistemic practice is defined by the application of analysis to problematic realities, including the problematic of power and the signifying practices that perpetuate it, then it is evident that Socrates' trial by the sophistic state represents the dawn of radical pedagogy—or perhaps the climactic moments of that long dawn, in which analysis was first used to critique power.

SOCRATIC INQUIRY AND THE POST-FREUDIAN TURN

As Peter Brooks observes in *Reading for Plot*, all narrative is an expression of desire, and many narratives reinscribe the psychoanalytic process, as both a return to a traumatic origin and a reworking of it toward more liberatory ends. Thus, in Plato's dialogues, and particularly in *The Apology* and *Phaedrus*, we see Plato returning to the scene of a crime, as it were, to the site of a youthful trauma (the trial and execution of his mentor), which is reworked continuously toward a more liberatory, healing, and humanizing end, insofar as it is objectified in art. This is why Socratic inquiry (and the Platonic inscription that enshrines it) invites interpretation from a psychoanalytic perspective, which can be particularly useful in informing its psychological origins. Platonic invention is rooted in the moment of the buried, yet living past"—is like the mandrake that sprouts from the blood of the gallows, from the traumatic terrain of Socrates' trial, his ears perhaps still ringing with the martyred mentor's prophesy of vengeance:

> Now I want to prophesy to those who convicted me.... I say gentleman, to those who voted to kill me, that a *vengeance* will come

upon you immediately after my death. . . . there will be more people to test you. . . . They will be more difficult to deal with and they will be younger. . . . (39c–d, my emphasis)

It is the troubled and traumatic ground of Socrates' trial that prompts the eternal return of Platonic invention, even as the excesses and abuses associated with sophistic power prompt the eternal return of Socrates' public interrogation. The trauma of a publically tried and unjustly executed master/mentor/exemplar requires that Plato "repeat, go over again, the ground that has been covered by his predecessor, the criminal" (Brooks 24)—like a detective intent on uncovering a crime and bringing to justice its perpetrators.

The eternal return of the Platonic word to the scene of a crime (Socrates' trial and execution) evidences a desire to "repeat and to 'work through' an as yet unmastered past" (293), to "uncover a moment of trauma, a scene of crime that makes sense of subsequent events, and his own development" (270). Plato, like Socrates and Hamlet, is "condemned to narrate the past, the world of ghosts which has fallen to his inheritance and which one can attempt to placate through acts of genealogical narration" (302). This retrospective gaze upon a traumatic past deeply informs the meaning-making process and the desire for knowledge, as evidenced not only in Plato's dialogues, but in the retrospective wisdom of Proust's *A la recherche du temps perdu*. As Brooks observes, "All desire aims at the future . . . is desire for a revelatory knowledge to come often first . . . experienced as the desire for the recovery of a buried memory, a lost trauma" (Brooks 312). Excavation of a traumatic past is as central to the meaning-making process in Plato as it is in Proust, whether it be the trauma of the trial and execution of a beloved exemplar/father figure or the trauma of separation anxiety induced by a mother's "goodnight kiss" and the incestuous, suicidal, and matricidal impulses it masks.

Platonic invention thus deconstructs itself in a most profound manner. For while advocating a knowledge that comes before languages, that exists as an a priori, transcendent signified, what Plato's dialogues dramatize is a knowledge that not only comes after language, through dialectic discourse, but comes after experience through memory—that is, an a posteriori knowledge that is either socially constructed or retrospectively excavated. As Brooks asserts, all narrative, including Plato's dialogues, "as a system of meaning, must conceive itself as essentially retrospective" (301). To the extent narrative inflects meaning, narrative and meaning are retrospective, are not *a priori* but *a posteriori* processes.

Thus, Platonic invention un-writes its central thesis regarding the nature of knowledge. The claim it makes is contradicted by the educative process it dramatizes. In Platonic invention, there is an inherent disconnect between knowledge as signified and knowledge as dramatized. What Plato signifies is an a priori Knowledge; what he dramatizes is an a posteriori knowledge that comes after language through dialectic discourse and the selective excavation of traumatic memory. As Brooks observes, "only the end can determine meaning" (22).

Socrates' own pedagogy of recantation performs the retrospective nature of meaning, consuming its previous positions "as it projects itself forward, retracting as it extends, calling for its end from its beginning, toward a finality that offers retrospective illumination of the whole" (53). Thus, Platonic invention is a discursive (pre)cursor of Proustian invention, whose paradigm of retrospective wisdom it prefigures by two and a half millennia. This comes as no surprise, given the profound influence of Plato on Proust's education, as evidenced by a narrative that not only gives voice to a deterministic "ideal hunger," which repeatedly enacts the drama of disappointment between the ideal and the real, but dramatizes as well a retrospective wisdom that recants itself from beginning to end. If the radical pedagogies of Socrates and Frere are genealogical relatives with respect to their origins, then similarly the *Phaedrus* and *A la recherche* share a common genealogy with respect to their vision of retrospective meaning.

This has profound implications for "re-reading" what has perhaps been the greatest critical crux of Platonic scholarship: the oppressive violence of a Truth that is an a priori, transcendent signified. Recent critics have misunderstood and misrepresented the *Phaedrus*, as an "organizing dynamic of a specific mode of human understanding" (Brooks 7). I will revisit this critical crux, and the implications of Plato's vision of knowledge, in "Plato and the Tyranny of the Transcendent."

Like Freirean signification, Platonic invention is deeply liberatory, in an individual and collective sense, insofar as it liberates the Athenian subject from the objectifying effects of sophistic signification and liberates the artist from the traumatic effects of experience, embedded in a "buried, yet living" past, whose effects, like the bones of an unquiet grave, refuse to remain buried. Freire's liberatory discourse is similarly aimed at excavating a traumatic colonial past by which the colonial present is held captive and is an attempt to liberate the political present from the colonial past through an educative process that is always and already political, whether colonial or liberatory. I will develop the genealogical and pedagogical implications of this political wound in greater detail in the next section.

Platonic invention gives voice to this buried yet eruptive past. Socratic inquiry, particularly in the *Apology* and in the *Phaedrus*, reflects a similarly recursive impulse, insofar as Socrates returns again and again to the written deposition of Meletus in the *Apology* and to the written text of Lysias in the *Phaedrus*, each of which he views as a "crime" against a genuinely, honorific, if not beautiful, rhetoric, grounded not in manufacturing belief but in unveiling reality. Phaedrus' uncritical idolatry of Lysias' text is a metonym for the collective blindness of the Athenian citizenry, and the 500-member trial jury in particular, toward the manipulative effects of sophistic discourse. Socrates' discourse throughout *Phaedrus* not only returns to the original scene of the crime (Lysias' text) but repeatedly returns to his own discourse, which it self-reflexively reworks toward liberatory ends, prefiguring a psychoanalytic process of retrospective analysis of a problematic reality through discourse with an Other.

Freire's discourse similarly foregrounds dialogue with the oppressed Other as a means of unveiling the problematic realities of power. Platonic invention similarly dramatizes an effort to "actualize the past in symbolic form, so that it can be replayed to a more successful outcome" (Brooks 270): the acquittal of Socrates and the condemnation of his accusers; the immortal resurrection of Socrates and the eternal oblivion of sophistry in the symbolic trial that Plato re-stages in the *Phaedrus,* as a sequel to the trial of sophistry Socrates stages in his defense in the *Apology.*

By virtue of their recursive nature, both Socratic inquiry and Platonic invention demonstrate their enduring relevance to the contemporary composition workshop, insofar as they model a process of meaning-making through analytical inquiry that is not only dialogic but recursive: that reworks what has been written or argued, plowing new words and fresh arguments into an existing text, which is never fixed and unalterable, but always and already a work in progress, tending through its successive unveilings and revisions toward a more edifying if not transformative end. Each confronts the wounds of Power, and the problematic realities they give rise to, whether in texts or in public forums, whether in the legal texts of Meletus and Lysias or in the academy, the marketplace, or the courtroom, as part of a written and oral interrogation that unveils the effects and mechanisms of power. In this, the radical praxis of Plato's Socrates is a precursor of contemporary social epistemic praxis, and of Freire's liberatory pedagogy in particular.

FREIRE AND THE POST-FREUDIAN TURN: THE WOUND OF EDIFICATION

To what extent does Freire's radical pedagogy share a common origin with Socratic inquiry, insofar as its critical Word is rooted in the wound of state power, is the spade with which he excavates a "buried, yet living past" in solidarity with the victims of it, in order to expose the violence of colonial domination on the colonized subject? To what extent does Freire's radical pedagogy similarly use analysis of power and its effects to free the subject from those effects, naming a problematic reality as a first step toward transforming the relationship between the subject and that reality, as a first critical step toward a recuperated participation in that reality?

Freirean praxis seeks the same thing as Socratic inquiry and Platonic invention, insofar as it enacts a return to the origins of trauma, that is, the wounds of colonial power on the colonized subject, and seeks to liberate those internalized effects by objectifying them in the realm of the symbolic, in a radical and pedagogical "talking cure" of its own invention—which fosters in the subject a transformative agency with respect to a problematic reality, made less so by the ability first to name it and subsequently to participate in it. As with Plato and Plato's Socrates, Frere's critical/analytical Word is born of a political wound.

As with Socratic inquiry and Platonic invention, Freire's radical pedagogy signifies the eternal return of the critical word to the scene of a collective crime, in order to mitigate the traumatic effects of that crime by unveiling them. The "crime" in Freire's case is not the excesses of sophistic power and signification, but of the excesses of colonial domination. In *Pedagogy of the Oppressed,* he systematically unveils the traumatic and dehumanizing effects of colonial domination as the most ethical site for critical inquiry, modeling a praxis as dialogic in its methods and as political in its ends as Socrates' elenchus. His analysis reveals the "historical reality" of "dehumanization" (27), fostering its "recognition" by pupils and readers alike, as a result of his strategic unveiling of it. This statement is significant because it underscores the mutual preoccupation of the radical pedagogies of Socrates and Freire with the historical, with a "dead, yet living past" which exerts a debilitating effect on the present. The ethical orientation of Freire's praxis is underscored by his assertion that "this . . . is the great humanistic, historical task of the oppressed" (28), and for those who teach amidst the problematic realities of dehumanization.

What then are the wounds of power that have historically dehumanized Freire's students? Freire, like Socrates, commences his inquiry into power by systematically unveiling through analysis its dehumanizing effects on the colonized. One of the first effects of domination that Freire unveils is the co-option of identity, whereby the oppressed is recruited into the ranks of the oppressor and even into his or her own self-oppression. This, naturally, co-opts from the beginning any liberatotry resistance, any struggle for liberation, for "almost always, during the initial stage of the struggle, the oppressed, instead of striving for liberation, tend themselves to become oppressors" (29–30). Another dehumanizing effect is the "'fear of freedom' which afflicts the oppressed. A fear which may . . . bind them to the role of the oppressed" (31).

Freire, like Socrates, similarly notes the extent to which the masses have internalized their oppression and the implications this has for the struggle for freedom. "The oppressed," Freire observes, "having internalized the image of the oppressor and adopted his guidelines, are fearful of freedom . . . which is the indispensable condition for the *quest for human completion*" (31, my emphasis). The final words are significant because they underscore the mutual goal of Socratic and Freirean praxis: the liberation of the Self into a "more fully human" participation in reality.

Freire continues situating inquiry at the site of historical trauma, cataloging the wounds of domination:

The oppressed suffer from the *duality* which has established itself in their inmost being. They discover that without freedom they *cannot exist authentically*. Yet although they desire authentic existence, they *fear* it. They are at one and the same time themselves and the oppressor, whose consciousness they have *internalized*. The *conflict* lies in the choice between being wholly themselves or being *divided* ... between being *spectators* or actors; between acting or having the illusion of acting ... between speaking out or being *silent, castrated* in their power to create and recreate, and in their power to transform the world. This is the *tragic dilemma* of the oppressed which their education must take into account. (32–33, my emphasis)

Freire's pedagogical vision of this "tragic dilemma" is significant, insofar as it coincides with Cornel West's vision of a "prophetic pragmatism," which similarly foregrounds awareness of the "tragic" as the generative point of departure for postmodern pragmatism. In "Pragmatism and the Tragic," West asserts that "a sense of the tragic is an attempt to keep alive some sense of possibility" (32). In looking with hope toward the future, a critical eye must forever be kept on the past, whose dehumanizing evils generate the desire for a re-humanizing good. West's notion of the tragic includes not merely the dehumanizing evils of the past but the death of hope for (and in) the future, which often attends the traumatic violence of the past.

Desire for a future different from a dehumanized past is bred from awareness of historical tragedy. This is the collective wound whose violent effects are mitigated by the winding shroud of words at the point of contact with this wound. The healing effect of language gives rise to a hope that further heals, like a wound in the fresh air of fresh realities. Thus are the historically and politically maimed healed, wound-to-wound through their dialogic words. A "talking cure" with political overtones, in which those maimed by history "talk back" to it and by talking back are able to turn their collective back to it, having escaped the colonizing effects of it—while forever keeping an eye trained on this tragic history. The circumstances, collectively, are akin to those of the individual who moves beyond the traumatic violence of the past through a dialogic discourse of "analysis" that fosters freedom psychologically as a precondition for fostering it politically, insofar as a reality named can more easily be claimed. Loss of hope is the collateral damage of historical tragedy, perpetuated by forgetfulness of the past, by a collective amnesia that serves the interest of domination, prolonging both the collective tragedy and its collectivizing effects.

Freire continues his systematic unveiling of the traumatic effects of historical domination of one people by another, noting that the oppressed "have been unjustly dealt with, deprived of their voice, cheated in the sale of their labor" (35). As he further observes, one of the "gravest" effects of domination is its tendency "to submerge men's consciousness," to dull, numb, or subvert their capacity for critical awareness, through the machinery of its propagandistic discourse and demonization of dissident discourse—an effect repeatedly noted by Socrates as well. Indeed, the whole purpose of dialogue in the *Phaedrus* is to transform the subject's relation to reality from a state of uncritical estrangement to one of critical engagement.

Each of these conditions "hinders [the] pursuit of self-affirmation," which is the goal of radical pedagogy in its ancient and contemporary incarnations. The "terror" and "violence" (41) of these conditions denotes them as a site of mass historical trauma, necessitating the intervention of a counter-hegemonic pedagogical narrative to heal and liberate the victims from these dehumanizing effects. This is what denotes the radical pedagogies of Socrates and Freire as a "humanist and libertarian pedagogy" (40). Signification amplifies and sediments the traumatic effects of domination, further hindering the liberatory struggle of its victims, whose reaction to the "violence of oppressors" is itself labeled 'violent,' 'barbaric,' 'wicked,' or 'ferocious'" (41), reinscribing the characterization of Socrates as "wicked" in his trial. Thus are the effects of domination misconstrued as the cause of it, used to rationalize further domination. The role colonial signification plays in Freire replicates the role of sophistic signification in the *Apology*, where Socrates is similarly demonized as a practitioner of witchcraft and a trafficker in the occult. As humans, the victims of oppression are reduced to the "object[s] of its domination" (44): "the earth, property, production, the creations of men, men themselves, time—everything is reduced to the status of objects at its *disposal*" (Freire 45, my emphasis). Lest we question the relevance of Socrates and Freire's radical critique of power to our own historical moment, it is useful to recall Naomi Klein's observations regarding the "planned misery" of radical, free-market capitalism,

> [which] erases the boundaries between Big Government and Big Business. [This] is not liberal, conservative or capitalist, but corporatist. Its main characteristics are huge transfers of public wealth to private hands, often accompanied by exploding debt, an ever-widening chasm between the dazzling rich and the *disposable* poor and an aggressive nationalism that justifies bottomless spending on security. For those inside the bubble of extreme wealth created by such an arrangement, there can be no more profitable way to organize society. (*Shock Doctrine* 18)

In this corporatist state, the middle as well as the lower class are considered "disposable." The wealth of the few is predicated on "throwing millions of people overboard: public sector workers, small business owners . . . trade unionists. . . . They are the disinherited, those described by the German Poet Rainer Maria Rilke as 'ones to whom neither the past nor the future belongs'" (350). The problematic realities of American radical capitalism are ideally suited for critical inquiry in a problem-posing, Freirean praxis that enacts the eternal return of the word to the wounds of the world and to the causes and effects of the economic wounds currently being inflicted in keeping with the "planned misery" of the corporatist state, whose fortunes are predicated on the willed misfortunes of the citizenry.

Yet another "wound" of domination catalogued by Freire is a collective "fatalism . . . interpreted as a docility that is a trait of national character," not an effect of domination. As Freire observes, fatalism "is almost always related to the power of destiny or fate or fortune—inevitable forces . . . under the sway of magic and myth, the oppressed . . . see their suffering, the fruit of exploitation, as the will of God," when in reality it is "the fruit of an historical and sociological situation, not an essential characteristic of a people's behavior" (48). Thus, another effect of domination is misconstrued as a cause and justification for it.

A further, and grimly ironic, effect of colonial domination is the victim's idolatry of his or her historical victimizer, toward whom they feel "an irresistible attraction" that extends to the oppressor's "way of life" (94): they fall prey to a desire "to resemble the oppressor, to imitate him, to follow him" (49). This is accompanied by a tendency to deprecate the self, a by-product of the crisis in self-esteem which is yet a further effect of domination. This "self-deprecation," as Freire notes, "is another characteristic of the oppressed, which derives from their internalization of the opinion the oppressors hold of them. So often do they hear that they are good for nothing, know nothing and are incapable of learning anything—that they are sick, lazy, and unproductive-that in the end they become convinced of their own unfitness" (49). Consequently, "they are reluctant to resist, and totally lack confidence in themselves. They have a diffuse, magical belief in the invulnerability and power of the oppressor" (50). Socrates similarly calls into question Phaedrus' uncritical idolatry of sophistic signification, as embodied in Lysias' text. Freire's critique of power, like that of Socrates, is liberatory insofar as it uses analysis to free the colonized citizen from the dehumanizing effects of oppression. Unless and until they recognize weakness in those wielding power over them, "they will continue disheartened, fearful, and beaten" (51).

By unveiling the limiting conditions of power, Freire was able to convert this self-defeating idolatry of power into a liberatory critique of it, enabling a fuller participation in realities, which had until then confined its members to a victimized spectatorship. The truly transformative possibility of Freire's pedagogical analysis of power resides in its potential to transform the passive objects of power into the active agents of their own self-affirmation, arising from a new awareness of the Self's authentic status, not an "emotionally dependent" ward of the state, but a self-signifying agent of his or her own social and political affirmation.

This is the historical landscape of collective trauma that Freire excavates with his radical, dialogic praxis, to which he returns, as if to a "buried, yet living past," or to the scene of a "crime." Freire's radical critique of power constructs a humanistic, counter-hegemonic history, which, like psychoanalytic discourse, desires to "repeat, go over again" the site of a trauma, unearthing the eruptive realities of its unquiet ground in order to free the subject from its captivity to a problematic if not dehumanizing past—toward a new reality, empowered and transformed by the participation of those formerly victimized by it. Even as Plato's dramatic dialogues revisit the traumatic terrain of Socrates' tribunal and execution in the *Apology* and *Phaedrus*, so does Freire's radical praxis similarly seeks to "actualize the past in symbolic form, so that it can be replayed to a more successful outcome"(Brooks 270).

THE ART OF EDIFICATION: THEORIZING A GENERATIVE "VITALISM"

At the heart of Socrates' trial lies a tragic irony. The state tries and executes a dissident scholar whose individual beliefs and philosophic practices are assumed to be subversively at odds with its own collective ideology, when in reality they are perhaps the most sublime expression of it. To what extent then is Socrates' dialogic practice rooted not just in a deeply personal religious ideology, but in the collective ideology of classical Greece? To shed light on the collective origins of Socratic inquiry, I want to turn to the theories of Freud's dissident protégé, Otto Rank, whose life-long study of the psychological origins of the creative impulse does much to unveil and demystify those origins. This is not to dismiss the contributions and relevance of Freudian theory to understanding the origins of the creative impulse, and of classical art in particular, as evidenced by the influence of the Oedipal complex (Freud's theory of a sublimated sexual impulse) and indeed by the relevance of the psychoanalytic process itself to our understanding of the narrative impulse. That said, the psychological origins of Socratic inquiry are rooted not just in the calling of his personal "daemon," nor merely in a personal desire to rework a "buried, yet living past" to mitigate the effects of a political wound, but equally in the collective ideology of classical Greece—as is Platonic Invention. As such, they reflect the influence of a collective aesthetic "vitalism," largely overlooked by criticism, as Hawk has usefully observed.

Normally, education and art are represented as distinct signifying practices, rooted in impulses whose origins are distinct. Yet, in ancient Greece might the two have informed one another? Was Socratic inquiry not only an expression of the creative urge, but also its highest expression? If we posit the edifying impulse as a manifestation of the creative impulse, might we also posit the artistic urge as a genealogical descendent of the educative impulse? Do teaching and art, particularly as practiced in Plato's Greece and as exemplified by Plato's Socrates, share a common psychological origin? What is the connection between eros, logos, and creativity, as evidenced in the

Greek master-pupil paradigm? To what extent are the artistic and educative impulses alike rooted in a desire to disseminate the self in space and time: in a desire for immortality? Was the educative model of ancient Greece indeed the prototype for all creativity: the art-of-all-arts? Can we fully understand the goal of mutual edification that defines Socratic inquiry without also more fully appreciating its collective origins and its aesthetic roots? What, finally, are the implications for social-epistemic praxis of this collective aesthetic ideology? To the extent the edification of Self and Other is prompted by the desire to shape and re-shape both toward a "more fully human" ideal, is this consistent with the goals of Freirean liberatory praxis?

No theorist to my knowledge has more usefully informed the origins of the creative urge, including their roots in the educative impulse, than Freud's heretical disciple, Otto Rank (*Art and Artist*, 1933). As opposed to Freud, who focused exclusively on the role of sublimated sexuality in his search for the origins of the creative urge, Rank proffers a much more comprehensive analysis of those origins: theorizing the role of morbid suffering in the artiste manqué, of the desire for immortality, of the need to replace something that is lost, of an ideology of sacrifice, and of the master-pupil educative dyad.

As Rank observes, the dialogic, master-pupil model of education developed by the Greeks, and refined by Socrates, transcended the mere pursuit of knowledge, insofar as it not only shaped the personality and identity of teacher and pupil, but became a path to their immortality. Thus, the pursuit of knowledge was absorbed into the identity politics and spirituality of the dialectic dyad; that is, it occurred within the mutual shaping of Self and Other toward a "more fully human ideal," defined in terms of the Beautiful and the Civic, in which love of a beautiful form grew into love of a beautiful idea, expressed in beautiful discourse, involving the dialectical alliteration of eros, logos, and ethos. This mutual fashioning of a shared identity fulfilled a host of desires: not only satisfying desires for edification, immortality, and love, but fulfilling as well the soul's "mirror hunger, ideal hunger, and merger hunger" tendencies (Kohut *Search* 378). Master and pupil alike were the plastic medium wherein the Self was shaped through the process of mutual edification toward a "more fully human" Greek ideal, in a process that was not only akin to the art of Greek sculpture, but was a likely origin of that three-dimensional art, where the Self could see the effect of the "knife's work" upon it in the shaping of this mutual ideal of humanity. Rank's observations on the artistic underpinnings of the master-pupil dyad in classical Greece are instructive:

> [B]eing a pupil did not mean the mere acquiring of a certain discipline and the mastery of a certain material knowledge . . . but the *forming* of a personality, which begins by identification with a master and is then "artificially" developed and perfected on the pupil's own lines . . . Socrates is the best known of many examples of this. . . . (54)

The relevance of Rank's observations is borne out by the ubiquity of this educative paradigm in classical Greece, as evidenced not only by the Aspasia-Socrates and Socrates-Plato dyads, but by the Plato-Aristotle, Aristotle-Alexander, Gorgias-Isocrates, Isocrates-Timatheus, Protagoras-Anaxagoras, and Anaxagoras-Pericles dyads. In other words, it isn't just dialectical knowledge that Socrates bequeaths to Phaedrus, but this desire to shape the Self and Other toward an ideal Beauty, physically and intellectually, in which the beauty of eros, logos, and ethos were mutually dependent. Further, Beauty is not just defined in physical or intellectual, but in political terms, involving in its most ideal form civic action for the common good. Socrates isn't interested in the mere dissemination of philosophic knowledge, but in the dissemination and reproduction of his ideal Self in an Other-as-pupil/statesman/philosophic lover.

Before he "creates works of art," the master-as-artist creates an Other in the image of himself. This is his first (and perhaps greatest) creation—and the first means by which he evidences his creative genius. The Self begets an ideal Other-as-work-of-art, as the living embodiment of the immortal soul and the ideal of Beauty. Santas notes "that in Socrates' view specific eros is essentially connected with *begetting or creativity*, and that it extends beyond sexuality" (18, my emphasis).

In Plato, this creative tendency to objectify the ideal Self in the Other shifts that objectification to the symbolic realm of art: in the dramatic dialogues, in particular. Thus, the process has come full circle: an artistic impulse expressing itself in the educative molding of an Other, in Plato turns back to art to objectify and immortalize itself. If Socrates' art occurs in the material realm, in the plasticity of the Self-Other dyad, then the art of Plato's writing returns it to the realm of the symbolic. Creative impulses objectified in the mutual shaping of Self and Other within an educative context are subsequently displaced into the symbolic realm, in works of art that immortalize the ideal, "fully human" soul of writer and teacher. Thus, an artistic impulse given material representation in Socrates' teaching is given symbolic representation in Plato's writing.

Rank then raises a provocative question: was the artistic impulse of the Greeks a mere "by-product" of this educative ideology, in which the "education of men" was viewed as the *truest* of all living arts, in which men "should try themselves to become as beautiful and perfect as the statues around them" (54, my emphasis)? Rank continues:

> Seen in this light, [the master-pupil dyad], which, as Plato tells us, aimed perpetually at the improvement and perfection of the beloved youth, appears definitely as the Classical counterpart of the primitive body art on a spiritualized plane. In the primitive stage it is a matter of physical self-enhancement; in the civilized stage, a spiritual *perfecting in the other person*, who becomes transferred into the worthy successor of oneself here on earth; and that, not on the basis of the biological

procreation of one's body, but in the sense of the *spiritual immortality-symbolism in the pupil*, the younger. (54–55, my emphasis)

In other words, did the mentor-pupil dyad comprise not only the highest form of art in classical Greece, but the point of origin for Greek art, insofar as the material it used to express its sublime ideal was neither marble, nor dramatic poetry, nor epic myth, but the body, personality, intellect, and soul of a chosen Other, molded in the image of ideal Beauty by a mentor, whose Self is similarly perfected by the hand of beauty, embodied in the Other? Did Greek art then arise from the desire to concretize this living emblem of the ideal, defined in terms of full human naturalness: in sculpture, mosaics, and frescos, in poetry, drama, and epic myth? Was this educative paradigm the fount of Greek art and, as such, not only an additional but perhaps the most significant origin of the artistic impulse in Greece, and in Plato in particular, who enshrines this master-pupil dyad in his dialogues as the defining feature of his aesthetic ideology, as the only living, plastic art form, and therefore the prototype of all Greek art? Is the beloved "golden one" (Phaedrus) not only a symbolic representation of the beautiful, if untutored, student, but also the prototype for the subject of Greek art, of which Achilles and Theseus, the marble figures of Praxiteles and Phidias, and the dramatic characters of Sophocles and Aristophanes were the symbolic incarnations. Finally, does the Freirean educative impulse arise from a similar desire: to not only to liberate the subject, but to construct it along ideal, humanistic lines—as a critically aware, self-determining, civically engaged subject? Is Freirean praxis motivated not only by a desire to enable a more fully human participation in reality by its subject, but also by a desire to mold that subject toward the realization of this ideal, replicating in the process the educative impulse of the ancient Greeks and of Plato's Socrates in particular?

Rank's observation shed light on yet another psychological origin of the creative impulse, embodied in the educative ideology of ancient Greece: the desire for immortality. To the extent the Self begets itself in an Other, it perpetuates or disseminates itself in space and time. To the extent the pupil carries on the teachings of the mentor, as Plato does for Socrates, he immortalizes the soul of the teacher—or at least gives it a form of immortality. Thus, education fulfills the same desire for immortality as art. In other words, the origins of the educative impulse are rooted in a similar desire for immortality as the aesthetic urge.

Not only Greek art, but Christianity is deeply informed by this educative paradigm. As Rank asserts, "Christianity took over this ideal of personal character-formation in the symbol of the Exemplar-Master . . . [and] relieved the individual of the task of personal self-creation" (55). Rank situates the psychological origins of the mentor-pupil dyad in the impulses associated with primitive pagan art, insofar as it arises from a similar need to "glorify" the creative ego by "artistic idealization, and at the same time to overcome its mortality by eternalizing it in art"(56). Thus, Socratic inquiry is rooted not just in artistic impulses, but also religious ones. The religious impulses from which it springs are pagan in nature, as evidenced not only by Socrates' epiphany before the Oracle of Delphi, but by its reinscription of the religious nature of pagan art, insofar as the tendency to glorify the self through body art is displaced onto the Other, whose edification becomes a form of self-glorification.

Thus, art (and by implication, the art of teaching) is not only a means of self-edification and self-fashioning, but of self-eternalization. In primitive art, the body of the Self is the medium for its enhancement; in classical art and education, the idealized Other is the medium for the edification and eternalizing of the Self. As Rank affirms, the "tendency toward self-creation . . . is one of the essential components of artistic creation" (29). The ideal Self of mentor and pupil that is generated in the dialogic dyad evidences the synergy between the pedagogic and artistic impulse. The creative impulse is directed toward the edified Other-as-Self, which becomes its first creation. Instead of ornamenting his own body, like the primitive artists of old, Socrates "ornaments" the intellect of the Other: not only displaces this self-ornamentation from the physical to the intellectual realm, but from the Self to the Other. Self-ornamentation toward an ideal beauty and the immortality of the soul is the impetus of classical art, as it was for primitive art, including the classical art of education. A heightened appreciation of pedagogy's creative origins extends our critical understanding of the educative impulse beyond the rigidities of the cognitive-expressivist-social epistemic categories and into spheres of enabling complexities, as Hawk observes. Instead of Invention being posited as a neglected aspect of composition pedagogy, the educative impulse itself is posited as being always and already a manifestation of the creative impulse. Rank's theory of a classical educative impulse informed by artistic tendencies reinforces Hawk's theory of "vitalism" and his critique of a history of rhetoric and composition that marginalizes the role of the creative impulse, not only in composition, but in the teaching of it, which is as central to the composing process as it is to composition pedagogy, to writing as to the teaching of writing.

Rank's theory on the origins of the creative/educative impulse similarly underscores the dialogic nature of it. To "disseminate" this ideal Self requires its objectification in an Other. Like a sculptor crafting an idealized self-portrait, the Self "impresses and enforces a dominant form on the natural material of bone, flesh, and blood *as an assertion of its own independence,* so that art in this application of it to man himself achieves or seeks to achieve a truly *new creation*" (29, my emphasis). Freire's attempt, pedagogically, to fashion a new political subject is inherently an act of creation, precisely replicating in this sense the creative nature of Socrates' dialectic elenchus. The creative impulse in an educative context paradoxically signifies the assertion of the Self and its dependence on an Other. In the *Symposium*, Plato dramatizes this creative educative process, conjuring a new human type molded in accordance with the ideological ideals of his philosophy and as an immortal objectification of his own soul—even though this utopian self devolves into a dystopian subject.

The classical artist merely displaces the sight of self-assertion in primitive art from the body of the Self to the Other, whose soul, mind, and personality it shapes in the image of its ideal self. The shift from primitive to classical art merely dramatizes the shift in self-assertion from the Self to the Other, who is appropriated as a sign of the ideal self and whose growing beauty nurtures that self. This "formative plasticity" of the Other in the hands of the creative, disseminating Self, "urged . . . by an idealized instinct of will to style" reinscribes the self-directed plasticity of the body in primitive art. Socrates is intent on "tattooing" the soul of Phaedrus in his own image. As Rank observes, "the Tahitian word 'tatu' is derived from 'ta,' which means mark or sign" (30). Socrates' "tattooing" of Phaedrus' soul reincribes pagan tribal customs insofar as it "indicates membership of a particular totem, and is therefore in a sense a collective badge of the individual which robs him of his personality . . . [and] yet . . . does not merely label him, but enhances his individual significance by marking him off from others" (30). Socrates' desire to edify Phaedrus is an attempt to "mark him off from others," to signify Phaedrus as a sign of the ideal Self, to philosophically "tattoo" his intellect, thus signifying his membership in a select, totemic clan, embodied in the dialectical dyad.

Moreover, the dynamics of this dyad have less to do with resolving a sexual, as opposed to a creative, problem, as Rank observes: "The fact that an idealized self-glorification in the person of another can take on physical forms . . . has actually nothing to do with the sex of the beloved, but is concerned only with the struggle to develop a personality and the impulse to create which arises from it" (56). Rank's observations have profound implications for our understanding of the Greek educative paradigm, for they reveal not only that sexual desire was trumped by an impulse toward mutual edification, but that both were absorbed by a creative impulse, arising from the effort to shape a personality toward an ideal of Beauty. Education, far from being distinct from the creative urge, was an expression of it—given its preoccupation with the mutual shaping of Self and Other.

If the Other's beauty awakens the memory of beauty in the beholder, objectified in the sculptures of Praxiteles and Phidias, then it similarly awakens the desire of the beholder to participate in this sculpting of this ideal beauty, in the form of dialectics. Dialectics then is the intellectual counterpart to the marble by which Socrates seeks to give shape to this ideal of beauty in the Other. Friere's dialogic learning similarly becomes the medium for this transformation of the Other into an image of the ideal Self. It is the medium in which he practices his art, perfecting this ideal in the Other as a means of perfecting it in himself. If Phaedrus would erect a statue on Mt. Olympus in honor of Socrates' beautiful discourse, Socrates similarly seeks to sculpt a living statue of the Other as a monument to this ideal of Greek humanity.

Distinctions between Self and Other become blurred: indeed, it is just this initial resemblance, or alliteration, between Self and Other, evidenced in their mutual love of beauty, incarnated in discourse and in Phaedrus' physical appearance, that arouses the "merger hunger" tendencies, the desire for the two-in-one, concretized in the shared identity of their mutual edification, under the sign of the "philosophic lover," the "mark" of dialectics, which signifies their totemic membership in a select group: in which eros, logos, and ethos are harmonized under the "ta" (or sign) of Beauty. A profound mirroring between Self and Other occurs, in the fulfillment of ideal hunger and merger hunger tendencies, in what evolves into a Self-Self alliteration. In Freirean praxis, this mirroring is evidenced in the deep sense of solidarity that develops between teacher and student, similarly grounded in "evolutionary" and "revolutionary" love (West 57, 180).

In molding the Other as a semblance of the ideal Self, it is as if Socrates is erecting a living statue in his own honor—not on the remote heights of Olympus but in the realm of the everyday, as a mirroring offspring of the Self. The chosen Other, as Rank observes, is a manifestation of the ideal, spiritually as well as physically:

> This impulse is at bottom directed toward the creator's own *rebirth in the closest possible likeness,* which is naturally more readily found in his own sex.... But the likeness to himself will not only be found in the bodily form of his own sex, but also be built up with regard to the spiritual affinity, and in this regard the youthfulness of the beloved stands for the bodily symbol of immortality. In this manner does the mature man, whose impulse to perpetuate himself drives him away from the biological sex life, live his own life over again in his youthful [pupil]; not only seeking to *transform* him into his intellectual counterpart, but making him his spiritual ideal, the symbol of his vanishing youth. (56, my emphasis)

The creative urge, operating through the mentor-pupil dyad, is deeply informed by the need to mitigate the destructive forces of Time, is driven by the desire to immortalize not only the ideal Self but the ideal and beloved Other. This is as true of Plato's dialogues as it is of Michelangelo's sculptures and Shakespeare's sonnets, each of which evidences the artist's "intention of immortalizing his friend's beauty ... if time is bound to destroy his bodliness" (57). Art is the objectification of a desire to see this "beauty ... incorporated into eternity," side-by-side with the creator's soul and, as such, satisfies the desire for the "two-in-one" in the hereafter, as does the experience of philosophic love in the here and now. As Rank states, "the matter is at bottom one of self-immortalization expressed in another (in the ideal)," though the works of all three artists (Plato, Michelangelo, Shakespeare) have also "expressed with great clearness . . . the idea of oneness with the friend" (58)—the desire for the "two-in-one."

If nothing else, Rankian theory establishes the deep affinity between educative, creative, religious, and political impulses, for which the *Phaedrus* is an apt case study. As Rank confides, "I had . . . sought to establish as the primary ideology the belief in immortality. . . . this individual urge to eternalization of the personality, which motivates artistic production, [as] a principle inherent in the art form itself, in fact its essence" (9, 11). Thus, the creative urge is, respectively, a cause and an effect of educational and spiritual desires: for if, on the one hand, it prompts the urge to shape the personality of Self and Other in a process of mutual edification, then on the other it fulfills the soul's desire for immortality by objectifying it in art. The dialogic education of the Other is not only an expression of religious and artistic impulses, but of political impulses as well, insofar as the desire to realize the fully edified, human ideal embodied in the pupil-as-ideal-statesman, which prompted Socrates, Isocrates, and Plato to undertake the dialogic education of Alcibiades, Critias, Charmides, Timotheus, Dionysus II, and Dion, respectively, in an effort to make this ideal real (which, save for Timotheus, largely failed).

The cult of the beautiful, to which classical Greek art is devoted, is a displacement of the impulse in religious art to give concrete representation to the soul. As Rank notes, "the concept of the beautiful, which inspires the works of art of a period is derived . . . from its concretization. That is, the religious art portrayed the idea of the soul in concrete form . . . in the shape of gods" (12–13). In *Phaedrus,* as in many examples of Greek art, the idealized human figure is posited as a "god," as evidenced by the many passages where Socrates likens the beloved youth to a god. The desire to give concrete form to the abstract concept of the soul is perhaps the oldest origin of the creative impulse. The Greek master-pupil dyad was but a means of giving concrete form to the concept of the soul, in the idealized beauty of Phaedrus' form and in the idealized beauty of philosophic discourse. As Rank observes,

> this close association . . . of art and religion, each of which strives in its own way to make the absolute eternal and the eternal absolute. . . . [this] idea of the soul . . . arises from the problem of death. . . . [T]he redeeming power of art . . . resides in the way in which it lends concrete existence to abstract ideas of the soul. (13)

The ends served by art and the Greek educative model "are abstract and spiritual," transcending a mere idolatry of the beautiful or pursuit of knowledge for its own sake—or for the mere gratification of sexual desires. The beautiful in classical Greece is viewed as the incarnation of the immortal. The most significant effect of the Self's edification of an ideal Other was the further edification of itself—toward the realization of an immortal ideal. Edification of the Other thus becomes a form of self-edification: possessing the ideal Other a means of possessing the immortal Self.

Art made possible the development of religions through its objectification of the soul, giving the abstract concept of god concrete form. The Greek educative paradigm appropriated this use of art as a means to individual immortality. Religion depends on art to give material representation to the abstract concept of the soul (God) in the generation of belief. The history of art thus reinscribes the generative tensions of the master-pupil dyad, insofar as art had to wage the same liboratory struggle against the master discourse of religion in order to give concrete representation to its own soul, as opposed to being appropriated as a mere vessel for the representation of God.

The religion-art dyad reinscribes the master-slave dialectic of the teacher-pupil, artist-apprentice, father-son dyads, which commence in servitude and culminate in rebellion. Art's refusal to serve religion, as Rank's refusal to serve Freud, and indeed, as Socrates' refusal to serve the sophistic Athenian state, often results in the violent backlash of the once dominant ideological discourse against its nascent upstart, by whose liboratory project its sovereignty is threatened. This backlash of the ideological orthodoxy may take the form of censorship, persecution, exile, and/or execution, as it did not only for Socrates and the other dissident scholars of his time (Aspasia, Anaxagoras), but for Rank, who was banished from the Vienna circle for his heretical views relative to orthodox Freudian theory, and Freire, who was exiled from Brazil as a result of his liboratory praxis. The irony is that Art, as Rank observes, "though born from the same spirit of religion, appears not only as outlasting it, but as fulfilling it"—insofar as it not only supplants religion as a source of spirituality and as vehicle for immortalizing the artist's soul, but for immortalizing the collective soul of the culture, which seizes it as a symbol of its own immortality. Thus, religion comprises a "transition[al] stage in the development of art" (16). As Rank concludes (and the *Phaedrus* evidences), "man himself—in his own full naturalness, yet in idealized beauty too—had become the vehicle of the immortal soul"(16). Thus, artistic creation in ancient Greece (whether in the concrete realm of the master-pupil dyad or in the symbolic realms of sculpture, painting, mosaics, poetry, drama, and epic myth) may be seen as "a deified incarnation of masculine reproductive power" (20). This desire to teach, this impulse toward the mutual edification of Self and Other is but the effect of a creative impulse, seeking to objectify the soul through the mutual shaping of Self and Other, in a dialogic praxis whose intellectual, spiritual, and political ends are expressive of a collective aesthetic ideology. Political, as well as aesthetic, ideologies inform the origins of Socratic inquiry and Freirean praxis, insofar as each is rooted in a political wound whose violent effects on Self and Other are mitigated by their mutual edification. Having theorized the psychological origins of Socratic inquiry, Platonic invention, and Freirean praxis, I want to extend the genealogical bounds of their radical pedagogies by mapping their respective goals and assumptions.

3 A Radical Genealogy
Mapping Goals and Assumptions

> It is not necessary to read [the dialogues] closely to be impressed with [Plato's] intense interest in the correction of social and political abuses ... to grasp fully what he intended to say ... the dialogues must be understood as *acts of knowing*, examples of *how knowledge is acquired*.
> —Cairns (xiv–xviii, my emphasis)

THE RADICAL CRITIQUE OF POWER: A (PRE)CURSIVE PRECURSOR

A pedagogy is defined by its goals, assumptions, methods, "program content," and ultimately by the consequences of it for the individual and the society. Do the radical pedagogies of Socrates and Freire share a common genealogy, not only with respect to their origins but with respect to their goals, assumptions, methods, and "program contents"? Is the pedagogy of Plato's Socrates indeed radical, according to the criteria by which we understand the term "radical pedagogy"? Where in Plato's *Phaedrus* do we find evidence of this convergence between Socratic inquiry and social-epistemic praxis? Finally, to what extent might advocates of radical pedagogy discover a theoretical warrant in the ancient elenchus of Plato's Socrates?

Far from being an antiquated, irrelevant mode of teaching, the radical praxis modeled by Socrates in Plato's *Apology* and *Phaedrus* deeply informs the assumptions, goals, and methodologies that define radical, social-epistemic praxis, by virtue of its fourfold conflation of the ethical, the political, the educational, and the rhetorical. As radical, dissident scholars offered exile by states whose power and signifying practices they interrogated, Freire and Socrates share an intellectual and pedagogical heritage: one that privileges the generative relation between thought and language, analysis and action, interpretation and intervention.

Perhaps nowhere in the entire canon of Platonic dialogues do we discover a more succinct articulation of the goals or compelling dramatization of the methods of Socratic inquiry than in the *Apology*, which occurs within the context of Socrates' defense of his elenchus, or critical inquiry. His defense of dialectic philosophy is concomitantly a prosecution of sophistry and sophistic signifying practices; it is always and already a "trial" of sophistry that performs the agonistic nature of his elenchus: a live-action, "show and tell" demonstration of dialectic philosophy in "combat" with sophistry, in which Socrates is simultaneously defendant, prosecutor, and judge.

His defense is a critique of power and the power of sophistic persuasion through which it circulates and by which it corrupts the ideals of justice and democracy that it purportedly embodies. In his defense, Socrates unveils the hidden mechanism by which this corruption occurs, focusing on the affective power of sophistic signification. Thus, he turns the tables on his accusers, whose legal writ indicts the affective power of his own philosophic discourse as an instrument for "corrupting the youth of Athens," particularly those students who have become oligarchic statesmen (Alcibiades, Critias, and Charmides). These former student-statesmen are Socrates' absent defendants at the trial, who are similarly being tried in absentia and posthumously, as he has been "tried and convicted" in absentia in the court of public opinion, through the opinion-manipulating effects of sophistic rhetoric, as a result of a long campaign of public demonization broadcast through the forensic oratory of his sophistic accusers.

If the trial were held in modern times, there likely would have been a change of venue, due to the sensational and prejudicial publicity surrounding the defendant. Thus, the outcome of the trial was determined before it even commenced, its verdict a foregone conclusion, given the "witch-hunt" circumstances in which it was conducted and the defendant's own self-destructive, martyr complex: his willingness to die to kill sophistry. Rhetoric has corrupted the ideal of Athenian justice both outside and inside the courtroom, in a tightly circumscribed world where the opinions of jury, judge, and prosecution are subject to rhetorical control.

The trial of Socrates and the immortal monument to it that Plato erects in the *Apology* is a radical indictment of power and the power of persuasion that perfectly embodies the symbiosis between the Word and the World, analysis and action, insofar as Socrates' words are always and already actions that effect the ruin of power. His dialectic enacts the deed, fulfills the destructive wish implied within it—like the vengeful Greeks within the Trojan horse. The lethal irony at the heart of the *Apology* is that in bringing Socrates before them on charges of impiety and corrupting the youth, his sophist-accusers have opened their well-guarded gates to the Trojan horse that will destroy them. The defendant is the agent of their own destruction. Of everyone in that courtroom, only Socrates foresees this, as evidenced by the climactic curse he pronounces upon his accusers. His courtroom dialectic deconstructs the myth of sophistry's absolute control over the legal system: a myth his sophistic accusers believe and perpetuate, as if drugged by the pharmakon of their own manipulative discourse, unaware they are being led to their ruin by the one they are leading to ruin.

The *Phaedrus,* as Derrida rightly observes, restages this "trial of writing"—or rather, continues the polemic initiated by Plato's Socrates in the *Apology,* by reversing the roles of defendant and prosecutor. It is not surprising that Socrates articulates the goals, assumptions, methods, and focus of his elenchus, for his defense is always and already a defense of his teaching, his philosophy, and his life. He practiced his elenchus not only in the search for knowledge, but in the search for the Self, insofar as he came to know himself through it. Hence, the relevance of Cairns' aforementioned observation, which applies equally to Socrates or Plato: "to grasp fully what he intended to say . . . the dialogues must be understood as acts of knowing, examples of how knowledge is acquired." He literally practiced what he preached, dedicating his life to philosophic eros, to the search for mutual edification within a relationship of love. The ontological and epistemological focus of Socratic inquiry and Platonic invention on the meaning-making process underscores not only the modernity but the postmodernity of both.

The trial is at heart a duel of rival discourses (philosophy and sophistry) argued by their respective advocates (Socrates vs. Antyus and Meletus), waged in the public arena of a courtroom, which attests to the social-epistemic nature of Socratic inquiry, inasmuch as it foregrounds inquiry into the opposed *signifying practices* of sophistry and philosophy. Further, as Socrates reveals in his defense, his praxis is always and already social-epistemic in nature insofar as it seeks the edification of Self and Other through heightened powers of critical analysis for the common good. Given this twofold emphasis on critical reflection and civic engagement, Socrates' ancient elenchus is entirely consistent with the *goals* of education in general (as evidenced in the mission statements of many universities, academic departments, and post-secondary programs), with the goals of the postmodern writing workshop, and with the goals of social-epistemic praxis in particular.

Socrates' radical praxis, like that of Freire's, is always and already social, political, and ethical. It seeks edification not through analysis for its own sake, but as a necessary precondition for social and political action, aimed at mitigating the excesses of the dangerous marriage of rhetoric and power, and the corruption of the political and justice systems; the end result is a "more fully human," equitable, free, and civically engaged polis. He pays tribute to the civic nature of his elenchus early in his defense in the *Apology*, in words that underscore its socio-political roots:

> I was attached to this city by the god . . . as upon a great and noble horse which was somewhat sluggish because of its size and needed to be stirred up by a kind of gadfly. It is to fulfill some such function that I believe the god has placed me in the city. I never cease to rouse each and every one of you, to persuade you and reproach you all day long and everywhere I find myself in your company. (30e–31a)

Socrates' statement is significant inasmuch as it underscores the transformative goals of his civic discourse relative to the prevailing reality, which needs to be "stirred up," "rouse[d]," from its "sluggish" status quo through a ceaseless critique, acting like a "gadfly" on a "sluggish horse." This series of dramatic verbs ("stirred up," "rouse," "persuade," "reproach") attests to the active nature of his civic discourse, each in itself an action upon a reality it seeks to transform—here offered in the context of a tribunal, as a defense of his teaching against trumped up charges, as the culminating act of a life-long inquiry into the "dangerous" affects of sophistic rhetoric. In his defense, Socrates performs the active nature of his discourse, literally interrogating the foremost practitioners of sophistic discourse (Antyus and Meletus), whose dangerous signifying practices he calls into question, publically unveils, in a face-to-face intervention, which, if not immediately transformative, nevertheless results in a transformative backlash after his martyrdom, when Antyus and Meletus are respectively exiled and executed, and sophistry is consigned to oblivion for 2,500 years by Plato's dialogues.

Socrates' defense is not only emblematic of his life-long inquiry, but Freirean in nature, insofar as it "unveils" a problematic reality (in which public opinion is manipulated by sophistic discourse) in order to transform that reality. The very charges that have been brought against him and the guilty verdict that follows are Exhibits A and B in evidence of his claims relative to sophistic discourse. The problematic reality Socrates unveils in his discourse during his defense is the corruption of the Athenian justice system by sophistic, forensic signifying practices. The abuses, as Will Durant observes, were ubiquitous, including, as follows:

> [P]ersonal abuse in forensic debate. The diffusion and weakening of judicial responsibility, the susceptibility of jurors to oratorical displays ... these are the black marks against the system of law.... the irresponsibility of the Assembly, that may without check or precedent or revision vote its momentary passion on one day, and on the next day its passionate regret ... the disorderliness of faction perpetually disturbing the guidance and administration of the state—these are vital defects, for which Athens will pay the full penalty to Sparta, Philip, Alexander, and Rome. (262)

Durant's view is significant as a corrective to the appreciative, useful, and ground-breaking "re-reading" of sophistry advanced by recent scholars, such as Susan Jarratt. Jarratt's rescue of sophistry from the historic trashbin of Platonic invention, while warranted, should nevertheless not obscure the abuses associated with the excesses of sophistic signification or power during Socrates' embattled career or the violence of the blood feud between sophistry and philosophy, which was also a war of signification between their respective discourses, of Persuasion versus Dialectics. In the *Apology*, the courtroom becomes the climactic arena for this ancient war of discourses, for the rhetorical combat between prosecutor and defendant, in which the "deck is stacked," the system rigged, the verdict prejudiced in the state's favor. Realizing this, Socrates literally dies to expose it. Only his death will ensure that the violence done to him will return upon his accusers. He literally speaks and dies with a vengeance. This illumines the possible origins of his elenchus (and perhaps of Platonic invention, as well), both of which were rooted not just in the impulse to edify, but in the urge to avenge unjust injuries inflicted, past and present.

Socrates' cross-examination of Meletus is intent on exposing the corrupt nature of the Athenian justice system under the sway of sophistic forensics within the courtroom, even as his public inquiry sought to "unveil" the problematic aspect of sophistic reality, and the signifying practices that perpetuated it, beyond the courtroom: in the marketplace, the academy, and the Assembly. The dominance of sophistic discourse in the Athens of Socrates' final years is characterized, as Field observes, by its intolerance of "dissident opinion": an intolerance that "converted prejudice into persecution" (140). Field continues:

> [F]ears and suspicions of such an attempt [to overthrow Athenian democracy] did not disappear. Isocrates expresses alarm lest in criticizing any act or policy of the people he should lay himself open to suspicions of oligarchic tendencies. And Lysias shows us again and again how useful insinuation of such tendencies could be if it was desired to discredit any enemy or political opponent. (110)

Aristotle confirms this climate of "fear and suspicion," "prejudice and persecution," as Stone observes:

> As Aristotle tells us, one of Dionysus' predecessors, Hiero, used agent provocateurs as well as spies to ferret out "any chance utterance or action" that indicated dissent. Women called "sharp ears" were sent out "wherever there was any gathering or conference." Their assignment was not only to report any dangerous utterance, but by their known or suspected presence, to inhibit critics of the regime. "When men are afraid of spies of this sort," Aristotle observes, "they keep a check on their tongues." Tongues wagged freely in Athens; none more freely than that of Socrates. (133–134)

These are the problematic realities of sophistic power and discourse Socrates seeks to "unveil" in his dialectic elenchus. Not only did Athenians "love good oratory to their ruin," but this oratory seems to have taken a particularly partisan turn toward prejudice and persecution during the rhetorical blood feud between the advocates of sophistry and philosophy, democracy and oligarchy that characterized the three decades from Pericles' death to Socrates' trial. As Glenn observes, the fields of "politics, philosophy, and rhetoric" became "male intellectual battlegrounds," as part of a fiercely partisan war of words that was "vocal, virile, and public," in which the marketplace, the Assembly, and the courtroom became arenas of "masculinist display" (14). Refusing to relinquish the freedom, the right, and the necessity to speak truth-to-power, Socrates thrills to this rhetorical combat, knowing full well the perils of it. There is in his defense an unmistakable tone of willful martyrdom to a just cause. The "unveiling" of this problematic reality in order to transform that reality is central to Freirean praxis, as well, and establishes a pedagogical alliteration between Socratic and Freirean inquiry that bridges the classical/postmodern divide.

The social and ethical nature of Socrates' inquiry is further evidenced when he speaks directly to the public, noting that "I was always concerned with you, approaching each one of you like a father or an elder brother to persuade you to care for virtue" (31b). The patronizing tone does not obviate the social nature of his inquiry. Indeed, it underscores the solidarity he feels with the Athenian citizenry, in this prefiguring Freire's solidarity with the Brazilian peasants.

Socrates defends the ethical nature of his discourse, noting that unlike his accusers he has never practiced it for money, having never "received a fee nor asked for one" (31c). The fact that this is his "first appearance in a law court, at the age of seventy" underscores the conjunction of the ethical and the dialectical, even as he shrewdly plays upon the emotions of the public, whose empathy for an elderly, law-abiding citizen he seeks to arouse—in this perhaps evidencing as well his own mastery of (if not implication in) a sophistic discourse of manipulation. It can equally be argued, however, that here Socrates evidences his understanding of the affective power of rhetoric in Aristotelian terms, by virtue of his effective use of appeals to logos, ethos, and pathos in his defense.

Socrates further evidences the deeply ethical and social goals of his praxis when he observes that in contradistinction to the sophists' "eagerness to possess as much wealth, reputation, and honors as possible," philosophic inquiry seeks "wisdom or truth, or the best possible state of your soul" (29e). Its concern with detecting genuine "goodness" and unveiling pseudo-goodness evidences both its ethical and its Freirean nature:

> I shall question him, examine him, and test him and if I do not think he has attained the goodness that he says he has, I shall reproach him ... and more so the citizens because you are *kindred* to me. ... For I go around doing nothing but persuading both young and old among you not to care for your body or your wealth in preference to ... the best possible state of your soul ... *and everything else good for men, both individual and collectively.* (30a–b, my emphasis).

Socrates' defense is significant for it illumines the ethical and social nature of his inquiry, which is concerned only with what is good for the individual and the community, by unveiling equally the good and the pretense of good. This unveiling of the difference between putative and authentic wisdom, between the pretense and the practice of genuine goodness, is achieved through critical inquiry, which is potentially transformative "both individual[ly] and collectively." It also alliterates with Freire's distinction between false consciousness and "authentic" thought, which is validated by its consequences, as evidenced in his notion of "conscientization," or "consciousness-as-action" (64, 101).

Socrates bears further witness to the social-epistemic nature of his inquiry when he describes himself as a "man who really fights for justice," whose critical inquiry into a problematic reality seeks to "prevent the occurrence of many unjust and illegal happenings in the city" (32a). Socrates' inquiry, like Freire's, poses reality as a problem to be analyzed and transformed through critical intervention: the problem being the dangerous affective power of sophistic discourse. Socrates further evidences the ethical nature of his praxis when he asserts that "my whole concern is not to do anything unjust or impious" (32d), citing his refusal to participate in the Council's public lynching of ten generals for their actions in "the battle of Arginusae . . . in 406 b.c. . . . when a violent storm prevented [them] from rescuing their survivors" (36n). His refusal then underscores his ethical character, as one who "will not yield to any man contrary to what is right. . . . I have never come to an agreement with anyone to act unjustly" (32b–33a).

Socrates' refusal to beg for mercy or recant his discourse in the face of execution further evidences the integrity of its ethical stance, its concern for doing what is right or good, both individually and collectively: "I will not beg you to acquit me" (34e), for "as long as I draw breath and am able, I will not cease to practice philosophy . . ." (29d). Even on the threshold of execution, Socrates not only refuses to recant the practice of philosophy, but at this dramatic eleventh hour uses it to "teach and persuade" the public (35c)—right up to his first sip of the hemlock. Again, his refusal to recant here stands in dramatic juxtaposition to his pedagogy of dialectic recantation. This seeming contradiction disappears, however, when we understand that his dialectic recantation of pseudo consciousness was merely the means to a higher end: philosophical knowledge. He is as unwilling to recant this, and the pedagogical method of generating it, as he is willing to recant the pseudo wisdom of sophistry, which he does with pedagogical precision in his dialectics of recantation.

One by one, Socrates rejects the offer of a fine, imprisonment, and exile—if he will only recant the practice of philosophy, which would be tantamount to committing suicide, insofar as "the unexamined life is not worth living" (38a). For Socrates, knowledge is life—and knowledge of Self the goal not only of education but of life. As he asserts, "I would much rather die after making this kind of defense than live after making another kind," his only crime being that he "lacked . . . shamelessness and the willingness to say to you what you would most gladly have heard from me" (42e). Better to be caught by an honorific death than by shameful "wickedness"—like his accusers. Better to be "condemned to death by you" than "condemned by truth to wickedness and injustice" before a jury of posterity, their heads hooded in immortal shamefulness. Whereas Socrates feels honored by sophistry's condemnation of him, he sees shame in the verdict they have passed upon themselves—and feels confident posterity will share his verdict of sophistry, while acquitting his guilty verdict on appeal. His martyrdom is his appeal to posterity, which Plato litigates posthumously.

Dialectics is for Socrates the political weapon par excellence, as well as the means by which he avenged the injustices perpetrated against his oligarchic peers, the Athenian citizenry, and, in the end, his own slandered reputation. The very public nature of Socrates' elenchic defense underscores the social nature of his discourse in what is tantamount to a trial of one discourse by another. The transformative effect of Socratic inquiry upon sophistry is foreshadowed in the penultimate and prophetic words of his defense, when he prophesizes that "vengeance will come upon you immediately after my death." Socrates continues:

> [A] vengeance much harder to bear than that which you took in killing me. You did this in the belief that you would avoid giving an *account* of your life, but I maintain that quite the opposite will happen to you. There will be more people to *test* you. . . . They will be *more difficult to deal with* as they will be *younger* than you. . . . You are wrong to believe that by killing people you will prevent anyone from *reproaching* you for not living in the *right* way. To escape such *tests* is *neither possible* nor *good*. . . . With this *prophesy* to you who convicted me, I part from you. (39c–e)

The "feasibility" of this death-bed prophesy will be "tested" by Platonic invention in writing—even as the verities of Socratic inquiry and Platonic invention relative to sophistry will be successfully "tested" by posterity. In the final chapter, I hope to "test the feasibility" of a radical pedagogy predicated on a Socrates-Freire genealogy, moving into a neo-humanist pragmatism. With these prophetic words, however, Socrates is already damning his sophistic accusers (and sophistry) from beyond the grave, as if he has already foreseen those who will rise in his wake to carry on his work, holding sophistry to "account," continuing to "test" its claims, to hold its effects up to public scrutiny, to interrogate its dangerous implications, "reproaching" them for the excesses of power and discourse: tests it will be impossible to escape, conducted by people who will be even "more difficult to deal with," being "younger."

Socrates has already foreseen the career of Plato, whose presence he acknowledges during the trial, whose role as rightful heir he correctly intuits, as the nephew and cousin of two of his most infamous student-statesmen, Critias and Charmides, as the son of a woman, who like Aspasia, was a leading voice in his political cause. It is the passing of the torch from oral to written inquiry, each enacted under the sign of dialectic edification. From a Rankian perspective, the Socrates-Plato dyad evidences multiple dynamics of the master-pupil relationship on which Greek education, and our subsequent western educational system, is predicated. Those dynamics deeply inform the origins of the artistic impulse, and the educative impulse that is an expression of it. The dynamics of this master-pupil relationship also deeply inform the rebellious impulse to overthrow the master, in order to fulfill the imperatives of the pupil's own religion of genius. I will return to this theme in Chapter 7, "Plato and the Tyranny of the Transcendent," in an effort to open a "dilatory space" between pupil and master, that in effect severs the hyphen of Plato-Socrates, calling into question their respective views of an a priori knowledge that "comes before" language and memory. As Field observes, "even when actual physical danger was not a threat, the first sophists were assaulted by Socrates in an intellectual battle taken up with a vengeance by his student Plato—a battle with far-reaching social and political consequences" (63), as well as ontological and epistemological implications.

THE *PHAEDRUS* AS SOCIAL-EPISTEMIC PRAXIS

Commentary on the *Phaedrus* similarly reveals the social-epistemic nature of Socratic inquiry. Socrates' radical pedagogy is similar to Freire's with respect to its emphasis on analysis-into-action. Through critical analysis, his praxis seeks not just the mutual edification of Self and Other, but the exposure of rhetorical and political excesses as a means of resisting and reforming those excesses. Socratic and Freirean inquiry, alike, are characterized by the dialogic "unveiling" of a problematic reality, not as an end in itself, but as a first, necessary step toward transforming that reality toward a "more fully human" engagement with it. As Freire observes, "the more the people unveil this reality which is to be the object of their transformation, the more critically they enter that reality" (38). Civic engagement transforms political realities that are immutable sans such engagement, that serve the interests of ruling elites to the determinant of the common good. If for Socrates, the problematic reality his dialectic analysis sought to unveil was the manipulative effects of sophistic discourse and the excesses of sophistic power enabled by sophistic rhetoric, then for Freire the problematic reality to be unveiled and transformed was colonial oppression of the Other, and the signifying practices that enabled it. In the radical praxis of both Socrates and Freire, the goal was to transform subjugated objects into active subjects through inquiry into a problematic reality that fostered civic engagement with it, as a means of mitigating or eliminating its dehumanizing effects.

Freire's pedagogy is similarly focused on unveiling the manipulative effects of discourse, which perpetuate the oppression of people by providing the means for both the circulation and consolidation of power. His inquiry focuses on the complicity and corruption of the education system itself by unveiling the extent to which ruling elites use "'educational methods' . . . [to] deny pedagogical action in the liberation process . . . us[ing] propaganda to convince" (55). For Freire, the goal of dialogic praxis is twofold, insofar as "teachers and students . . . co-intent on reality, are both Subjects, not only in the task of unveiling that reality, and thereby coming to know it critically, but in the task of re-creating that knowledge" (56). This dual goal is deeply consistent with the aims of Socratic inquiry, which in the *Apology* and *Phaedrus* is intent on unveiling the problematic nature of sophistic discourse as a means of mitigating its dangerous effects, not merely individually but collectively, not merely in the agora, but in the courtroom, in the pursuit of "authentic" wisdom.

Freire's description of "teachers and students" as "Subjects" is significant insofar as it underscores the mutual agency relative to reality that is recuperated through his dialogic inquiry and insofar as it resonates with the mutual edification and agency that characterize the transformative master-pupil dyad in Socratic dialectics. The intent of Freire's liberatory praxis reinforces the thrust of Socrates' dialectic inquiry, insofar as it privileges a mutual engagement "in critical thinking and the quest for mutual humanization" (62), in which objects "acted upon" by reality become Subjects who act upon that reality in turn, through civic engagement. Here it is useful to recall Griswold's definition of dialectical inquiry, which seeks to determine the nature of a thing by unveiling its "capacity for acting on something else." Thus, Freire's "problem-posing education," like Socrates' interrogation of sophistry, "involves a constant unveiling of reality"—not as an end in itself, but toward the "*emergence of consciousness* and *critical intervention* in reality" (68).

Socrates' life-long critique of sophistry, culminating in his trial, constitutes a continuous "critical intervention" against the dehumanizing effects of a problematic reality, embodied in the propagandistic effects of sophistic rhetoric. Given its intent to liberate the objects of this discourse into an active, humanizing, signifying status as Subjects, it similarly configures "education as the practice of freedom" (69). To the extent Socratic inquiry rescues people, individually and collectively, from an inauthentic life as objects of domination (acting through sophistic discourse) to an authentic life as Subjects "engaged in inquiry and creative transformation" of their reality, it prefigures Freirean liberatory pedagogy (71).

In the *Apology*, as in the *Phaedrus*, Plato's Socrates "presents the very situation" to the people and the pupil respectively, "as a problem . . . an historical reality susceptible to transformation"—as evidenced in the language of his prophetic closing remarks, in which he foresees a reality transformed by those who will rise in his wake, in which his sophistic accusers will be held accountable, subject not only to further "testing," "reproaches," scrutiny, and analysis, but to "a vengeance much harder to bear" than that to which they have subjected him. "The object of action," for Socrates as for Freire, "is the reality to be transformed ... with other men" (83).

The linguistic nature of Socrates' analysis evidences its powerful alliteration with Freirean liberatory education: "Consistent with the liberating purpose of dialogical education, the object of the investigation is not men, but rather the *thought-language* with which men refer to reality ..." (86, my emphasis). Socrates, like Freire, seeks to unveil through analysis the "thinking" embodied in discourse, whether it is the debased intent of sophistic discourse to manufacture belief or Phaedrus' idolatrous view of sophistry. The thought-language of each is held up to critical analysis.

In the final analysis, the goal of each educative paradigm is liberatory. The "fundamental theme of our epoch" is the same as it was in Socrates' Athens: "that of domination—which implies its opposite, the theme of liberation, as the objective to be achieved" (93). To the extent they privilege critical inquiry and transformative intervention relative to a problematic, dehumanizing reality, the pedagogies of Socrates and Freire deeply inform one another.

Unveiling and intervention are the two defining aspects of each praxis. If we assume that the unveiling of reality is an intervention upon it, then analysis is not merely a precondition of action, but always and already an action in itself—in a pedagogy that is inherently an act of freedom, from its inception to its culmination, from the classroom to the community, insofar as the mere act of unveiling reality co-opts its ability to subjugate: draws a liberatory line in the sand between the Self and the signifying realities that would subjugate it. Critical analysis of a subjugating reality creates a liberatory firewall against its dehumanizing effects. Hence, the liberatory and transformative nature of Socratic inquiry and Feirean praxis: these kindred pedagogies of humanizing analysis, which integrate liberatory struggle against domination across 2,500 years.

The praxis of each proceeds from the assumption that the reality of domination, whether assuming the form of mass-manipulative signifying practices or structures of colonial oppression, is not a fixed situation that has unalterably closed upon itself to preserve and perpetuate itself, but a malleable and mutable complex of circumstances, subject to transformation, offering hope for a "more fully human" engagement with them. This is as true for Socrates as for Friere. Socrates would not have undertaken his life-long dialectic inquiry of sophistry if he did not believe it was subject to resistance, modification, or even eradication. The fact he had witnessed sophistry's growth from an emergent, if marginal, discourse during Pericles' reign to the dominant discourse of his middle and old age evidenced that it was subject to historical processes—not an unalterable given of reality. If the ideal of enlightened monarchy had become real during the reign of Pericles, it could become so again. Political reality is not immutable, but subject to change, as his own era had shown, as evidenced in the violent fluctuations in political reality from 427 to 399 BC, when three of Socrates' oligarchic pupils (Alcibiades, Critias, Charmides) rose to power, were corrupted by it, and were overthrown by their sophistic rivals. Thus, the cyclical nature of history belies the myth of its immutability.

Socrates, like Freire, commences with an analysis that unveils reality, that exposes it "not as a fixed entity, as something given—something to which men, as mere spectators, must adapt," but as a problem that can be solved, as a set of circumstances that can be engaged civically, in which reality is "perceived in the complexity of its constant 'becoming'" (Freire 99). Thus, the material conditions of oppression are unveiled not as immutable, but as malleable and therefore subject to actions arising from critical reflection upon them. As Freire asserts, "the starting point for organizing the program content of education or political action must be the present, existential, concrete situation. . . . we must pose this existential, concrete, present situation to the people as a problem which challenges them and requires a response . . ." (85): civic engagement. For Socrates, the "existential, concrete, present situation" that he poses to the people in his trial and to his pupil in the *Phaedrus* is the manipulative nature of sophistic discourse and its dangerous implications for the common good. This ancient focus has disturbing implications for our own historical moment in post "flash-crash" America, where we struggle with the effects of "disaster capitalism" so compellingly described in Naomi Klein's *Shock Doctrine,* including the manipulative effects of the discourse that enables its dehumanizing practices, the most violent of which is perhaps the diminished access of millions of citizens to the material benefits of democratic life: jobs, health care, and education.

Though the goals of Socratic praxis are as political as they are personal, as edifying as they are erotic, the centrality of the impulse to educate, of the desire for mutual edification, is evidenced throughout the *Phaedrus*. As Griswold asserts, "Socrates speaks repeatedly here of teaching (277e) and learning (277a, d)" (215). The educative model he practices, grounded in the master-pupil dyad, had philosophical, political, spiritual, and aesthetic connotations, inasmuch as it was not only a means of intellectual edification, political reform, and personal immortality, but it also gave to the artistic impulse its most sublime expression: in the mutual molding of Self and Other toward a living ideal of Greek humanity, which occurred within the educative paradigm. In a culture that valorized above all arts, the plastic mediums of sculpture and drama, education was seen as the most plastic art of all: its goal being the mutual shaping of Self and Other toward a sublime ideal of Beauty and civic duty. Griswold succinctly defines the focus and intent of dialectic analysis, which is

> to reflect on the nature of anything . . . and determine both its natural capacity for *acting on something else and its way of doing so.* . . . The steps of this rule-governed procedure are to be followed in a set sequence, that one must do this if one wants to make others scientific . . . and that the art is teachable. (191, my emphasis)

Sophistic discourse is analyzed in *Phaedrus* for its "capacity for acting on something else": public opinion, and through its manipulation of public opinion, to enable the actions of the state—and the various apparatuses it came to control: political, legal, military, ceremonial, and educational. Socrates' first two discourses in the *Phaedrus* are nothing if not an effective "knock-off" of sophistic discourse and a scathing analysis of its affective power relative to public opinion, of its "capacity for acting on something else and its way of doing so." The goal is to "make others scientific" as a means of arming them against the manipulative effects of sophistic rhetoric, wherein the state produces the support and approval it requires for its political and self-interested actions through a rhetoric of persuasion, grounded not in realities but in "resemblances" and perceptions. Socratic inquiry is a genealogical precursor of Freirean praxis insofar as it posits dialogical edification as the means of mitigating the subjugating effects of signification upon the subject.

The goal is not merely personal edification through rhetorical analysis, but political agency, insofar as such analysis mitigates the manipulative effects of sophistic rhetoric. Griswold underscores the centrality of analysis to this educative paradigm, noting that "in practice, analysis and (literally) education are inseparable" (200). Thus, education is always and already critical and political, as evidenced not just in our own time, but by Socrates' career, and by the *Phaedrus* in particular. As Griswold attests, Phaedrus "loves rhetoric but does not understand its deeply political function," as a means of shaping public opinion, and as the circulatory system for sophistic power (38). For Socrates, Phaedrus is a surrogate for the Athenian citizen, whom he would arm with the tools of critical analysis, by way of defending the polis from the dangerous affective powers of sophistic discourse. His praxis is truly radical insofar as it aims to subvert the unholy marriage between sophistic power and the power of sophistic persuasion.

Sophistic rhetoric is, as Griswold contends, the vehicle of the "tyrannical desire for power" (62)—it is the means by which the state controls its subjects, through the artful, mass manipulation of public opinion. Thus, dialectic analysis of rhetoric within the classroom acts as a check on its manipulative excesses beyond the classroom. As a pedagogy focused on the signifying practices of powerful elites and the adverse affect of sophistic discourse on the citizenry, relying on dialectic analysis to mitigate those effects, Socrates' radical pedagogy could not be more social-epistemic, either in its assumptions, goals, or methods. Sophistic rhetoric is the means par excellence of "social control" of the masses, through the skillful manipulation of public opinion.

In effect, Socrates takes the product of sophistic rhetoric (Phaedrus) and turns him back upon the sophists, as a surrogate philosopher, to disarm it. He knows Phaedrus is an "impressario" of discourse, signifying his acute sense of audience, who is as susceptible to a flow of rhetorical oratory as Socrates is to philosophic discourse. Phaedrus is a lightning rod for sophistic orators and thus an ideal choice for disseminating Socrates' resistant discourse at its point of contact with sophistry. The conversion to dialectic philosophy of an idolater of sophistry serves to underscore the superiority of the former to the latter. Socrates fights fire with fire, writing with oratory, and rhetoric with philosophy, first by giving a sophistic speech himself and second by converting a sophist into a philosopher in order to counter the effects of sophistry. Phaedrus' conversion metonymically signifies the conversion of the Athenian polis from an uncritical idolatry of sophistry to a philosophical critique of it, which, by shielding public opinion from the manipulative effects of sophistry, preserves the integrity of public opinion, as well as its grounding in realities as opposed to perceptions. As Griswold observes,

> Phaedrus is to serve as an intermediary between Socrates and the "opinion makers" of the city [the sophists]. Phaedrus must therefore be educated and equipped with the proper teaching to take back with him. Socrates would wish to upgrade the rhetoric of the opinion makers in order to save philosophy (and so himself) from condemnation by the city. . . . On this interpretation in sum, a strong political undercurrent prevails in the *Phaedrus*. (27)

Griswold's observations are instructive, for they illumine one of the central dramas of the *Phaedrus* and the era: the lethal political blood feud between democrats and oligarchs, sophists and philosophers: between Lysias, Meletus, Antyus et al. on the one hand, and Anaxagorus, Aspasia, Alcibiades, Critias, Charmides, Socrates, and Plato on the other, not one of whom was spared trial, exile, or execution. Even Plato's self-imposed exile to Syracuse in the wake of Socrates' trial and execution attests to the violence of sophistry—and his desire to distance himself from it.

Griswold's observation underscores the extent to which education was implicated and conscripted into this partisan political feud—as well as the extent to which sophistic rhetoric and philosophic discourse were alike inseparable from the political. There is, however, a personal as well as a collective aim to the political goals of Socrates' pedagogy. For Phaedrus represents not just the means of mitigating the excesses of sophistry, but of strengthening Socrates' own position philosophically and politically. As Griswold concludes: "Phaedrus is useful to Socrates as a conveyor to the city of a partial, politically useful defense of philosophy" (27).

The erotic theme of Lysias' speech is intended to dramatize the unethical nature and dangerous affective powers of sophistic rhetoric. The dialectical nature of Socrates' counter-arguments is intended to model the means by which the manipulative effects of sophistic discourse may be mitigated. Thus, by nature of its resistant, subversive, polemical, and liberatory orientation relative to sophistry, Socrates' pedagogy is not only inherently political and ethical, but decidedly resistant and radical.

This calls into question one of the primary critiques of Platonic discourse: that it serves the interest of the individual, not the polis, insofar as it is concerned exclusively with the pursuit of the truth and the edification of the Self. The truths it demonstrates, however, are always and already political, insofar as it seeks to dramatize the unethical and dangerous effects of the dominant discourse of the period, sophistry, and to liberate the citizen from the manipulative effects of this discourse. Socrates' own trial and execution is "Exhibit A" against the lethal effects of sophistic discourse, operating through the manipulation of public opinion: a fact of which he was no doubt aware and which undoubtedly fueled his impulse toward martyrdom, knowing it would do more than all his words combined to effect the ruin and damnation of the sophists and sophistic discourse. Socrates' life-long mission as a dialectical "gadfly" relative to the beast of the state evidences the synergy between the philosophical, the political, the spiritual, and the educational. His educative paradigm is not concerned with political ends alone, however.

The principal aim of Socrates' dialectic engagement with Phaedrus is neither erotic nor political, but the mutual edification of Self and Other. In countering Lysias' profane Eros, Socrates contends that "genuine love has a different goal: neither friendship as such, nor (still less) sexual gratification, but . . . the *common good* of the lovers" (94, my emphasis). Mutual edification is every bit as much the aim of dialectics as the pursuit of philosophic eros or the political transformation of reality. Yet, as Ferrari observes in *Listening to the Cicadas: A Study of Plato's Phaedrus*, the nature and terms of this "common good" are defined exclusively by Socrates, the dialectical master, and correspond precisely to his own self-interested desires for love, wisdom, and immortality, seemingly irrespective of the interlocutor's desires. This same critique has been leveled at practitioners of radical pedagogy, and though already addressed in Chapter 1, will be revisited in Chapter 8. The ethical concern for pedagogy is evidenced in Plato's subtitle to the *Phaedrus:* "on the Beautiful, Ethical." As Griswold observes, "the true teacher will aim for long term growth in the soul of the beloved" (214), not immediate sexual favors as does Lysias.

Thus, Socrates' dialectical workshop is configured to fulfill all three goals that define higher education today: personal edification or enrichment, preparation for a profession, and participatory citizenship. Like Isocrates, the profession for which his educative model prepared students was enlightened statesmanship, in the service of the common good—and in the spirit of the leader who was the living embodiment of the ideal Greek statesman and to whose inner circle Socrates belonged: Pericles. If in the mock trial of the *Antidosis,* Isocrates proudly cites the career of his prize pupil, the statesman-general Timatheus, to ennoble his pedagogy, Socrates distances his teaching from the oligarchic atrocities of his prize pupils, Alcibiades, Critias, and Charmides, with whose guilt he is nevertheless associated by the sophists, as evidenced by the accusation of "corrupting the youth of Athens": a corruption they attribute to his radical pedagogy. Socrates was very possibly mentored by Pericles' courtesan-muse-political mentor, Aspasia, as evidenced by the advice she gives to Plato's Socrates for gaining the "favors" of Alcibiades under the sign of philosophic eros. The centrality of the other two goals of Socrates' praxis (edification and participatory citizenship) is abundantly evidenced throughout *Phaedrus*.

SELF-KNOWLEDGE AND MUTUAL EDIFICATION

What is less clear, though no less significant, is the mutual edification that occurs within the dialectic, master-pupil dyad, and the edification of Socrates in particular. What form does this edification assume? As Griswold observes, "Socrates' desire to converse with Phaedrus stems from his desire for self-knowledge," which is the by-product of the violent struggle touched off in his soul by the profane and sacred desires awakened by the spectacle of the sublime, as embodied in Phaedrus' beauty and his love of beautiful discourse (214). Through his dialectical engagement with Phaedrus, Socrates comes to know the nature of his own divided soul, is precipitated into a violent struggle between the sophistic and philosophic, debased and honorific, profane and sacred halves of his soul. Hence, the immortal image of the "winged chariot," which dramatizes the divided nature and epic struggle that is waged anew in Socrates' soul as a result of his desire to edify: a desire prompted by the affective power of Phaedrus' beauty and love of beautiful discourse, whether as an orator or appreciative listener.

Under Socrates' tutelage, Phaedrus undertakes a dialectical journey from the baser to the loftier realms of his soul, which commences on the low road of the erotic in Lysias' discourse and his uncritical mimicry of it, and culminates on the high road of dialectical philosophy: into which the erotic, political, intellectual, and spiritual are absorbed in the harmonizing flight of dialectical discourse and the philosophic life it consecrates.

Through this epic struggle, precipitated by the beauty of the Other, Socrates comes to know himself anew: as one capable of living up to (and dying for) his philosophic ideals—as one who has mastered the baser impulses by which sophistry is driven: sex, violence, and power—all operating through a debased rhetoric of artful deception: which his dialectical analysis ruthlessly and relentlessly exposes, in the interest of the common good. Through dialectic discourse, Socrates does not merely argue the hierarchical oppositions between sophistry and philosophy, he acts them out, lives them out, for they are each deeply embedded in his divided soul. This is the central drama of *Phaedrus*, played out in the divided soul of Socrates and between the opposed discourses of sophistry and philosophy. This primal conflict between good and evil, sacred and profane, honorific and debased, philosophic and sophistic impulses within Socrates' divided soul, and between philosophy and sophistry, gives the dialogue its dramatic impetus: even as it shifts the locus of violence and conflict from the polis, the courtroom, and the battlefield to the human soul and the realms of discourse, from the military to the rhetorical arena, reinscribing the partisan blood-feud between sophistry and philosophy, democrats and oligarchs, Antyus, Meletus, and Lysias on the one hand and Critias, Charmides, and Socrates on the other. The conflict is resolved by the absorption of sophistic impulses into the philosophic life, and by the absorption of eros and logos into ethos, by the assimilation of the Beautiful in body and word into the Good, characterized by the mutual edification of Self and Other.

Despite the lofty aims of Socrates' dialectical analysis (edification, political reform), one can't help but wonder if it was driven by a darker agenda: for personal vengeance upon the sophists, for having destroyed his friends, ruined his reputation, and trampled underfoot the sophistic ideal of participatory government and the oligarchic ideal of enlightened monarchy. If Socrates' soul was indeed divided between profane and sacred impulses, as his trope of the "winged chariot" suggests, then an interesting question arises: to what extent was the ennobling philosophic impulse profaned by a desire for vengeance upon the sophists, and to what extent was his philosophic discourse tainted by sophistic signifying tendencies? If pedagogy is, as Freire asserts, always and forever political, to the extent it either perpetuates or resists the dominant ideology of the state, then to what extent were the reformist, altruistic goals of Socrates' radical pedagogy profaned by a personal and politicized desire for vengeance? I will revisit the ethical implications of his elenchus in "Love in a Time of War: The Ethos of Eros" (Chapter 8). For now, I want to extend the bounds of this genealogical map. Having mapped a genealogy of origins, goals, and assumptions, is it possible to map a genealogy of methods in the radical pedagogies of Socrates and Freire?

4 The Dawn of Analysis
The Method of His Madness

> Anal-y-sis: separation of a thing into the parts or elements of which it is composed, from Greek, from *analyein* to break up, from *ana* (up) + *lyein* (loosen).
>
> —*Webster* (43)

> Socrates: "There it is, Phaedrus! Do not listen to me any longer; let my speech end here."
> Phaedrus: "But I thought you were in the middle of it, and would say as much about the non-lover as you have said about the lover, to set forth all his good points, and show that he ought to be favored. So now, Socrates, why did you stop?"
>
> —*Phaedrus* (241d)

Of the *Phaedrus*' many critical cruxes that have incited debate, none is perhaps more problematic than its abrupt ruptures and discontinuities, and none of these is more striking than the sudden and significant shift from rhetoric to rhetorical analysis that occurs in the midst of Socrates' first mimetic speech. This abrupt rupture deeply informs the methodology of his elenchus inasmuch as it prefigures a generative sequence of recantations, each privileging a retrospective analysis. This method of analytical recantation is a defining feature of Socrates' radical pedagogy, operating as an internal meta-discourse within the broader discourse of philosophy's recantation of sophistry. Its radical critique of sophistic signifying practices is always and already a critique of sophistic power, which announces its genealogical affinity to Freirean praxis across two-and-a-half millennia insofar as it grounds the role of analysis, and particularly analysis of signifying practices, in the recantation of power that is the humanistic thrust of each radical pedagogy. Thus, in mapping the genealogy of Socrates and Freire, we discover affinities across the spectrum of their radical pedagogies: from their respective origins and assumptions, to their goals, methods, and "generative themes." Inquiry into their respective methodologies significantly extends the boundaries of this genealogical map.

A nexus of questions guides this inquiry into the respective methodologies of their radical pedagogies. To what degree does the methodology of each privilege *dialogic analysis of problematic realties* as a precondition for liberatory *transformation* of those realities? More specifically, what are the respective realities subjected to dialogic analysis in each praxis—and, finally, what are the *implications* of their respective interrogations for contemporary social-epistemic praxis?

This radical shift from rhetoric to rhetorical analysis, from sophistic discourse to analysis of sophistic signifying practices occurs when Socrates abruptly abandons his first speech as a work in progress. In mid-sentence, he drops the guise of sophist and becomes once again the dialectic philosopher, deconstructing the speech he has just delivered in a sophistic mode, exposing its numerous flaws: its plethora of clichés; its want of definition, division and classification, effective arrangement, and sound logic. This shift from imitation to interpretation performs in a metonymic moment the movement from sophistry to philosophy, prefiguring the broader protrepticus (or gradual turning of Phaedrus toward philosophy), of which it is a part. This abrupt shift from rhetoric to rhetorical analysis creates a rupture, or "dialatory space" as Brooks observes, in which critical reflection can occur—as it does in Freire's analysis of colonial pedagogy, which similarly leverages a liberatory space between colonizer and colonized through dialogic analysis of oppression and its effects. It further demonstrates the liberatory efficacy of the Word that names a problematic World, insofar as naming reality recuperates a measure of agency relative to that reality.

Socrates' radical rupture signifies not only the dawn of analysis, but the dawn of textual interpretation. It signifies as well a liberatory moment in the practice of freedom, insofar as it mitigates the affective power of signification with analysis of it, frees the citizen from the affective chains of signification into a liberatory agency relative to it. Analysis that disarms signification arms the citizen against it affective power, which is why such analysis is as humanistic as it is political. Socrates' radical pedagogy, like Freire's, posits the intellectual as a public intellectual, who uses analysis of problematic realties to speak truth-to-power on behalf of the common good.

Before he can convert Phaedrus from a sophist to a dialectic philosopher, Socrates performs his own conversion, models the protrepticus (the "gradual turning toward") on himself: mimicking Phaedrus' idolatry of sophistry by giving a sophistic speech, as a precondition for modeling dialectic analysis of it. A false Other-Other resemblance sets the stage for a genuine Self-Self alliteration under the sign of philosophic eros. This is also the essence of Freirean praxis, which similarly converts a self that is always and already political from its status as a silent, inauthentic object of power into an authentic signifying subject relative to power (and the power of persuasion). Enhanced participation in reality commences with the naming of it.

THE TRIAL OF SOPHISTIC SIGNIFICATION

Though Socrates' Grand Inquisition into sophistry commences in earnest when he prematurely ends his sophistic speech, it has been foreshadowed from the start—indeed, from his first words, which herald the movement from sophistry to philosophy: "Where do you come from, Phaedrus my friend, and where are you going?" (227a). The question not only establishes the interrogative mode of the dialogue, in a dialogue that will interrogate the nature of sophistry, love, madness, knowledge, the soul, and rhetoric itself, but the movement from idolatry of discourse to analysis of it, from an erotic rhetoric to dialectic Eros, from sophistry to philosophy. Finally, Socrates' opening words foreshadow his final words: "Let us be going" (279c): signifying the solidarity of master and pupil, the mutual edification of self and other in their movement toward a dialogic philosophy, which is always and already a process of self-becoming, a work-in-progress, whose birth has been depicted but whose final destination is implied rather than dramatized. The *Phaedrus*, as a model of radical pedagogy, is more concerned with the dramatization of the process of critical edification rather than with the product of it—which is why it is of such pedagogical import to contemporary educators, and to social-epistemic praxis in particular. The edification it models is never depicted as an outcome, but always and already as a *becoming*. In this, it prefigures Freire's recantation of colonial domination through analysis of its mechanisms, signifying practices, and effects.

Perhaps most significantly for the first-year writing teacher, this rupture between rhetoric and rhetorical analysis, and the opening question that hints at this critical movement, allegorizes the desired movement of the first-year student from a similar uncritical idolatry toward a critical interpretation of texts (and rhetoric). In the *Phaedrus,* the most critical moments of the dialogue occur in those ruptures between rhetoric and rhetorical analysis, each enacting an ironic and transformative recantation of what has been written, spoken, or signified: a series of recantations, all the more ironic given Socrates' repeated refusal to recant his elenchus in the *Apology*. If in his trial, he refuses to recant the philosophic for the sophistic, in *Phaedrus* he does just the reverse: recants the sophistic in favor of the philosophic. This strategy of recantation is fundamental to the rhetorical and pedagogical strategy of the *Phaedrus*.

If in the *Apology,* Socrates turns his trial into a trial of sophistry, in the *Phaedrus* he continues this prosecution. His early and effective use of irony, satire, and imagery prefigures the dialectical critique of the second speech, launching the progression of recantations that spiral upward in a gyre of critical cognition. The diverse signifying practices that reinforce the dialectic recantation of sophistry (myth, meta-drama, mimicry, history, irony, allegory, satire, and erotic innuendo) evidence the rich rhetorical complexity of the *Phaedrus*. Polemically, Plato is rectifying the injustice of a real trial with the avenging justice of a fictional trial, in which those who executed Socrates for the unethical ("corrupt" and "impious") effects of his teaching are themselves depicted as using the education of youth for unethical ends (the seduction of Phaedrus by Lysias). Moreover, Plato "probably had personal knowledge of many of the cases of bribery, confiscation, and judicial murder preserved for us in the orations of Lysias" (Shorey 5). As Shorey observes,

[Plato] was entirely willing to parody and satirize the Philistine banality and poverty of ideas of the successful lawyer and popular logographer. This he does in the *Phaedrus*, probably written soon after Lysias' death. . . . Plato associated this degeneracy with far-reaching philosophies of *negation*. (32, my emphasis)

This statement is significant for it underscores the high stakes of Socrates' and Freire's counter-hegemonic analyses of power, which undertake to convert the *negation* of the self into an affirmation of the self, by altering the material conditions of reality that inhibit self-affirmation, including the affective power of sophistic persuasion and colonial signification.

The movement between rhetoric and rhetorical analysis is the dominant pattern of the *Phaedrus* and commences when Socrates, after listening to Phaedrus recite Lysias' text from memory, delivers his own critical analysis of it, systematically dismantling Lysias' text, narrating a litany of its rhetorical abuses. His, "Oh, noble Lysias!" is an ironic critique of the sophist's thesis that "favors ought to be granted rather to the non-lover than to the lover" (237b). Lysias' discourse is a not only a shining example of the debased ends sophistic rhetoric serves (sexual seduction), but a compelling example as well of its affective power on the audience, as evidenced by Phaedrus' idolatry of it: a metonym for the affective power sophistry exerts on the Athenian citizenry, who "loved oratory to their ruin." Socrates clearly has his work cut out for him.

He begins by observing that Lysias repeated himself "two or three times, as if he did not find it easy to say many things about one subject," due to a damning paucity of ideas (235a). Socrates argues that his rival's speech lacks invention and originality, consisting as it does of clichéd, "inevitable arguments" that praise "the non-lover's calm and blame the lover's unreason" (236a). He then proposes to give a sophistic speech that trumps Lysias'. Having already used satiric irony and imagery, Socrates resorts to an allegory, which rips away the lamb's guise of the Lysian "non-lover" to reveal the wolf of the lover for what he really is. He begins his own first speech by shrewdly allegorizing Phaedrus' wooing by Lysias: "there was once upon a time a boy . . . of *great beauty*: and *he had many lovers*. And among these was one of peculiar *craftiness* [Lysias] who was as much in love with the boy as anyone, but had made him believe that he was not in love [in order] that favors ought to be granted rather to the non lover than to the lover" (236c).

Socrates' argument is all the more ironic given the trumped-up charges of "corrupting the youth of Athens" for which he was tried and executed. What could be more "corrupting" than using rhetoric to seduce a youth one purportedly does not love, than using rhetoric not for ethical but erotic ends? In the *Phaedrus*, Socrates puts Lysias on trial, bringing the same charge that was brought against him: using rhetoric to corrupt the youth of Athens—as if indeed, *Phaedrus* was written with a vengeance by a pupil to effect the eternal acquittal of his philosophic exemplar and the immortal damnation of his sophistic accusers, fulfilling Socrates' prophetic curse in the climactic moments of the *Apology*.

Socrates' opening critique of Lysias' sophistry is significant for multiple reasons. First, to the extent Socrates is allegorizing Phaedrus, it underscores Phaedrus' "great beauty," which is furthered evidenced by the fact "he had many lovers." Second, the charge of "craftiness" sustains the critique of sophistry as the practice of rhetoric for debased ends (manipulation of public opinion, gratification of erotic desires, etc.), again dramatizing the hypocrisy of the accusations made against Socrates during his trial, whose discourse was similarly faulted for its "craftiness." It further exposes the hypocrisy of Lysias' discourse, insofar as it puts the lie to Lysias' claim of being a "non-lover," whereas in fact "he was as much in love with the boy as anyone" (237b).

This rhetorical unmasking prefigures not only the intent, but the strategy of the entire dialogue, insofar as Socrates' dialectical discourse not only unmasks the ethical and logical limitations of sophistry, but does so through a series of masks adopted by Socrates, which are subsequently and sequentially removed to heighten Phaedrus' powers of dialectical analysis. Finally, in its unmasking capacity, dialectic analysis prefigures the "unveiling" of reality by dialogic analysis in Freire's liberatory praxis.

Socrates exposes his rival's speech as a masterpiece of debased deception: debased because its end is mere physical seduction and the means it uses to achieve this end is deception, is false representation of oneself (as a non-lover). Yet, in his own first speech, Socrates dons the mask of sophistry to "woo" Phaedrus away from Lysias—even as Plato has donned the mask of Socrates' persona. Though Socrates indicts the deceptions of sophistic rhetoric, he is not above using deception himself, even to the point of donning the mask of sophistry to expose its flaws. This calls into question the ethos of his own discourse, an issue I will take up at greater length in chapter 8 "Love in a Time of War: The Ethos of Eros." As Socrates asserts, Lysias advocates a debased rhetoric that uses reason to sate sexual appetites, observing that "when desire irrationally drags us toward pleasures and rules within us, its rule is called excess." Further, it is the precise opposite of philosophic "love," which Socrates defines as the "victory" of rationality over pleasure by virtue of a "self-restraint" that leads "toward the best," not the debased (238a–b). This epic struggle between rationality and pleasure, restraint and impulse is the central conflict of the dialogue, even as it reinscribes the war in Socrates' divided soul between the light and dark horses of reason and passion. Socrates continues his critical dissection of Lysias' text. As a form of persuasion, it lacks both "clearness and consistency" as a consequence of failing to define key terms, such as "love" and "madness." A want of division and classification ("dividing things . . . by classes," 265e), contributes to its confusion and discontinuity.

Abruptly switching hats from rhetoric to rhetorical analysis, Socrates models the centrality of division and classification to analysis by analyzing the nature of madness, in support of his counter-argument that, with respect to love, madness is a blessing, not a curse. He breaks madness down into "two kinds . . . one resulting from human ailments, the other from a divine disturbance" (265a). He then breaks down the second "kind" into "four types": consisting of the madness of the "prophet," the "mystic," the "poet," and the "lover." In keeping with the true nature of the Greek concept of "analysis," Socrates "loosens up" fresh, contradictory meanings from Lysias' reductive notion of madness as pathological derangement. He reinforces his analysis of madness with his analysis of "types of soul," again demonstrating the centrality of division and classification to analysis. In this analysis, Socrates will

> Classify the types of discourse and the type of soul, and the various ways in which souls are affected . . . suggesting the type of speech appropriate for each type of soul, and showing what kind of speech can be relied on to create belief in one soul and disbelief in another, and why. (271b)

Socrates' crash course on analysis is edifying both personally and politically to the extent it fosters self-knowledge and collective resistance. Socrates proceeds from an analysis of the nature of madness and love to an analysis of the nature of justice (272d). To the extent it fosters analysis ("the breaking down of a whole into its constitutive parts"), division, and classification is fundamental to critical thinking in the western cognitive tradition. Unfortunately, teachers have "over-learned" this aspect of classical rhetoric, resulting in pedagogies that place a reductive emphasis on division and classification (thesis and subheads) to the exclusion of rhetorical complexity. The writing that often results is but a reductive caricature of its ancient, analytical precursor, sans the effective use of the diverse tropes that comprise the *Phaedrus'* sophisticated web of signification: figuration, mask-wearing, erotic innuendo, peroration, and climactic arrangement, to name but a few. Each reinforces the dialectic recantation, in a signifying web that enriches the polemical complexity of the *Phaedrus*. Yet in its translation into the first-year writing sequence, this rhetorical complexity is often reduced to an emphasis on division and classification and the tripartite emphasis on invention, arrangement, and finish. Yet, the fault lies less with classical rhetoric than with the appropriations of interpretation.

In his breakdown of Lysias' text, Socrates further observes that it lacks "arrangement," insofar as "the parts of the discourse are thrown helter-skelter" (264b). As such, it violates virtually every aesthetic principle of effective composition, whether written or spoken. In this regard, Lysias' text bears an ironic, uncanny resemblance to Plato's composition of the *Phaedrus,* which similarly breaks every Socratic rule of "beautiful" composition—signifying the eruptive tensions between master and pupil. Here again, the *Phaedrus* deconstructs itself: its logic is Socratean, but its composition is Lysian, as it veers erratically among contradictory discourses, at times employing the sophistic signifying practices it purportedly critiques.

In his analysis of love and madness, Socrates argues that Lysias proposes a kind of "left-handed love, which is very justly reviled" (266a), inasmuch as it is divorced from passion, of which the lover's madness constitutes genuine proof of love. Further, it is predicated on "the big lie": that it is better to love a non-lover than a lover. The fact that Phaedrus is holding Lysias' speech in his left hand reinforces Socrates' characterization of it as a "left-handed love." As a symbol, the left hand was traditionally associated with thieves and liars: the left hand of thieves was cut off, while the sinner to the left of the crucified Christ was unredeemed. In pagan nature-worshipping societies, such as ancient Greece, occult rites of purification required some talisman of the victim, such as "the criminal's hand . . . called the 'Hand of Glory' . . . derived linguistically from mandragore," (Firor 113), and further associated with the mandrake, believed to sprout beneath the gallows, nourished by the victim's blood. Similarly, to purify Phaedrus from the corrupting influence of sophistry, Socrates requires some talisman of the "defendant/criminal" (Lysias). This he finds in the sophist's speech, not only consecrating a "left-handed love," but held in the left hand of Phaedrus. Lysias' speech thus becomes an emblem of the "pharmakos," whose poison is introduced into Phaedrus' psyche through the ear, by the cunning tongue of Lysias. As a talisman that possesses the "magical efficacy of anything connected with" the sophistic word-wizard, the text of Lysias' speech replicates the role of artifacts in pagan "corpse cures": the "hangman's rope, pieces of gibbet, gravestone chips, graveyard mold, pieces of shroud" (Firor 112).

The "pharmakon" of Lysias' text is used by Socrates to effect the philosophic awakening of Phaedrus through a ritual of analytical purification, replete with ceremonial gestures (covering of the head, invocations to the gods, displays of "divine frenzy," etc.). Lysias' text alliterates with these pagan talismans of purification and regeneration in another sense. As Firor observes, "[l]egends of the mandrake and of the 'Hand of Glory' are closely connected with love potions"(115). This is significant insofar as it is principally as an instrument of Phaedrus' seduction, as a kind of love potion (exploiting Phaedrus' love of beautiful discourse, and especially discourse about love) that Lysias deploys his sophistic rhetoric. As a species of "left-handed love," Lysias' text profanes the alliteration between Eros and Logos, corrupting both to satisfy sexual desires.

The seeming inscrutability of the *Phaedrus* is due to its rhetorical complexity, to its blurring of the bounds between sophistry and philosophy, erotic and philosophic love, honorific and debased rhetoric, and finally, Socrates and Plato. Socrates' discourse dramatizes the dialectic, oppositional tensions between two rhetorics—indeed, it embodies the conflict between sophistic and philosophic rhetoric: at times emphasizing dialectics, at times giving voice to a full-throated eroticism, at times proceeding by reason, and at times seemingly bent on revenge. Throughout the *Apology* and the *Phaedrus,* Socratic discourse dramatizes the violent fluctuation between analysis and passion, between the loftier and baser impulses of his divided soul, between the sacred and the profane: between impulses oriented toward mutual edification, philosophic love, and humanistic reforms, on the one hand, and impulses fueled by eroticism and revenge on the other, evidencing the very sophistic signifying practices he is indicting. Socrates' tendency toward rhetorical overkill in both dialogues evidences this fall from rhetorical grace, dramatizes perhaps the central conflict in each (the violence of Socrates' divided soul), even as it informs the "dilatory space" opened by the tensions between master and pupil.

The portrait of Socrates that Plato hands down to posterity in the *Apology* and *Phaedrus* is not entirely flattering. On the one hand, this may be nothing more than an effort to humanize the exemplar, by portraying him to posterity with "warts and all"—may reflect nothing more than a desire to embody the ideal in the real, to achieve a more balanced, true-to-life portrait. On the other hand, it might signify something darker, that has deeper implications for our reading of both texts, that indeed opens a "dilatory space" between Plato and Plato's Socrates, in which Plato's immortalizing defense of Socrates is always and already a critique of his elenchus, evidencing a philosophic split between master and pupil that deeply informs the themes of guilt, shame, and recantation that course through the dialectic discourse, shedding fresh light on "Plato's" attack on writing, and on the sophistic tendencies of Socrates' polemic and Platonic invention. This turn toward rhetorical overkill merits closer scrutiny.

REVENGE AND RHETORICAL OVERKILL: THE MEGALEGORIC TURN

At this stage, Socrates' critique gives way to rhetorical excess, or overkill. In his divided soul, the balance tips from reason to passion (and particularly, to a passion for vengeance upon the sophists), as dialectical analysis devolves into a megalegoric rhetoric of boastful arrogance or "big talking," reinscribing the rhetorical excesses of his defense in the *Apology.* The reasoned constraint of the light horse is supplanted by the eruptive passion of the dark horse of his soul. As critics assert, this "unbecoming," "boastful," "arrogant," "imprudent," and "ill-considered" tone violates one of the foremost principals of effective rhetoric: "kairos," in which the word is suited to the circumstances. This "megalegoria" or "boastful arrogance" is evidenced in the tone with which Socrates confronts his accuser, Meletus, in effect shaming him before the public jury.

In his interrogation of Meletus, Socrates takes off the rhetorical gloves, adopting a combative, accusatory, even bullying tone. Meletus' accusation of "corrupting the young" is tantamount in Socrates' view to malicious prosecution, to "dealing frivolously with serious matters [and] irresponsibly bringing people to court" (24c). He calls out his foremost accuser directly: "Come here and tell me, Meletus . . . you say you have discovered the one who corrupts them, namely me, and you bring me here and accuse me to these men" (24d). Socrates continues his cross-examination, which sustains his life-long critique of sophistic power, operating through the power of persuasion. His blood is up for the rhetorical combat: "You see, Meletus, that you are silent and know not what to say. Does this not seem shameful to you and a sufficient proof of what I say?" (24e).

Critics have argued that Socrates commits a tactical blunder in this interrogation, whose combative rhetoric is counter-productive to a verdict of acquittal. As Stone observes, "the tone he adopted . . . was offensively boastful and arrogant. That is what *megalegoria* ('big talking') meant" (184, my emphasis): a term that "Fielding renders as 'unbecoming and imprudent'; Todd as 'rather ill-considered.'" As Stone concludes, Socrates "looks more like a picador enraging a bull than a defendant trying to mollify a jury" (186).

Perhaps blinded to the pitfalls of his interrogation by "megalegoria," Socrates presses Meletus with his cross-examination: "And I alone corrupt them? Is that what you mean?" To which Meletus calmly responds, "That is most definitely what I mean" (25b). In classic dialectical style, Socrates tries to use Meletus' own words against him, by deploying an analogy. He asks if Meletus' reasoning applies as well to horses: "that all men improve them and one individual corrupts them" (25b). By virtue of his respectful, if grandstanding, ripostes to Socrates' bellicose and bullying questions, Meletus appears to come off the better for the exchange. Socrates' conclusion to this cross-examination, perhaps delivered as an aside to the jury, strikes the same tone of rhetorical overkill: "He seems to have made this deposition out of insolence, violence, and youthful zeal" (27a).

It is not difficult to imagine the jury's empathy swinging from the defendant to the accuser, further eroding Socrates' chances of acquittal. As Brickhouse and Smith observe, "it is not uncommon for scholars to suggest that this argument is in some way unfair to Meletus" (117)—and therefore counter-productive in the quest for a verdict of acquittal. They find Socrates "guilty" of rhetorical excess. Brickhouse and Smith continue:

> There is virtual unanimity in [scholars'] assessments of Socrates' interrogation of Meletus: Socrates, they say, makes no attempt to refute the specific charges, but demonstrates his own dialectical ability to "entrap" Meletus into confusion and contradiction. . . . the discrediting of Meletus seems to be all that Socrates intends to achieve through the interrogation. . . . Moreover, the interrogation is unmistakably similar to the elenctic refutations Socrates has always employed with such devastating efficiency against others who claim to be wise when

they are not. . . . And if the elenchus is taken to demonstrate only a contradiction in his opponent's assertions, and not the truth or falsity of individual propositions, it is difficult to see how the interrogation could possibly result in a proof of Socrates' innocence of the formal charges. (112–113)

—or how philosophic rhetoric is any different from sophistic rhetoric, serving the debased ends of vengeance, as Lysias' text serves the debased ends of sexual desire and Meletus' deposition the debased ends of a malicious prosecution. Socrates, it appears, is more interested in publically "discrediting" his opponent than he is in arguing the merits of the case, in refuting the charges against him, in speaking truth to power. By engaging in these "slick dialectical skills," he only reinforces the jury's prejudice regarding his reputation as a "clever speaker": in other words, as a sophist in the guise of a philosopher, as a wolf in lamb's clothing.

If nothing else, Socrates' "megalegoria" evidences the intensity of the struggle in his divided soul between reason and passion, between the search for knowledge and the thirst for vengeance, between its honorific and debased, sacred and profane impulses—again embodied in his own trope of the winged chariot of the soul, whose charioteer is struggling to reconcile the opposed strengths of the light and dark steeds. The violent struggle in Socrates' soul, incited from the moment he lays eyes on Phaedrus, hiding under his cloak a sophistic text, quickened by the effect of Phaedrus' beauty upon his beauty-loving soul, is perhaps the central drama of the *Phaedrus*, reinforcing the rhetorical combat between sophistry and philosophy waged between Lysias and Socrates. His megalegoric outburst in the *Apology* may signify the eruptive force of repressed passions, through the constraining force of his reason, even as Freire's interrogation of colonial power may signify the eruptive force of the "political unconscious" (Jameson), enervated by an insurrectional, vengeful, liberatory impulse embodied in his dialogical analysis of colonial domination.

RE-DIRECT: IN DEFENSE OF SOCRATES' MEGALEGORIA

Having recapitulated criticism's indictment of Socrates' "megalegoria" in the *Apology*, Brickhouse and Smith proceed to problematize and refute it, in a compelling argument that demonstrates the ways Socrates' interrogation of Meletus is entirely consistent with a direct defense of the formal accusations, with an assumption that he took "the charges seriously," as evidenced by his repeated avowals to the jury that he is "hopeful that his defense will succeed" (19a2–4). As Brickhouse and Smith assert,

Such behavior would not only be impudent in the extreme, it would constitute an unnecessary incitement to the jury to follow prejudice instead of the law, and thus to come to a verdict that was both inappropriate and immoral. It would make little sense, then, were Socrates to dismiss the formal accusations and to use his opportunity to question Meletus only to make an ironical or rhetorical point, having already expressed his recognition of the danger posed to him by the formal accusations and his desire for his defense to be successful. Yet such verbal trickery is precisely what the established view portrays Socrates as employing in his interrogation of Meletus. (114)

Further, by using the occasion for any purpose other than "to convince his fellow Athenians"—especially those of the jury who confuse philosophy with sophistry—that he has done no wrong, "he would convict himself of impiety for having disobeyed the command of the god" that inspired his dialectic mission: in essence, proving one of the charges against him.

Brickhouse and Smith then delve below the "boastful arrogance" of Socrates' megalegoria to evidence the efficacy of his dialectical defense of the charges during his cross-examination of Meletus. His reasoning against the charge of "corrupting the youth," conveyed through the metaphor of horse training, in effect implicates all Athenians in the charge. As Brickhouse and Smith conclude, "if the jury is to convict Socrates on this ground, they must convict virtually all Athens as well" (118). Brickhouse and Smith show how, point by point, Socrates deconstructs Meletus' accusations, evidencing not the sorcery of sophistic discourse, but the efficacy of dialectical reasoning. If the tone is, in places, megalegoric, the reasoning is purely dialectic; if the former violates a sense of ethos, the latter is a successful appeal to logos.

Is there not perhaps a third way to "read" Socrates' megalegoria, which reconciles the seeming incompatibilities of these two interpretations—that rejects the seeming binary opposition they proffer between dialectics and "boastful arrogance?" To what extent do these two rhetorics of Socrates (megalegoria and dialectics) cancel each other out—and more significantly, to what extent are they the inevitable expression of a divided soul: of a soul halved by its sacred and profane tendencies toward philosophy and passion, edification and eroticism, reason and revenge?

Indeed, the conflicting discourses to which Socrates gives voice in the *Apology* evidence the deep division in his soul to which his discourse gives voice in the *Phaedrus,* with which it is entirely consistent. His entire philosophical polemic is an attempt to embody, if not reconcile, these deep divisions in his soul between logos and eros, reason and passion, sophistry and philosophy. Under the sign of philosophic eros, the profaned eroticism of Lysias' sophistry is absorbed into the sacred eros of Socrates' philosophy—in which the path to logos leads to and through eros, in which knowledge is the by-product of love: a love inseparably yoked to the liberatory edification of the Other, for Socrates, as for Freire.

This conflict is dramatized in the *Apology* and the *Phaedrus*. Time and again, Socrates' reason gives rise to a bullying bravado during his defense that gives back the ground he has gained. Indeed, Socrates' rhetoric in his interrogation of Meletus seems driven by two competing desires: to defend and to avenge the self. Indeed, Socrates' cross-examination of Meletus replicates the rhetorical circumstances of the *Phaedrus* insofar as it evidences his deeply divided soul, which is forever waging a struggle to reconcile its lowest and loftiest, its profane and sacred impulses. The temptations of revenge upon the sophists in the *Apology* are as affective as the temptations of eroticism, posed by Phaedrus' beauty and love of beautiful discourse in the *Phaedrus*, and an equally affective impulse toward revenge upon Lysias. As evidenced by the dual rhetorics of his interrogation of Meletus, Socrates is torn between the opposing agendas of acquittal and vengeance. Hence, the fluctuation between megalegoria and dialectics: the one giving vent to the anger in his blood, the other perpetuating his dialectical mission in defense of the accusations against him, which is intent on interrogating, if not destroying, sophistry.

The opportunity to avenge himself directly against his sophistic accusers in public is too good to resist: it is itself a kairic moment, par excellence. Socrates seizes the moment to reverse the tables and put sophistry on trial, then suits his rhetoric to this contingency. Though perhaps megalegoric and anti-kairic with respect to his immediate audience (the jury and the Athenian public), it is intensely kairic with respect to his absent audience: posterity—upon which he demonstrably keeps one eye throughout his defense.

As in the *Phaedrus*, the profane desire for revenge is too violent to control, gains mastery of his soul in these megalegoric moments, only to be reined in anew by the impulse toward dialectics. The rhetoric of the interrogation enacts the same central drama of the *Phaedrus*, insofar as it prefigures the conflict between the soul's profane and sacred desires, for political revenge and dialectic edification respectively, as well as between eroticism and edification. That Socrates' polemic in the *Phaedrus* is also an attempt to work off the sexual impulses aroused by the beautiful and beloved pupil is evidenced by the erotic imagery that proliferates when he performs his "divine frenzy" as evidence of his genuine love—speaking of course in general terms, regarding the affective power of the erotic sublime on the lover. The phallic overtones of the plumed quills figuratively dramatize the violence of the erotic sublime on Socrates, prefiguring by two-score centuries the dual affective power of the sublime, to incite terror or ecstasy in the beholder, as theorized by Grey, Wordsworth, Ruskin, and Proust.

These passages of the *Phaedrus* evidence the tension between the profane and sacred impulses of Socrates' soul, embodied respectively in a rhetoric of seduction and of dialectics, inspired respectively by his passion and his reason, by desires that are by turn erotic and edifying. In the *Apology*, Socrates unmasks the debased rhetoric of his accusers with the right hand of dialectics, even as he gives the dagger-thrust a twist with the left hand of "megalegoria." One soul-steed is not given its head at the expense of the other; both alternately assert their strength in a discourse that reflects and dramatizes the eternal tension in his soul between reason and passion, philosophic and erotic love.

Socrates' speech, like Hamlet's, is a double-speaking discourse, adapted to the lethal and vengeful circumstances of the tribunal. Like Hamlet's discourse in the meta-dramatic trial of The Mousetrap, and in the perpetual interrogation he conducts into the crimes of Claudius, Socrates' megalegoric dialectics in the trial-within-the-trial he stages is similarly intent on avenging the truths it unmasks. Hence, the symbiosis between megalegoria and dialectics, vengeance and logos.

Thus, in contradistinction to the "either-or" interpretations of Brickhouse and Smith and the earlier critical tradition they problematize, I prefer a "both-and" reading of Socrates' cross-examination of Meletus, which is informed by the dual discourses of revenge and dialectics, whose alternation dramatizes the duality of Socrates' soul and the contradictory division within it. The rhetorical pendulum swings from the dialectics of Socrates' interrogation to the vengeful elements of it, in a reading that both recuperates and revises the interpretations of two earlier critical traditions. Far from being "committed to promoting the jury's performance of its proper legal function by telling the truth relevant to the question of his guilt or innocence of the charges," as Brickhouse and Smith contend (115), I believe Socrates realizes the jury is rigged from the outset, as a consequence of the long-standing prejudices against him, which have gone unchallenged most of his life. Therefore, any attempt at earning an acquittal from this jury is futile. He is intent, not on arguing the merits of his case, but on exposing the perfidy of his accusers' sophistic rhetoric and the extent to which the justice system has been corrupted by it: by its ability to sway opinion to serve its own debased partisan ends, to rig the system so that a defendant has no chance to confront his accusers directly, and so that charges may be brought and verdicts attained with virtually no evidence to justify either accusation or verdict.

This is the problematic reality that Socrates' dialogic analysis in the *Apology* seeks to "unveil," as a lethal precondition for radically transforming it. It is the reality of injustice, of a corrupt legal apparatus, that his dialogic analysis "unveils" and that the act of martyrdom transforms. He suffers injustice at the hands of the sophists to kill sophistry and injustice. The action that flows from this analysis is the sole act capable of fulfilling its liberatory promise and is as ruinous to these sophistic realities as it is redemptive for their victim. Socrates' interrogation of power in ancient Athens signifies the dawn of radical pedagogy, insofar as problematic realities are "unveiled" in order to be transformed by the civic engagement awakened from the transformation of public awareness.

If an acquittal is impossible due to the corruption of the Athenian justice system by the sophists who control every facet of it (who are prosecution, judge, and jury), why waste his breath—even in a dialectical critique? The answer is simple and reconciles the seeming contradiction in Socrates' rhetoric that has sparked such lively critical debate. Demonstrating the superiority of dialectics in direct rhetorical combat with sophistry not only is tantamount to a performative defense of his entire life, but it enacts his revenge as well. In other words, it satisfies both the profane and sacred desires of his soul for revenge and dialectics, by using dialectics as a medium of his revenge, while at the same time defending himself from the formal charges lodged against him. His interrogation of Meletus is indeed a controlled, deliberate, cunning execution of his dual desires for vengeance and truth, in which he gives free reign to one and then the other, giving vent by turns to a hot-blooded megalegoria and to a cold-blooded dialectical inquisition.

Indeed, at times in his megalegoric moments, Socrates is almost baiting the jury to render a guilty verdict, which he already knows to be a foregone conclusion, given the corruption of the Athenian justice system:

> I am unpopular with many people. This will be my undoing . . . the slanders and envy of many people. This has destroyed many other good men [he adds, thinking perhaps of his mentor, Anaxagoras, similarly tried and exiled on a charge of impiety] and will I think, continue to do so. There is no danger that it will stop at me. (28a)

His efforts to win an acquittal have been fatally handicapped by his inability to confront his accusers, to "bring one of them to court to refute him"—in short, by the impossibility of bringing to bear upon these "first accusers" the one weapon that might win his acquittal: dialectics. Instead, he "must fight with shadows, as it were in making one's defense, and cross-examine when no-one answers" (18d). Given his awareness of these prejudicial conditions, and his prescience of the outcome, why would he condescend to seek an acquittal—or to grovel for mercy by recanting his views? Instead, he uses his defense as an opportunity par excellence to indict the corruption of the Athenian justice system by sophistry and sophistic signifying practices, in the process "unveiling" it for the citizens present in the audience and the 500-member jury. He speaks truth to power, knowing it will not win him an acquittal, but knowing as well that it will effect the ruin of sophistic power once his words are converted to action in martyrdom.

If he can't defend himself with dialectics against these absent "first accusers," he can use dialectics to defend himself against the more immediate charges of his "second accusers"—though not to win an acquittal, which is further handicapped by two facts: the long-standing nature of the jury's prejudice against him and the want of time to reverse it. As Socrates observes, he has but a "short time" with which to "uproot from your minds . . . the slander that has resided there so long" (19a). Given these realities, acquittal is never his goal. Since acquittal with honor is not possible, and acquittal with dishonor is beneath him, acquittal can never be the goal of his defense: only the vengeful unmasking of his accuser's perfidy, which he enacts through a rhetoric of megalegoric dialectics. The defense he mounts has two objectives, is the narrative of two desires: to unveil with dialectics the "wickedness" that has injured him and to avenge it with a rhetoric of megalegoria, intent on giving his accusers "their just deserts," in person and in public.

Thus, the inquisition of sophistry that Socrates conducts at his trial is merely the continuation of his life-long mission, which it brings to a fitting and dramatic climax. In the public tribunal they mount against him, the sophists have unwittingly handed Socrates the weapon of their own mass destruction, as well as the moral high ground in the ancient blood feud between sophistry and philosophy, between a corrupted democracy and a marginalized oligarchy.

As further evidence of his rhetorical complexity, Socrates uses myth metaphorically to claim the high moral ground in his trial, further demonstrating the vengeful nature of his elenchus in general, and his trial defense in particular. In his defense, Socrates invokes a mythical hero who is vengeance personified, Achilles. He does so within the context of a refusal to recant from his beliefs to gain a more favorable sentence, situating himself firmly in this ancient tradition of the revenge-minded protagonist: "He despised death and danger and was much more afraid to live a coward who did not avenge his friends" or give "the wrongdoer his just deserts ... a laughingstock by the curved ships, a burden upon the earth" (28d). Socrates boldly confronts his accusers as vengeance personified, resurrecting the ghost of Achilles, before hurling down at them from this moral redoubt the thunderbolts of his prophetic curse. Thus, even the evocation of Achilles evidences the megalegoric turn, adding a mythical twist to it. One can only wonder what effect these words had on his accusers. By resurrecting before their collective gaze the specter of vengeance personified (Achilles), Socrates may indeed have sent a shiver of premonition up their collective spine, reinforced by the courtroom spectacle of Socrates-as-the-incarnation of Truth-Speaking-to-Power, and prophesying its ruin.

As in the *Apology*, Socrates' polemic of sophistry in the *Phaedrus* is guilty of similar rhetorical excesses, or megalegoric overkill, which undermines somewhat the credibility of his dialectic analysis. Yet, even in this, Socrates' argument is instructive for composition students and teachers alike, insofar as it dramatizes the dangers of arguing extreme positions—which by definition resist the rationale. His tendency to use sophistic signifying practices to destroy sophistry evidences the predatory, if not hypocritical, irony of his argument. It perhaps evidences, as well, a sadic impulse toward his sophistic rivals, rooted in a desire to do violence to those who would do violence to him—and who did violence to his former mentors and pupils (Anaxagoras, Aspasia, Alcibiades, Critias, and Charmides).

In the *Phaedrus*, as Socrates' critique of Lysias' text proceeds, analysis similarly gives way to rhetorical excess. A dialectics, which until now has served the light horse of reason, is usurped by the dark horse of revenge, as philosophy is prostituted by sophistic impulses in a rhetorical bloodletting.

Socrates asserts, for example, that sophistry reinforces "effeminate" qualities by privileging a beloved who is "not used to manly toils and the sweat of exertion" but "accustomed to a delicate and unmanly mode of life" (239c). Moreover, he argues that such a love will not only emasculate, but impoverish the beloved, by keeping him "bereft of the dearest and kindest and holiest of possessions" (239e). Further, this jealous and possessive Lysian lover, masquerading as a non-lover, will not only impoverish and emasculate, but also isolate the beloved by depriving him of "father, mother, relatives, and friends," keeping him "unmarried, childless, and homeless" (240a). In this manner will the old, lecherous, sophistic lover seek to control every facet of the youthful beloved's life. Resorting to rhetorical hyperbole, Socrates constructs Lysias as a paragon of the sophistic-lover-as-monster, warning that "he does not leave [the beloved] day or night," while being "suspiciously guarded in all ways against everybody" (240d–e)—the very incarnation of possessive desire. By virtue of these possessive behaviors, the sophistic lover is "not only unendurable, but disgusting" (240e). Effeminancy, sexual perversion, lechery, monstrosity, enslavement, stalking, and physical ugliness: Lysias as a sophistic lover is castigated under the sign of each.

Moreover, Socrates delivers this critique in the guise of the non-lover, who speaks with contempt of the Lysian lover, for he has pierced Lysias' pretense of indifference. Thus, he kills Lysias twice over: as an unethical non-lover and as a monstrosity of a lover, with a lethal impersonation of Lysias as both non-lover and lover. With violent brush-strokes, intended to frighten the beloved, Socrates continues his hyperbolic portrait of the old sophistic lecher-as-lover, who is given an "old, unlovely face" (240b–d) that is not only "unendurable, but disgusting" (240e). His portrait of the sophistic-lover-as-monster continues unabated. Who would want to be associated with such a "horrid creature [for] such creatures [are] extremely disagreeable to live with [being] driven by the sting of necessity [which produces] the utter most disgust" (240b–d). They are "unendurable," "wearisome," "faithless, irritable, jealous, and disagreeable, harmful to his property, harmful to his physical condition, and most harmful by far to the cultivation of his soul" (241c). In this scathing portrait of the sophistic lover, Plato's Socrates reveals the depth of his antipathy for Lysias' thesis and, by implication, for sophistic signifying practices. He reveals as well the rhetorical depths to which he will sink to give his rival his "just deserts," the rhetorical excesses to which he will resort to recant sophistry.

In this grotesque caricature of the sophist-as-lover, Plato exacts a measure of revenge against those who set themselves above Socrates at his trial, depicting their physical ugliness as an expression of an inward, ethical ugliness—hence the rhetorical excesses of Platonic vengeance, so evident here in Socrates' first speech. Socrates' rhetorical overkill is further evidenced by the fact he ranks "a sophist" near the bottom of his hierarchy of souls, on a par with a "demagogue" and just above a "tyrant" (248e). His hyperbolic attack on sophistic monstrosity reaches new heights (or lows) when

The Dawn of Analysis 77

he adds the accusation of sexual practices that range from the beast-like to the perverse, depicting the sophist as one "who gives himself up to pleasure and like a beast proceeds to lust and begetting; he makes license of his companion and is not afraid to pursue pleasure in *violation of nature*" (251a, my emphasis). If the monstrosities of the sophistic lover are not enough to dissuade Phaedrus, Socrates depicts the dangers of such a liaison for the beloved, which will damn him in the hereafter, by consigning his wingless soul "after three successive periods of a thousand years [and] . . . after the judgment . . . to the place of correction under the earth [to] pay [its] penalty" (249b).

In his megalegoric rhetoric, Socrates demonstrates that the affective power of philosophic discourse is no less violent than the affective power of sophistic rhetoric, in this evidencing its sophistic tendencies, its "peculiar intimacy" with sophistry—indeed, the extent to which it is indebted to sophistry for its own affective force. Philosophic discourse, no less than the sophistry it indicts, is not above hyperbolic fear-mongering to achieve it ends. Socrates, as evidenced by his megalegoric dialectics, is not above adopting a "stoops to conquer" strategy to defeat sophistry.

Perhaps Socrates' mimicry of sophistic discourse in his first speech, in order to woo Phaedrus away from his idolatry of it, infects his second speech, insofar as he deploys sophistic signifying practices in analysis of sophistic signifying practices. The guise of the sophist is not so easily shed, not so easily recanted. While recanting sophistry, he continues to use sophistic signifying practices, continues to use rhetoric for debased as well as honorific ends, for vengeance and erotic pleasure as well as for mutual edification and philosophic eros—for the erotic is never abandoned in Socrates' elenchus, but merely absorbed into philosophic eros. The sacred absorbs the profane. Thus, the megalegoric tendencies of Socrates' elenchus in the *Phaedrus* echoes the rhetorical overkill of the *Apology*, even as it calls into question the pupil's idolatry of the exemplar.

THE THEORY OF RESEMBLANCES: SOPHISTRY UNVEILED

> It follows, that anyone who intends to mislead another . . . must discern precisely the degree of resemblance and dissimilarity between this and that. . . . [W]hen people hold beliefs contrary to fact, and are misled, it is plain that the error has crept into their minds through the suggestion of some similarity or other.
>
> —Socrates (262a–b)

As in the *Apology*, Socrates' discourse in the *Phaedrus* alternates between the impassioned and the reasoned, between megalegoria and analysis, in his sustained indictment of sophistry's dangerous affective power. Having given voice to his megalegoric impulses, the rhetorical pendulum now swings back to dialectic analysis: to an examination of how sophistic signification works, of how it acts upon subjects to reduce them to the objects of its manipulative, partisan ends. He uses analysis to unveil the nature of sophistic discourse and the mechanisms by which it achieves its ends. Foremost among these is its mastery of a rhetoric of resemblances, which is used to persuade the multitude "to do evil instead of good"—as in the trial of Socrates (260c). He continues: "then he whose speaking is an art will make the same thing *appear* to the same persons at one time *just* and at another, if he wishes, *unjust*" (261c, my emphasis).

The statement is significant for it evidences Socrates' abiding concern with social justice and ethics, with the good and evil effects of rhetoric: a focus entirely in alignment with the tripartite focus of social-epistemic praxis on social justice, ethics, and signifying practices. Freire, for example, is similarly concerned with the way multitudes are reduced to objects who are acted upon to serve the interests of the state: "our advanced technological society is rapidly making objects of most of us and subtly programming us into conformity to the logic of its system" (14). Socrates thus attempts to educate the untutored Phaedrus regarding the affective power of the sophist, who endeavors to "lead his hearers on with sportive words" (262d), as if arming Phaedrus against its seductive power. Guided by his analytical precepts, which aim to discover the nature of a thing, what it acts upon, and how it acts upon them, Socrates applies these principles of analysis to sophistic rhetoric in an effort to discover and unveil the means by which it manufactures belief from opinion. His *Theory of Resemblances* unmasks the hidden processes by which sophistic persuasion operates, and through the teaching of it he arms the untutored citizen/pupil against the dangerous affective power of sophistic rhetoric.

As Socrates demonstrates, sophistic persuasion uses deceptions grounded in resemblances to the truth to manufacture the consent it needs for the policies and actions it favors, without regard for the public good or the truth. Deception in discourse is the art of making opinion resemble truth and making belief seem like knowledge. Such opinion or belief arises from its "similarity" to the truth. Where there is great and obvious dissimilarity between truth and opinion, the truth cannot be mistaken for opinion, and deception is therefore difficult to achieve. As Socrates notes, "in the case then of those whose opinions are at variance with the facts and who are deceived, this error evidently slips in through some resemblances" (262b).

Socrates' insights into the mechanisms of sophistic rhetoric are relevant to our own times, to the extent these same rhetorical strategies of plausible dis-information and mis-information are used to shape public opinion for state policies. For example, the government's argument to rally public opinion for the Iraq war made effective, if immoral, use of this rhetoric of resemblance, manufacturing "evidence" of the nuclear rods and "intelligence" of Iraqi informants to make it seem as if Iraq indeed possessed weapons of mass destruction or was intent on manufacturing them, though no evidence of either was ever presented or discovered. To rally public opinion for the claim that Iraq intended to use such weapons against America, a false resemblance was created between the "terrorist" state of Iraq and Al Qaeda, between Saddam Hussein and Osama bin Laden, the mastermind of the 9/11 terrorist attack—though in fact no evidence existed to support this claim. Yet, so effective was this false "resemblance" between Hussein and bin Laden that years later, a majority of citizens believe it is true.

This is but one example of the dangerous affective power of rhetoric across 2,500 years and the enduring need to analyze the claims and supporting evidence before assessing the validity of such rhetoric, given the catastrophic effects and implications for uncritically accepting such "belief" as "knowledge," whose toll can only be measured in blood and billions. The ubiquity today of this unholy alliance between power and the power of persuasion, operating through a rhetoric of resemblance, evidences the acuity and relevance of Socratic inquiry for our own representative democracy. The signifying practices of the state, operating through every form of media (print, television, radio, and Internet) and in every public forum (political, economic, religious, and educational), cannot be permitted to operate uncritically. To do so is not only to risk, but to guarantee a repetition of the catastrophes of the past, from the stock market crash of 1929 to the "flash crash" of the banking industry in 2008, from Vietnam to Iraq, from Watergate and Iran-Contra to Guantanamo and Abu Ghraib. It is the right and responsibility of every citizen, and every form of media, to subject this rhetoric of resemblance, its claims and evidence, to critical scrutiny, in an effort to distinguish "belief" from "knowledge" and "resemblance" from "reality" toward the practice of a democracy rooted not in resemblances but in realities. In this, citizens and educators can profit from the career of Socrates, whose public scrutiny and interrogation of state signifying practices (embodied in sophistic rhetoric) served a deeply civic ethos, as a rhetorical firewall against the excesses and abuses of power and the power of persuasion.

Ironically (and perhaps even hypocritically), the effective deception of Socrates' first speech is a function of its resemblance to Lysias' sophistic speech. The close resemblance between them facilitates the immanent deception. In fact, does not the efficacy of Socrates' protrepticus rely on a system of "resemblances" to turn Phaedrus from sophistry to philosophy: not only by giving a first speech that resembles Lysias' sophistic speech, in which a non-lover, Lysias, "resembles" a lover, after which Socrates will act in a manner that "resembles" madness to convince Phaedrus of the authenticity of his own love, in contradistinction to Lysias' counterfeit love. Thus, Socrates is not above using this same rhetoric of "resemblances" which he condemns in sophistic discourse, as practiced "in the courts ... public assemblages ... and political gatherings" (261b–d). Doesn't his very mastery of the sophistic tropes he decries put the lie to his assertion that "I possess no art of speaking" (262d)? For example, he castigates Isocrates (Lysias), while adopting in the *Phaedrus* Isocrates' definition of an effective rhetor, to whose "natural endowments [are] added knowledge and practice" (262d). As Ferrari observes, it is just this "deceptive resemblance" between sophistic and philosophic concepts of love that "allows Socrates to become so deeply engaged in his own emulation of Lysias' speech" (95). Their "peculiar intimacy" quickens his "antic" discourse, as an expression of the predatory aggressions of the self, for there is a "menace" to his mimicry, to borrow a phrase from post-colonial discourse coined by Homi Bhabha (qtd. in Griffiths et al. 75). Socrates' mimicry of Lysias' speech is the Trojan horse that penetrates Lysian discourse as a (pre)text for destroying it.

Socrates' critique of sophistry is systematic. Sophistic discourse is not only corrupt by virtue of the sexual perversion it serves and by its unethical tendency to argue either side of an issue, but by its mercenary nature: "pay them a royal tribute" (266c). It is a debased form of discourse because "probabilities are more to be esteemed than truths" (267b). Yet, of its many disreputable features, it is its affective power that Socrates most stridently attacks, whether it is the ability of "tearful speeches, to arouse pity for old age and poverty . . . [or for] rousing large companies to wrath, and soothing them again by charms . . . devising and abolishing calumnies on any grounds whatsoever" (267c). This affective power of sophistry comprises the most immediate danger because it has already turned Phaedrus' head away from philosophy and toward sophistry, as evidenced by his uncritical idolatry of Lysias' speech, which he not only holds fast against his breast but which he has memorized. If not physically, he has already been seduced mentally by Lysias' crafty discourse. And this sudden turn toward sophistry is what poses the immediate threat to Socrates' project of mutual edification.

Lysias' text, clutched in Phaedrus' left hand, concealed under his cloak, functions as a talisman of revenge, insofar as it enacts a parricidal desire: "the perfect removal of that father [Lysias] whose censoring presence" is turned into an absence. It signifies the reduction of Lysias to object status, as a precondition for his complete erasure, in which a temporary absence is made permanent by the climactic turn toward dialectics. Socrates' dialectic discourse enacts the parricide of Lysias and, as such, constitutes a form of revenge for his trial and execution by the sophists. He seeks to kill Lysias and stand in his place. Socrates is competing with his rival in absentia and must attach his oral discourse to the written text that has come before, in this manner rewriting it, much as criticism attaches itself to the primary texts it appropriates. Socrates, in effect, reinscribes the predatory aggressions of criticism toward a text, models the interpretive act of critical thinking for his pupil, Phaedrus—and thus prefigures Plato's criticism of writing, which leaves itself vulnerable to just such interpretive aggressions.

Socrates is already performing the textual aggressions that Plato fears posterity will enact upon his own texts. Socrates takes his revenge on Lysias by attacking the writing of Lysias, which is just the opening salvo in his attack on writing. If Socrates' critique of Lysias' text inaugurates the move from rhetoric to rhetorical analysis, from idolatry to critical reflection, what, if any, are the flaws of his own analysis? Are there intentional as well as inherent flaws in his analysis, and might the reader, as much as Phaedrus, benefit from an analysis of his analysis?

RE-DIRECT: IN DEFENSE OF LYSIAS

Many critics have, not surprisingly, noted the deficiencies of Lysias' speech relative to Socrates' discourse, even noting the trial motif of the *Phaedrus*. As Griswold observes,

> the boy is put in the position of an impartial judge, the lover in the position of the defendant, and the non-lover in that of both prosecution and plaintiff. The speech [by Lysias] reads like a very sober legal brief, enumerating in an ostensibly logical manner the pros and cons of satisfying the nonlover and lover, respectively . . . The purpose of Lysias' speech is to solicit a ruling that will gratify the nonlover sexually. (45)

In the best tradition of sophistic discourse, the speech is forensic in nature, completely "lacking . . . in the rhetoric of love"—in contradistinction to Socrates' speeches, and particularly to his "hymn to love." Socrates' discourse performs love, insofar as it performs the soul's sacred and profane desires, whereas Lysias' speech performs a mere seduction. As such, the "nonlover needs rhetoric to survive," which is nothing more than the discourse of profane desire: be it for sex, revenge, or the manipulation of public opinion (47). Reason, in other words, is conscripted as an "instrument for the satisfaction of [sexual] desire."

Ferrari is one of the few critics who develops a more appreciative reading of Lysias' speech, arguing that Socrates' "reading" of it is really a "misreading." For example, Socrates criticizes Lysias' speech for its lack of "organic unity," failing to see the intentionality behind this discourse strategy: ironically, in a "dialogue [*Phaedrus*], which taken as a whole, is deliberately disunified in its structure," which intentionally uses disunity to "jar its readers and urging them thereby to reconstitute the living creature from its scattered limbs"—to re-member its disjointed parts (53). Thus, in modeling a criticism of sophistic discourse, Socrates lays his own discourse open to critique, by virtue of its ironic hypocrisy.

Ferrari raises a critical question: "why is it that Plato allows Socrates to skip over the subtler aspects of Lysias' speech, while nevertheless alerting the reader to their presence?" (53). The answer is simple: to acknowledge the "subtler aspects of Lysias' speech," to highlight its strengths, would be to validate "Lysias' way of life." And the *Phaedrus* is nothing if not an argument that touts the virtue of the philosophic life: defined as a dedicated search for self-knowledge through love and discourse with the Other.

The virtues of this philosophic life are juxtaposed to the vices of a life conducted along sophistic lines: dedicated to the pursuit of erotic desire, in which language is used as a tool of seduction—whether it is to seduce the body of a beloved in the quest for sex or the body of public opinion in the quest for power. Socrates' critique turns a blind eye to the strengths of Lysias' speech, focusing instead on what it lacks (definition, climactic arrangement, organic unity), opting instead to "pierce its ethical heartlessness . . . reacting instead to its parasitism . . . (55)—while conveniently ignoring the parasitism of dialectics that preys upon the limitations of other discourses (sophistry, myth, poetry, and ceremonial rhetoric) to nourish its own desires.

Ferrari concludes that "Socrates is misreading Lysias' text and failing to do it justice, for he is not appreciating those facets of the piece which its author would have most wanted to see appreciated" (56). Further, Socrates' critique of Lysias' text is prophetic:

> [for] what happens to Lysias' text in Socrates' hands is a perfect example of the danger to which Socrates himself will later describe all written texts as being susceptible: namely, that they circulate too freely among readers who fail to appreciate them, so that they are not self-sufficient but would benefit from some defensive explanation from their "father" or author. (279d–e) (56)

Yet, aside from Phaedrus' uncritical idolatry, there is no one at this "trial" to defend Lysias' text against its philosophic usurper, perfectly dramatizing the problem with the written word that Socrates cites at the close of the *Phaedrus*. What is wanted in the dialogue is a re-direct, a cross-examination, a genuine dialogue between equal rhetorical combatants, as in the historical trial. Instead, Lysias is tried in absentia. Thus, the trail of writing re-staged in the *Phaedrus* perfectly reinscribes the trial of Socrates, who similarly attacks his "first accusers" in absentia. For Socrates, "to enter into the spirit of [the text's] stylistic achievements as an appreciative reader is to risk becoming complicit in the process" (56). Ferrari's appreciative reading of Lysias' text provides this missing "re-direct" in the tribunal staged by Plato (Socrates)—in effect, (re)presenting Lysias to his accusers.

Ferrari's final observation is significant insofar as it prophesizes one of the most problematic aspects of Socrates' discourse in the *Phaedrus*: the extent to which it is complicit in sophistic discourse (the thing it seeks to destroy), the extent to which it is tainted by sophistry and, as such, responsible for the self-destructive effects it unleashes: in the form of guilt, shame, betrayal, and the further deceptions these produce in the quest for forgiveness, expatiation, and the immortality of the ideal soul (issues I will address in a subsequent chapter).

What precisely are the virtues of Lysias' speech overlooked by Socrates? Ferrari acknowledges a "certain magnificent audacity in the non-lover's suggestion" (92). In his appreciative reading of Lysias' speech, Ferrari notes that there is in Socrates' first speech none of the "zestful audacity that we found in Lysias' non-lover, nor his potentially refreshing straight-forwardness" (97). There is a disarming candor to Lysias' speech that somewhat redeems its unethical and base intents—an almost tongue-in-check playfulness that smiles at its own audacity. The rich artifice of Socrates' discourse, by contrast, masks its lethal intent and possessive desires. Thus, there is in Socrates' analysis of Lysias' text a "blind spot" with respect to its virtues and possible intentions—a hyper-critical tendency that ignores its strengths, revealing perhaps its own sadic, vengeful well-springs. The bold inventiveness of Lysias' text merits an appreciative re-reading of it. Yet Socrates commits the same error of omission in his analysis that scholars in rhetoric and composition have committed ever since, emphasizing the grammatical, logical, structural, political-ethical, the process, and the product of writing, while ignoring "invention" and "vitalism," which "almost disappears from the discourse of rhetoric and composition," as Hawk observes in *A Counter-History of Composition* (8).

(DIS)CLOSING ARGUMENTS: ANALYSIS AND THE SOCIAL-EPISTEMIC TURN

Socrates elaborates on his critique of sophistry, hoping in this manner to develop Phaedrus' own critical thinking skills, as an intervention against a problematic reality, embodied in the affective power of sophistic signifying practices, and its dangerous implications for the practice of freedom—in which Phaedrus is a stand-in for the Athenian citizenry. Through rhetorical analysis, Socrates in effect is arming that citizenry against those who would manipulate their beliefs for their own partisan ends. Analysis, as practiced by Socrates, is a form of liberatory self-defense, intended to awaken the multitude from its idolatrous slumber. The goal of his critique is to unmask the dangerous deceptions of sophistic rhetoric: "but those whom you have heard, who write treatises on the art of speech nowadays, are deceivers and conceal the nature of the soul. . . . For in *the courts, they say, nobody cares for truth* . . . but for that which is convincing and that is probability" (270c, 272e, my emphasis)—as evidenced by his own trial. With respect to an edifying rhetoric, Socrates concludes, "[s]o far as the art is concerned, I do not think the quest of it lies along the path of Lysias" (137). As Shorey observes, "Sophistic discourse is for Plato (Socrates) . . . rhetorical in a pejorative sense: it seeks to induce belief without regard for whether the belief is transcendently true. . . . [he] views the Sophists as moral relativists who therefore have no reason not to be manipulative, deceitful or downright corrupting in their use of discourse" (56).

Dialectics (as evidenced in the second and third speeches) then is the method par excellence for realizing the goal of self-knowledge, of mutual edification. Further, this methodology is inherently social, insofar as it relies on a dialogic "construction" of meaning between Self and Other, teacher and pupil. "Socrates endorses the notion," as Griswold asserts, "that he must come to know himself through the mediation of others, that is, through dialogue" (173). This effectively situates Socrates' radical praxis as a precursor of current dialogic pedagogies, drawing on the social-epistemic theories of Vygotsky, Freire, and others. The unveiling of a problematic reality through dialogic analysis, not as an end in itself but as an intervention focused on the transformation of that reality, is central to Freirean liberatory praxis.

Both advocate a problem-posing pedagogy to facilitate the practice of freedom: if in Freire's case the problem posed to students is the reality of their colonial oppression, in Socrates' case it is the affective power of sophistic signifying practices—particularly as they corrupt the justice system.

In each, analysis is undertaken to unveil an aspect of reality as problematic as it is specific, as an intervention against that reality. As Freire observes, "to surmount the situation of oppression, men must first critically recognize its causes, so that through transforming action they can create a new situation, one which makes possible the pursuit of fuller humanity" (31–32). Rhetorical analysis is the means by which Socrates enables Phaedrus to recognize the problematic aspects of sophistic rhetoric. Freire underscores the analytical focus of his problem-posing inquiry when he asserts that "this pedagogy makes oppression and its causes objects of reflection by the oppressed, and from that reflection will come their necessary engagement in the struggle for their liberation" (33).

Reflection on reality and action to transform it go hand in hand in the radical pedagogies of Socrates and Freire. Socrates' martyrdom was the ultimate translation of this analysis into action, even as his trial of sophistry during his tribunal was the penultimate act of intervention. The elevation of a marginal philosophic discourse to the status of a discourse that dominated western intellectuality for 2,500 years evidences the transformative effect of Socratic inquiry.

Thus, in both its analytical and transformative moments, Socratic inquiry is consonant with the "two distinct phases" of Freirean liberatory praxis: "in the first, the oppressed unveil the world of the oppressor and through the praxis commit themselves to its transformation. . . . it is always through action in depth that the culture of domination is confronted" (40). In the *Apology* and *Phaedrus,* Socrates directly confronts the sophistic "culture of domination," inscribed in writing in Meletus' deposition and Lysias' text, bringing to bear upon them analyses which expose the extent to which one has corrupted the Athenian system of justice and the other the use of rhetoric (to gain sexual favors).

Phaedrus' uncritical idolatry of Lysias' text, and with sophistry in general, reinforces Freire's observation that "at a certain point in their existential experience the oppressed feel an irresistible attraction towards the oppressor and his way of life. Sharing this way of life becomes an overpowering aspiration" (49). The Greek educative paradigm reinforced this tendency. In the *Phaedrus*, Socratic analysis intervenes to liberate the subject from its idolatrous servitude to sophistry—toward the realization of a "more fully human" critical awareness and agency. This humanistic goal of Socratic education also alliterates with Freirean praxis and its goal of "becoming more fully human" by humanizing historical circumstances—the immediate material conditions of reality. As Socrates' dialectic inquiry evidences, and as Freirean praxis reveals, analysis is always and already intervention, and "political action" always and already "pedagogical action" (53). Insofar as classroom interpretation of reality is an act of intervention upon it, the pedagogical is always and already political.

By virtue of its reliance on dialogic analysis to unveil reality, Socrates' methodology is deeply aligned with Freirean praxis, not just in the "task of unveiling that reality, and thereby coming to know it critically, but in the task of re-creating that reality" (56), which was the principle goal and primary effect of Socrates' life and death. Like Freire's interrogation of colonial oppression, Socrates' dialogic investigation into the affective power of sophistic signifying practices was a "restless, impatient, continuing, hopeful inquiry . . . pursue[d] in the world, with the world, and with [the] other" (58). Socratic thought rises to the benchmark set by Freire for all "authentic thinking" insofar as it too is "concerned about reality, does not take place in ivory tower isolation, but only in communication . . . has meaning only when generated by action upon the world" (64).

Any analysis of reality divorced from actions aimed at transforming that reality devolves into a mere academic exercise. Analysis is never meaningful in and of itself, but only as a transforming agent of reality. If in the classroom, analysis is conducted dialogically, not as an end in itself (for the purpose of fulfilling course requirements, taking tests, writing papers, or assigning grades), but an intervention on reality whose circulation among students is a springboard to its circulation beyond the classroom, to its dissemination in the world, in solidarity with Others, and with other disseminations that it joins, then such analysis rises to the Freirean benchmark for "authentic thinking."

To return to the original definition of "analysis" with which I began this chapter, derivative of the Greek "*ana* (up) + *lyein* (loosen)," Socratic inquiry can be said to "loosen up" alternative meanings regarding what is truly beautiful in discourse: that its beauty cannot be judged merely by its affective power, but must also be assessed by its ethical outcomes, which inherently ground the political as determined by the mutual edification of Self and Other. Socrates "loosens" up Lysias' reductive concept of "madness," freeing additional meanings, or kinds of madness. He "loosens up" Phaedrus' concept of the soul, deploying an image of a winged chariot drawn by unruly steeds to capture the violence of the struggle between sacred and profane impulses and the need to absorb the latter in the former. He "loosens up" Phaedrus' notion of beautiful discourse, introducing notions of definition, division, classification, and arrangement; of mutual edification, political reform, and a civic ethos that serves the common good. By breaking things down into their constitutive elements, Socrates "loosens up" or frees additional, even transformative, meanings, toward the transformation of problematic realities "unveiled" by those dialogically excavated meanings. For all of these reasons, Socratic inquiry may be aptly posited as a (pre)cursive precursor of Freriean praxis.

A GENEALOGY OF METHOD: FREIRE'S CRITIQUE OF COLONIAL POWER

Socrates' dialogic analysis of the problematic of sophistic power and the signifying practices that sustained it is an ancient precursor of Freirean praxis and the problematic of colonial power it poses to students. With respect to methodology, Freire's radical pedagogy similarly privileges a dialogic "mode of analysis" that foregrounds the material conditions of reality, which it poses to the students as a series of problems or "generative themes" to be studied, analyzed, discussed, researched, written about, and acted upon. As Freire asserts, educators "must abandon the educational goal of deposit-making and replace it with the posing of problems of [people] in their relation with the world" (66). Thus, this "problem-posing education involves a constant unveiling of reality" (68). Freire continues:

> The starting point for organizing the program content of education or political action must be the present, existential, concrete situation, reflecting the aspirations of the people.... [W]e must pose this ... to the people as a problem which challenges them and requires a response—not just at the intellectual level, but at the level of action [or application]. (85)

In this active-learning model of education, critical reflection and dissemination comprise a twofold intervention within the classroom, as a springboard for a broader dissemination beyond the classroom, yoked to civic intervention in the immediate community—in the spirit of applied learning. In other words, analysis is accompanied by application in some concrete form, in the immediate community—even if the application is only a broader dissemination of the classroom analysis to the community at large, in which students assume the role of co-educators, of public intellectuals, in which individual analysis within the classroom serves some broader, collective common good beyond it.

Thus, the first function of this "mode of analysis" is to "unveil" a reality that is problematic, is to (re)present it to the world, not as an immutable given, but as a problem that can be acted upon, mitigated, resolved. This spirit of critical analysis is "represented in its unmasking function" (Giroux 17). Freire, similarly, observes that "the more people *unveil this challenging reality* which is to be the object of their transforming action, the more critically they enter into that reality" (38, my emphasis). This view of the relation between theory and reality, analysis and material conditions establishes, as Giroux notes, a generative solidarity not only between Freire and Socrates but between Freire and the Frankfurt School (Adorno, Marcuse, Horkheimer et al.), "in which the ultimate purpose of critique should be critical thinking in the interest of social change. . . . in which critical thought becomes the precondition for human freedom" (18–19).

In this mode of analysis, reality is unveiled dialogically, as part of social inquiry into a problematic reality. Methodologically speaking, the teacher functions as a co-investigator of reality, not as the voice of authority on reality: as one who enables student inquiry, who assumes a developmental role relative to students "coming into voice" on the problem to be unveiled, as authorities in the meaning-making process, as the agents of their own signifying practices.

Dialogue is always and already the lifeblood of critical inquiry, whether in small collaborative groups or peer pairings (where students collectively discuss the reality unveiled or co-author an inquiry), or in macro group discussions, where a problem is unveiled and discussed collectively, perhaps in conjunction with a primary or secondary reading that serves as a springboard to the "unveiling," or in dialogue with others beyond the classroom, as part of an extended "unveiling"—whether with peers, stakeholders, or citizens. As Freire asserts, "the correct method lies in dialogue" (54). Once the "generative themes" of inquiry have been identified, related to the unveiling of reality, they are engaged dialogically. Freire continues:

> It is to the reality which mediates [people] and to the perception of that reality held by educators and people, that we must go to find the program content of education. The investigation of what I have termed the people's "thematic universe"—the complex of their "generative themes"—inaugurates the dialogue of education as the practice of freedom. *The methodology of that investigation must likewise be dialogical,* affording the opportunity both to discover generative themes and to stimulate people's awareness in regard to these themes. Consistent with the liberating purpose of dialogical education, the object of the education is not [people], but rather the *thought-language* with which [they] refer to reality. (86, my emphasis)

Freire doesn't posit the "decoding" of a problematic reality as occurring outside the dialogic process, but as always and already dialogic. Analysis of problematic realities occurs concomitantly with discussion of those realities in collaborative groups, by which the investigation is further shaped and informed. As Freire observes, these discussions "initiate decoding dialogues in the 'thematic investigation circles'" (110). Freire's method is significant insofar as it underscores not only the centrality of dialogue to every phase of the investigation, but of the collaborative group. This is tantamount to taking Elbow's feedback group and politicizing it, making not the betterment of the writer the sole aim of education, but the betterment of society through the enhanced efficacy of the student's writing, whose aim is not just personal enrichment, but social problem-solving through civic engagement. It is a methodology which not only seeks to enact social change, but which is always and already social, emphasizing not only the social ends of knowledge, but the social means of knowledge-making. As Freire asserts, it is reality alone that authenticates knowledge; divorced from reality, and particularly from application to its most problematic aspects, knowledge devolves into an ivory tower discourse.

Freire further underscores the dialogic nature of this student-centered investigation of problematic realities. As Freire observes, "as each specific project is discussed, the other [students] make suggestions. These may be incorporated into the project and/or may be included in the brief essays to be written on the theme . . . to which bibliographic suggestions are annexed" (113). Thus, investigation of a problematic reality is conducted within the framework of collaborative discussions and a written research project, whose ultimate destination and real audience is not the teacher, nor even one's peers, but the point of contact between a problematic reality and the community.

Once this "decoding" process is completed, the contents of the analysis must be "codified" according to "the best channel of communication for each theme and its representation" (114). In this dissemination/application phase, the investigator selects from the "channels of communication" available, the one that best codifies the analysis for its broader dissemination to the public: "the visual (pictorial or graphic), the tactile [hand-outs, flyers], or the auditive [presentations/lectures/speeches]" (114). Once "codified in the "best channel of communication," the "didactic materials" for the dissemination of the decoding are prepared: "photographs, slides, film strips, posters, reading texts, and so forth" (115)—a list easily supplemented with PowerPoint, overhead projectors, or whatever "didactic materials" facilitate the broader dissemination of the knowledge ("decodings"). This codification for dissemination of the analysis replicates Socrates' codified analysis of sophistic signifying practices, as well as its dialogic dissemination through dialectic discourse. I will further develop the pedagogical implications of Freire's methodologies for a neo-humanist pragmatism in the final chapter.

Dialogic analysis of problematic realities, including the problematic of power and persuasion, is the medium of Socratic inquiry and Freirean praxis. To the extent their radical pedagogies situate inquiry at the intersection of the personal, social, political, ethical, and rhetorical, they evidence Griswold's observation that "philosophy is not just private and educative, but public and political" (133). The mechanism of Socrates' dialogic analysis evidences the methodological complexity of his elenchus, even as the diverse signifying practices that reinforce his polemic evidence its rhetorical complexity. In the *Phaedrus,* Socrates' dialectic analysis operates within a broader strategy of serial recantations, including both the ironic and genuine recantation of philosophy by Plato's Socrates and Plato respectively. In the next chapter, I want to unveil the mechanisms of these serial recantations through a rhetorical analysis of a rhetorical analysis, mapping their ubiquity as well as their deeper and darker implications—with particular regard to the dynamics of the self-other, master-pupil, Socrates-Plato dyad, and the concerns of postmodern criticism.

5 The Signifying Hood
The Dialectics of Recantation

> Recant: to take back (something one has said) publically: make an open confession of error.
> —Webster (612)

> Thus then, dear god of love, I have offered the fairest *recantation* and fullest atonement that my powers could compass.... Grant me thy pardon for what went before.
> —Socrates (257a, my emphasis)

Two moments in the *Phaedrus* deeply inform Socrates' pedagogical methodology. The first occurs when he *hoods* himself before delivering his initial sophistic speech in imitation of Lysias' written speech. The second occurs when he offers a *poem of atonement* immediately following this speech. These rituals, which respectively commence and conclude his sophistic speech, herald the dialectic recantation of sophistry in the second speech. They bracket his first speech like rhetorical bookends of recantation, performing the recantation they prefigure.

They evidence as well the rhetorical complexity of the polemic, in which myth, mimicry, meta-drama, and erotic figuration all reinforce the dialectics of analytical recantation. If the ritual of the hood performs the recantation of sophistry in the midst of speaking sophistically, the poem of atonement recants this recantation of philosophy. Both rituals evidence the violence of Socrates' shame, even as they underscore his ancient pagan piety and the centrality of ethos to his elenchus. They evidence as well the centrality of Love to his educative craft: the inseparability of logos, ethos, and pathos from Eros. For it is the violence he does to Love that prompts both rituals, in a rhetorical analysis of a speech that itself profanes Love by virtue of its thesis (that it is better to "grant favors rather to a non-lover than to a lover"). If the sophistic speech Socrates gives demonstrates Socrates' stoops-to-conquer, ends-justify-the-means pedagogical strategy, the rituals that inaugurate and consummate it dramatize his faith and his philosophy, meta-dramatically deconstructing his sophistic speech, as a running critique of it. These "book-end" rituals leverage a "dilatory space" between word and gesture, sophistry and philosophy that fosters critical cognition, that gives birth to analysis in the midst of a seeming idolatry through a strategy of recantation. Thus, throughout *Phaedrus*, dialectic

The Signifying Hood 91

analysis occurs within a broader strategy of serial recantations, reinforced by diverse signifying practices (mimicry, myth, meta-drama, and figuration; satire, irony, allegory, and amorous innuendo), all of which attest to the rhetorical complexity of the polemic.

Logos, ethos, and Eros deeply inform this strategy of recantation, insofar as recantation is essential to the logic of analysis, even as the shame that often attends it necessitates its repudiation to recuperate an ethical Eros. The Self's ironic recantations of Love, necessitated by the polemic, do violence to the Self, which in turn are mitigated through the recantation of its recantations. Thus, the Self is prompted to pause and cleanse itself of the stain of sophistry and its own temporary repudiation of philosophy. The mingled feet of dialectician and pupil, dangled in the Ilissus, trope on cleansing effect of the discourse of atonement, whose currents are mingled with the powerful "tongue" of dialectic analysis that drives the polemic. Rhetorical eddies that cycle back into the "tongue" of the dialectic polemic, hydraulic reversals that "reverse" the shameful effects of "speaking in tongues" against Love—meta-whirlpools that pause the dialectic current, that swirls briefly upon itself, before resuming its inexorable flow.

The search for the significance and implications of this strategy of recantation is guided by a host of questions. To what extent is this polemic of recantation informed by other signifying practices, and particularly by meta-dramatic discourse, myth, mimicry, and erotic figuration? To what extent do these signifying practices evidence an ancient "vitalism" largely overlooked by criticism—and what might be the implications for contemporary writing instruction of this neglected "vitalism?" What are the implications of the recantation of philosophy, however ironic and ephemeral, for *Phaedrus'* overall polemic, and for the dynamics of the master-pupil, Socrates-Plato dyad in particular? Does it prefigure the eternal return of recantation and the ultimate recantation of master by pupil, orality by writing, and philosophy by art? To what extent then is the *Phaedrus* not only a critique of sophistry, but of Socrates' philosophical elenchus, as evidenced in the ironic and/or authentic recantations it dramatizes? Do we discover evidence in its rhetoric of recantation that the guilt, shame, and fear expressed by Socrates devolves onto his pupil—or is the violence of Socrates' shame a projection of Plato's? If so, what might be the origins of Platonic shame? To what extent is the *Phaedrus* an effort to work off this shame in the symbolic realm—and as such, a commentary on the origins of the creative impulse, on the relationship between morbid suffering and creativity, and on the career of the artiste manqué, or suffering artist? In short, does this rhetoric of recantation inform not only Socrates' elenchus, but the origins of Platonic invention: not only as a medium for fostering critical thinking, but for mitigating the effects of shame relative to the profanation of the ideal? What finally are the implications for social-epistemic praxis of an ancient pedagogy that grounds analysis-as-recantation in an effort to mitigate the violence of power circulating through the power of persuasion?

In the *Phaedrus*, ironic recantation is the medium of a dual conversion: of a philosopher into a pseudo sophist, and of a sophist into a genuine philosopher. The entire protrepticus is deeply informed by the dynamics of the self-other dyad, operating under the sign of philosophic eros. Inherent in that dyad are numerous generative tensions: between sophist-philosopher, master-pupil, and lover-beloved. The transformation of self and other through dialectic discourse commences with the false conversion to sophistry of the dialectic self (Socrates) as a necessary (pre)text for the genuine conversion of the sophistic other (Phaedrus) to philosophic eros. Deception is inherent to Socrates' polemic, calling its ethos into question, insofar as he uses the very signifying practice he critiques in sophistic discourse: *a theory of signifying resemblances*. Mitigating the problematic ethics of this practice is the polemical efficacy of first addressing the counter-arguments as a springboard into developing one's own argument: a practice composition teachers regularly instruct students to employ. Thus, masking is essential to the unmasking. Disguise is a precondition of Socratic dialectics. He impersonates the counter-arguments as preamble to his own: argues the false as a (pre)text for advocating the authentic—begins his defense of philosophy with a feint toward sophistry. In order to commence this rhetorical boxing match, he first has to create a sparring partner: convert an absence into a presence, which he does through his mimicry of sophistry. Through the rituals of the hood and the poem of atonement, he shows Phaedrus that sophistry is just a polemical prop. He sounds the bell on his false combat, retires to the corner to cleanse the blood from his face through a ritual atonement, then returns to center ring, this time with the gloves off, as a dialectician. Yet, sans his real opponent, Lysias, he is confined to shadow-boxing with Lysias' text, to having a symbolic combat in the realm of the symbolic: language—which is altogether fitting, insofar as the *Phaedrus* reinscribes the ancient war of discourses, the rhetorical blood feud between sophistry and philosophy waged since the reign of Pericles.

Through a sequence of recantations, Socrates first converts himself into a sophistic Other, establishing between master and pupil an inauthentic other-other alliteration under the sign of sophistry. This is but a mere pretense, however, for converting the sophistic Other into a philosopher, establishing a genuine self-self alliteration under the sign of philosophic eros, which doesn't negate the sophistic sign, but merely absorbs it into itself, even as sophistic eroticism is absorbed into philosophic eros. Even after Lysias' putative defeat by Socrates, philosophic eros is still informed by sophistic signification, evidencing the permanence of their "peculiar intimacy." Just as post-colonial discourse is always implicated in colonial signification, so does the philosophic discourse of Plato's Socrates forever bear the mark of sophistic signification. As a signifying system, it bears the signs of Derrida's "graft;" like all textual discourse, it can never entirely free itself from its inter-textuality, can no more sever the hyphen that conjoins sophistic and philosophic discourse than Socrates can escape the hyphen of Plato-Socrates. I want to delve more deeply into the methodological mechanism of Socrates' polemic, and particularly into the extent to which it relies upon and models a series of recantations, to effect the mutual edification of self and other.

If Socrates relies heavily on mimesis and meta-drama to effect the conversion of the Self into a sophistic Other, he turns from rhetoric to rhetorical analysis and a strategy of ironic recantation to realize the conversion of the sophistic other to a philosophic self. Socrates' mimicry of sophistry mirrors and allegorizes Phaedrus' idolatry of it. The medium of Phaedrus' conversion to philosophic eros is a dialectic analysis that not only recants sophistry in favor of philosophy, but recants it through the *performance* of philosophy. Moreover, the conversion that is depicted is not merely cognitive but holistic, insofar as it is not merely a conversion from sophistic to philosophic discourse, and from uncritical to critical thinking that is dramatized, but a conversion to a lifestyle dedicated to philosophic eros. This symbiosis between philosophic eros and the life dedicated to it is another source of its "vitalism," perhaps the most overlooked aspect of Socrates' elenchus: a "blind spot" in criticism, which underscores Hawk's critique of the under-theorized nature of "vitalism" in rhetoric and composition.

RITUAL AND RECANTATION: THE "SIGNS" OF RHETORICAL COMPLEXITY

Socrates' radical pedagogy is holistic, insofar as it embodies not only the historical and mytho-poetic, mimicry and meta-drama, but religion and dialectics. His discourse is never simply a univocal dialectics, but rather a polyphonic compendium of diverse signifying systems, operating in contradictory consort, un-writing their own unity and coherence with serial recantations that disrupt the narrative flow and complicate the dialectical polemic. As a multifaceted composition, whose diverse signifying systems complement and contradict each other, Plato's *Phaedrus* seems to anticipate Goethe's dictum, voiced through the Director in the theatrical prelude to Faust: "Write a ragout, you have a pen" (ln 100).

If mimicry, myth, and figuration enact the apostasy into sophistic discourse, then meta-dramatic signification, dialectic analysis, and ironic recantation signify the birth and rebirth respectively of Phaedrus and Socrates to dialectic philosophy. The rupture between Socrates' first and second speech signifies not only the rupture between sophistry and philosophy, rhetoric and rhetorical analysis, but the birth of his pedagogy of ironic recantation. Yet the recantation signified in this rupture is actually prefigured by an earlier, equally dramatic rupture that similarly opens a "dilatory space" in which dialectical analysis is born. Thus, the stage for the generative rupture between sophistry and philosophy has been set by an earlier, equally protean breach between Socrates' words and deeds: specifically, between the sophistic words he is about to mouth and his gesture of donning a hood before speaking. I want to further explicate the implications of this "dumb show," for it evidences that Socrates' seeming mimicry of sophistry is always and already a critique of it. The gesture also underscores the generative capacity of role-playing, further evidencing the rhetorical complexity of his polemic, even as it evidences the complicity of sophistic signifying practices in that polemic and his particular reliance on the very *theory of resemblances* he so stridently indicts in sophistry.

Socrates' donning of the hood is but one of two rituals, however, that respectively commence and conclude his first sophistic speech, even as they perform and prefigure his pedagogy of recantation. They also signify the rhetorical complexity of his polemic to the extent they dramatize the intertextuality of dialectic and religious discourse. In the midst of his argument, Socrates pauses to conduct a religious ritual of purification, evidencing not only the life and death stakes of the rhetorical circumstances, but the polemic's undercurrent of vitalism, its life-force, in which the word is ever returning to the world: dramatizing the symbiotic, generative dialectic between living and learning. The *Phaedrus*' enduring vitalism derives from this generative intimacy of living and learning, as well as from the rhetorical complexity of its dialectic inventions, in which the polemical is fueled by the historical-mythical-poetical, the analytic by the figurative, the philosophic by the sophistic, and the rhetorical by the religious.

Perhaps most significantly, the rituals associated with the hood and the poem of atonement evidence the violence of Socrates' shame, of his profanation of the philosophic ideal, casting perhaps as well a reflective light on Plato's shame. I want to further explicate the implications of these two rituals of recantation: the hood's recantation of sophistry, and the poem of atonement's recantation of his recantation of philosophy.

Socrates' mimicry of sophistry is ironic: in order to recant sophistry, he must first recant philosophy. This leads to a dual ritual: first, he hoods his head to conceal his shame for temporarily profaning the philosophic ideal by speaking in sophistic tongues; second, he performs a ritual of purification to remove the stain of sophistry from his soul. These two meta-dramatic rites both perform and prefigure the discourse of ironic recantation that launches the second speech (the palinode) and the turn from sophistry to philosophy. These rituals of recantation prefigure the analytical recantation, ritualize the logos of dialectic analysis, even as they sustain the meta-dramatic impulse, no longer profaned by the affectation of sophistry, but consecrating the rebirth to philosophy. They underscore as well the rhetorical complexity of Socrates' polemic.

THE SIGNIFYING HOOD: THE DILATORY SPACE OF DIALECTICS

> I'm going to keep my head wrapped up while I talk that I may get through my discourse as quickly as possible and that I may not look at you and become embarrassed.
>
> —Socrates (237a)

The Signifying Hood   95

The specter of a hooded Socrates, like the *Phaedrus* itself, is layered with meanings whose complex interweaving not only attests to Plato's artistry, but invites multiple interpretations, while refusing to be enclosed within any single interpretation. Meaning in the *Phaedrus* is itself "hooded" with irony, allegory, figuration, mimicry, masking, meta-drama, and personification, thus problematizing any attempt to definitively "interpret" its meaning. Its rhetorical complexity mystifies the very interpretation it invites: ironic in a dialogue which dramatizes the interpretative act—the art of interpreting a text (Lysias'). The *Phaedrus'* signifying complexities are perhaps intended to resist the possessive aggressions of the critical gaze—to always and forever leave something of itself to itself, in this refuting Socrates' recantation of writing (a point I will develop at greater length in Chapter 7). William Covino's assessment is instructive: "Commentary on the *Phaedrus* writes a history of confusion. Since antiquity, those engaged and seduced by the dialogue ask the urgent question, 'What is it about?'" (10). Doubrovsky underscores the paradox at the heart of interpretation, whose possibilities encode its limitations: "in criticism there is something for everyone—as long as you see that whatever the meta-language used, there is no ultimate decoding of the metaphorical language of the work into a rigorously metonymic language that 'lays out' its meaning" (115). The effort to explicate the meta-dramatic implications of a hooded Socrates in the final analysis leaves those implications hooded.

On one level, the hooded head gestures toward the deceptions of sophistry, whose unethical, if not hypocritical, concealments Socrates is here performing. Sophistry is a hooded discourse, a wolf in lamb's clothing—in which Beauty's "favors" are gained through the artful deceptions of persuasive rhetoric, in which a lover poses as a non-lover to gain the "favors" he desires." The gesture tropes as well on Socrates' own complicity in this deception, in which he, like Lysias, pretends to be a non-lover in order to woo and win his beloved ideal, Phaedrus. He wears the hood to signify his hooded pretense as a non-lover. As Griswold asserts, "just as Lysias speaks through the dramatic fiction of the nonlover . . . so Socrates conceals himself as a nonlover who is pretending to be a lover" (48). He adopts not only Lysias' discourse, but his guise of the non-lover, in a performance that totalizes the mimetic impulse, further evidencing Socrates' artistry as a philosophic rhetorician. He not only adopts the words and deeds of a sophist, but the persona: as a persuasive, hooded, non-lover.

Yet, there is a double mimicry to Socrates' hooded sophistry, insofar as it tropes on Phaedrus' "hooded" cognitive abilities. In donning the hood, Socrates is again holding a mirror up to Phaedrus' uncritical idolatry of Lysias' discourse. The hood not only enacts his own shame, but calls Phaedrus' attention to the shameful nature of his own idolatry of sophistic discourse. Griswold's observation is instructive: "Phaedrus' deficiencies, as well as those of the contents of the [sophistic] speeches, are exhibited in *deed* and word" (56, my emphasis). Thus, with this hood, Socrates is already opening a "dilatory space" between sophistry and philosophy that prefigures the shift from rhetoric to rhetorical analysis in the palinode (second speech), in a gesture that comments critically on his pose and on Phaedrus' idolatry—that is a critical meta-text in itself, a form of talking-about-talking.

His gesture subverts his discourse, adds a layer of meaning that contradicts his sophistic words, introducing into his performance a dramatic ambivalence, which even in the sophistic moment opens up a dialectic space between word and gesture, sophistry and philosophy. It is as if in donning the hood, Socrates is giving Phaedrus a "wink and a nod," is cuing his own deception, by way of creating a space between his words and his critical judgment, between orality and interpretation. Even while mimicking sophistry, his recantation of it has commenced.

The dialectic recantation of the palinode (second speech) is thus prefigured by his meta-dramatic gesture. The dialectic Word, instead of preceding action, is preceded by it. As a meta-language, actions in the *Phaedrus* are as generative as words. There is thus, in the *Phaedrus* and in Socrates' pedagogy of recantation, a protean symbiosis between deed and word, in which each is implicated in the other, in a polemic that performs its meanings on the micro and macro levels, in its parts and in its entirety. The hood itself is a form of dialectic critique. Throughout the *Phaedrus,* its critique of sophistry is integrated across a rich complexity of signification in which mimicry, myth, and meta-drama reinforce the operation of irony, imagery, and satire, of history and dialectics, erotic figuration and sophistic signifying practices.

As evidenced by the hood, Socrates is already modeling the interpretive moment—and foreshadowing the interpretation to come. The hood jump-starts the protrepticus, to the extent it front-loads the critical gaze relative to a sophistic text—establishing a generative, dialectical opposition between mimicry and meta-drama, which until this moment have acted in consort to establish the Other-Other resemblance of sophistry. The hood enacts a first rupture with the sophistic pretense, like an actor who steps out of character to comment on his acting to the audience, with a wink and a nod. Thus, the hood subverts Phaedrus' suspension of disbelief relative to Socrates' esteem of sophistry.

Is Socrates' shame due not just to his having to give a sophistic speech, but to having to resort to deception to turn Phaedrus away from sophistry—itself a sophistic device? Is his shame due to the realization that he must profane the ethos of the philosophic ideal in order to establish the superiority of philosophy—that he must "speak ill of love" to convert Phaedrus to philosophic love? The hood is an early instance of the effects of shame, which are rooted in the profanation of the ideal, and which deeply inform not only the origins of Socrates' attack on writing, but also the origins of writing (and Platonic Invention) itself. As the *Phaedrus* proceeds, the reader comes to question the putative distinction between sophistry and philosophy, to suspect that the two discourses are always and already implicated in each other—that in Socrates' divided soul (and in Plato's), the sacred and profane (embodied respectively in philosophy and sophistry) dwell in restless cohabitation.

The hood comprises yet another mirror held up to Phaedrus' idolatry—inviting the pupil to share the master's shame regarding the taint of sophistry. It is a first, meta-dramatic attempt to get the student to abandon his idolatry of sophistry and assume a critical stance toward it. Yet, Socrates' hooded discourse mimes Phaedrus in another critical manner, which reinforces the alliteration between master and pupil. Again, Griswold's observations are instructive: Socrates is "imitating Phaedrus here. Both of them begin by attempting to conceal, under their cloaks as it were, the sources of their speeches" (27). Thus, the hood replicates the function of Phaedrus' cloak, concealing the author's true identity—and intent. This masking is essential to the recantation that follows—and which it here foreshadows.

Yet perhaps the greatest significance of the hood is ironic, insofar as it performs the recantation of sophistic discourse before that discourse even commences, prefiguring the analytical recantation of the palinode. As Griswold notes, "Socrates is concealed as he speaks, a visible ikon of his irony" (56). Socrates' covering his head before delivering his first speech serves to ironically deflate it, fostering in Phaedrus a critical detachment from the speech. His earlier, "Oh noble Lysias!" serves the same function. With this dramatic gesture, Socrates is already putting the pupil into the moment of critical analysis, by splitting his gaze between an idolatrous fixation on rhetoric and a rhetorical analysis of its shortcomings. With this simple if dramatic gesture, Socrates heralds the dialectics of ironic recantation.

This dramatic gesture deconstructs his own sophistic rhetoric, puts the lie to his own Lysian discourse, by hinting that Socrates doesn't really believe what he is about to say. The hood signifies the real beginning of his pedagogy of ironic recantation, even as it was prefigured by the myth of Oreithyia, which recants sophistry by allegorizing its affective power, as a species of seduction. Her kidnapping by the god of the north wind, Boreas, allegorizes the kidnapping of reason by sophistic discourse. Thus, like the hood, the myth recants the discourse it prefigures, further evidencing the rhetorical complexity of the polemic, whose signifying practices are as synchronous as they are diverse: fashioned from a rhetorical weave of myth and meta-drama, analysis and allegory, figuration and ironic recantation.

From a pedagogical standpoint, Socrates very effectively provides what was lacking in Phaedrus' response to Lysias' speech: a skeptical distance from which to assess its strengths and weaknesses. In a single gesture, he has launched the protrepticus toward critical thinking—encouraging Phaedrus to pay attention to "what I do, not what I say." Thus, the subtext of the gesture (covering his head) contains more critical truth than the entire text of Socrates' first speech, by which it is contradicted.

This aporea, or rupture, that Socrates creates between word and gesture, text and subtext, invites Phaedrus to fill in the gap with his own critical assessment: to become, in effect, the co-author of the text's meaning. With this gesture, Socrates is simultaneously speaking and commenting on his speech, establishing the critical distance that will enable Phaedrus to do the same: comment critically on the text. In a word, he is not only modeling critical discourse, but performing it. Critical consciousness, thus, implies the alienation of subject and object heretofore lacking in Phaedrus' idolatry of Lysias' speech, which collapsed the enabling separation of subject and object, conflating them in an uncritical and undifferentiated idolatry.

Critical thought enables the self to differentiate itself from the predatory aggressions of the sophistic Other. Socrates' first goal is to construct in Phaedrus a self differentiated from the sophistic Other, which he can only do through a dialectical discourse that separates the Self from the Other by virtue of its critical stance relative to the Other. By replacing idolatry with critical consciousness, dialectics gives birth to the authentic, free-standing self.

This birth to critical consciousness replicates the biological birth of the Self as a differentiated entity: a birth to thought achieved through language—even as the palinode to which the hood gestures signifies Socrates' rebirth to philosophy after his brief apostasy to sophistry. It is just one of the many generative gaps in *Phaedrus* that invite the play of meaning—which is precisely why, as Derrida asserts, the discontinuities in a text are often more generative of meaning than its coherences. To sever Phaedrus' idolatrous dependency on sophistry, Socrates must act as midwife to the birth of an independent self. Critical thought is the means (and the only means) by which Socrates can foster this Self independent of sophistry: a self differentiated from sophistry by dialectics.

Yet, there is darker significance to the hood as well. For it is not only an emblem of sophistic deceit, uncritical idolatry, and the critical gaze of dialectics, but an emblem of the profanation of the philosophic ideal and the morbid effects of this profanation on the soul of the philosopher. Of all the masks Socrates dons as part of his strategy of mutual edification, none is more signifying than the mask of sophistry. To speak in sophistic tongues, however, he must profane the philosophic ideal, and to express the shame this causes he covers his head. Socrates is performing not only the deceit of Lysias, the idolatry of Phaedrus, and the edification of dialectical analysis, but his own willing deceit in speaking like a non-lover and the shame of profanation associated with that deception.

The spectacle of shame Socrates presents to Phaedrus serves a critical pedagogical function. As Griswold asserts, "the feel of shame in the face of blasphemy" is one of the "pivots on which the transition from the low to the high discourse turns" (72). Shame is a fortunate, if not necessary, wound, however, insofar as it recuperates the ethical in the logical, by mitigating the shameful effects of the dialectic, which is always and already a form of violence—that does violence not just to the Other but to the Self.

Thus, we arrive at a significant formulation. Socratic dialectics (as well as the Platonic Invention that enshrines it) is rooted in a dual wound, one external and one internal: in the political wound of power and in the psychological wound of shame, arising from the violence it enacts on Self and Other in response to the violence of a political wound inflicted on the Self by the sophistic Other. It participates in the feedback loop of violence circulating between power and dialectics, in which analysis of power not only mitigates its violent effects, but ironically reproduces them in the violence it inflicts on the self and the other. Socrates cannot practice his elenchus without getting blood on his hand, without at times having to renounce dialectics, to speak-in-sophistic-tongues. The relish he takes in his life-long elenchus evidences the extent to which his own soul is marked by violence, participates in the violence it denounces. Is this then the source of the pupil's recantation of the master, of his critique of philosophy, of his apostasy to art, and the art of the written dialogue? Even more significantly, is his invention, like Socratic dialectics, also rooted in the dual wound of a master's martyrdom by sophistic power and his own profanation of the philosophic ideal: as evidenced by his critique of philosophy in writing and by his ultimate apostasy from philosophy to art? These are issues I will revisit in greater detail in Chapter 7.

The poem of atonement that interrupts the dialectic "occupies an intermediate position between low and high, or non-philosophical and philosophical, positions" (Griswold 72), evidencing as well the extent to which the philosophical is informed by the pious, and logos by ethos. The shame induced in Phaedrus by Socrates, by the "recognition of error" is necessary to the protrepticus: "although the language of ordinary opinion, poetry and religion are necessary to the ascent of knowledge, the recognition of error ... require[s] insight and introspection," which prepare the shift from idolatry to analysis. If the ritual of the hood signifies the philosopher's decent into sophistry, then figuration recuperates the philosophic ideal, signifying the ascent from sophistry to philosophy. A series of figures associated with the philosophical edification of Self and Other evidence this hierarchical relationship: the golden statue, Mount Olympus, the winged chariot, and the ladder of cognition.

Thus, before Socrates even drops the guise of sophistic rhetoric in favor of the rhetorical analysis that recants it, he has already introduced the pupil to the dialectic tension between rhetoric and rhetorical analysis, by donning a hood that is already a critical commentary on sophistic discourse, that physicalizes his critique of the sophistic discourse he mouths, in ironic counterpoint to it. Socrates performs the conversion from philosopher to sophist to philosopher on himself as a (pre)text for inaugurating Phaedrus' conversion from sophistry to philosophy, even as his mimicry of sophistry performs Phaedrus' idolatry of it, while allegorizing his own idolatry of Phaedrus.

This meta-dramatic (pre)text (a protrepticus-within-a-protrepticus) reveals the performative nature of Socrates' radical praxis, as well as the coherent diversity of his methods. His teaching evidences a "hands on," "live-action" approach to critical literacy that performs his logic, further infusing it with "vitalism." Indeed, Plato's *Phaedrus* (and Socrates' polemic within it) may be posited as an example of rhetoric that conjoins all three "types" of vitalism that Hawk theorizes: "oppositional, investigative, and complex" (5)—as evidenced by its adversarial relation to sophistry, by its investigation into the nature of love, madness, sophistry, philosophy, and perhaps most significantly, the relation between power and the power of persuasion, and finally by its rhetorical complexity. Oppositional. Investigative. Complex. As a "response to the question of life" (Hawk 5), it signifies its vitalistic roots in numerous ways: by virtue of the question it raises (is it better to love a non-lover than a lover); by virtue of its advocacy not just of dialectic philosophy, but of a life dedicated to philosophic Eros; and finally by its inquisition into the affective power of sophistic signifying practices upon the Athenian citizenry. Its vitalism, like that of Freire's praxis, is signified by the symbiosis between the word and the world, by the eternal return of the symbolic to the material. Its vitalism is signified finally by the numerous rituals that attend its rhetoric, in an effort to fulfill its dialectic wish, to embody its philosophic desire. The donning of the hood is but one in a sequence of generative rituals that vitalize the connection between word and deed: in which deeds are infused with the vitality of the critical Word and words are authenticated by the ethical and political acts to which they give rise, under the sign of philosophic eros.

Despite Socrates' recantation of poetry, epic myth, and epideictic (ceremonial) rhetoric, as a consequence of their affective power on the masses, which he saw as an assault on reason, his ancient elenchus possesses a similar "vitalism" by virtue of its reinscription of pagan oratory, which posits the magical, affective power (vitalism) of the spoken word, as emblematized in the numerous pagan rituals that attend Socrates' dialectic, as well as by the extent to which it is informed and revitalized by the myths of Achilles, Oreithyia, Stesichorus, and Theuth, and by the poetry of Sappho and the dramatists. Indeed, Plato's early ambition to write poetic verse for the stage is perhaps responsible for the inventive, multi-generic vitality that infuses his dialogues, as well as for the performative nature of those dialogues. Their vital link to life is further evidenced not only by the historical events they dramatize (the trial and death of Socrates), but the real people they were named after (Gorgias et al.). The vitalism of ancient rhetoric is evidenced as well in the collective Greek ideology, which posited education as the most plastic of all arts, ahead of sculpture, which represented a similar attempt to construct an ideal human type, under the signs of Beauty and Civic Duty.

The *Phaedrus*' rhetorical complexity is due in part to this undercurrent of vitalism that attends the dialectic polemic, evidencing its genealogical roots in pagan oratory, epic myth, poetry, and ceremonial ritual, as well as in the pagan art of body ornamentation and the plastic art of sculpture, by virtue of its wish to make the ideal real, and the symbolic material. The performative nature of Socrates' polemic (the role-playing and theatrical gestures) also infuse it with a vitality, insofar as they facilitate Phaedrus' conversion to philosophic eros. Dialectic, as Griswold notes, "cannot be taught verbally" but "learned only by the practice of it" (223). Thus, it "makes sense for Plato to *show* us what dialectic is" (223, my emphasis). The hood is the first instance of this "showing" in this theater of "show and tell," where the hood "tells" the truth of his sophistic lie—where his words "tell" of his sophistry, but the hood "shows" his philosophy, encouraging Phaedrus to believe the "show" and disregard the "tell." The dialectic is vitalized with actions that complicate and enrich its meaning, as acting becomes a meta-language that performs the meaning of the spoken word, often in counterpoint to it. The dialectic tension between word and deed reinscribes the dialectic critique of sophistry by philosophy.

The "vitalism" of Socratic inquiry "dialogues" with the vitalism of Freirean praxis, which flows from a similar conjunction of the educative and the political, of learning and life, insofar as it situates education in the "lived reality" of the student: which in Freire's case is the lived reality of colonial domination. His radical pedagogy is not only infused with the "vitalism" of the material world, of life but with the "vitalism" of his methodology, by virtue of its dialogic exchange and by its tendency to dissolve the barriers between the academic word and the material world. This it does by sending students out into the world to interview sources relative to the problematic reality being investigated, by inviting those sources into the classroom as guest speakers, to further unveil a problematic reality, and by the return of analysis to the world, as actions prompted by it. This dialectic communion between the word and the world infuses Freirean praxis with a vitalism redolent of the dynamism of Socrates' elenchus. Their respective vitalism derives from their humanistic and humanizing discourses. Their respective vitalism is a by-product of knowledge that flows from the "life of the area" through dialogic "conversation with inhabitants" (Friere 102–103). The mutual vitalism of Socratic inquiry and Freirean praxis is a result of the edifying symbiosis between "a subject (an I) confronting an object (reality)" (174). The vitalism of their radical pedagogies flows from the communion between inquiry and the "concrete, existential, present situation of real" people (82). The vitalism of their pedagogies derives from a knowledge that is local, circumstantial insofar as it "represents situations familiar to the individual" (106): a reality that is "decoded" dialogically, heightening the vitalism of the methodology. As with Socratic inquiry, the vitalism of Freirean praxis is heightened by the rich complex of signifying practices that characterize it: by the use of dialogue, field interviews, the transcription of interviews, "decoding" sessions, note-taking, research, presentations to peers and the public, visual signifiers ("pictorial or graphic"), by "tactile or auditive" signifying practices—by a diverse array of "didactic materials (photos, slides, film strips, posters, reading texts)" (114–115).

The vitalism of Freire's radical pedagogy reflects the synergy between the word and the world, between life and learning. Similarly, Socrates' "dumb-show" of sophistry is part of a "live-action" approach to teaching, in which philosophy's beauty relative to sophistry is not merely told, but performed, in what is tantamount to a trial-as-theater approach to critical literacy—in which the polemics of a mock trial are staged as theater, with a pedagogical theatricality that is not the least of the many methods Socrates uses in his radical praxis. Plato's Socrates doesn't merely espouse dialectics, but performs it—like an actor dropping the mask and stepping out of character to comment on the flaws of his own performance: an artist switching "hats" to an art critic.

In Socrates' pedagogy, creative impulses and critical tendencies exist in generative intimacy, further fueling the dialogue's vitalism. The creative impulse asserts itself not only in Socrates' "antic disposition," in the performative elements of his elenchus, whether as sophist, lover, or madman, but in the wonderful flow of imagery and figuration, whether in the service of playful, seductive, ironic, satiric, or dialectic impulses, whether speaking of the soul as a "winged chariot," of Phaedrus' beauty as something that "streams" into his soul through his eyes until it sprouts "feathers," or of Lysias as a "wolf" in "lamb's" clothing. Thus, the polemic is advanced as much through figuration, as through mimicry, myth, and meta-dramatic signification.

The impending shift from the art of rhetoric to rhetorical analysis is heralded as well by the detached tone with which Socrates delivers his first speech. As Griswold asserts, "the extreme impersonality of Socrates' first discourse reflects the importance it places on an abstract method of analysis" (58). Thus, there is even in Socrates' dry delivery of his first speech a meta-dramatic impulse, in which his voice subverts the meaning of the words, replicating the role of the hood—by putting the lie, as it were, to his seeming sophistry. Socrates' ritual hooding, however, is but one of two rites that underscore and prefigure the dialectical recantation.

THE POEM OF ATONEMENT: RECANTING A RECANTATION

If the ritual of the hood recants sophistry in the midst of mimicking it, the poem of atonement that follows his first speech recants Socrates' recantation of philosophy, mitigating the violent effects of his shame. Before Socrates can proceed with his philosophic critique of his own sophistic speech, he must first purify himself of the effects of it, of the "sin he has committed against the god" by speaking sophistically against Love.

In this rite of purification, myth and meta-dramatic gesture both prophesy the palinode, as a corrective discourse that recants the "error[s]" of sophistic signifying practices. Thus, as meta-dramatic ritual commences the apostasy to sophistry (the hood), so it concludes that apostasy (the bearing of the hooded head), and commences the redemptive turn to philosophy in the second speech. The un-hooding of Socrates' head prophesizes the dramatic un-hooding of sophistry for the debased discourse Socrates feels it to be, as well as the dramatic unveiling of philosophic inquiry—with its multiple analyses: of sophistic signifying practices, the nature of love, madness, and the soul, in a dramatic reversal of signification that rallies to the defense of philosophic Eros. As Socrates confides, "before *suffering* any *punishment* for *speaking ill of Love,* I will try to *atone for my recantation* with my *head bare* this time, not, as before, covered through *shame*" (243b, my emphasis).

The significance of this passage warrants further explication. The contrast of a head hooded and then bared reinforces the contrast between the effects of profanation and purification associated with the two rituals. The bearing of the head not only reverses the act of hooding the head, but reverses as well the effects of profanation associated with his hooded discourse. The bare head physicalizes his atonement, his "coming clean" before the gods, for the twofold sin he has committed: not only recanting philosophy to speak sophistically but, in the process, "speaking ill of love." The signs Socrates uses ("suffering," "punishment," "speaking ill," "atone," "recantation," and "shame") constitute a chain of signification that evidences the violence of his shame.

These violent effects are compounded by the fear associated with them: that he, like Homer and the mythic figure Stesichorus, will be struck blind for having "spoken ill of love" regarding Helen. The ritual thus reinscribes the vitalizing symbiosis between the philosophic and the pagan, word and deed, the mytho-poetic and dialectics, further attesting to the inscrutable rhetorical complexity of Socrates' polemic. As with the ritual of the hood, Socrates gives a performative turn to the myth of Stesichorus, not merely telling it but reciting "the poem, which is called a recantation" ('the saying is not true; thou didst not go within the well-oared ships, nor didst thou come to the walls of Troy') (243b). The punishment of blindness for "speaking ill of Love" is reversed for Stesichorus after his "poem" of recantation, in contrast to Homer, who was "stricken with blindness" for speaking ill of Helen, and who remained so for "being ignorant of the reason" (243a).

The restoration of Stesichorus' sight evidences the efficacy of atonement for sins committed, even as Socrates' desire to avoid a similar punishment for a similar crime attests to his piety—again in contradistinction to the accusation brought against him at his trial. The myth of Stesichorus also is a polemic commentary on the "blindness" associated with sophistry, and with speaking in sophistic tongues, versus the "sight" associated with philosophic wisdom. It also reinscribes the magical, pagan world-outlook regarding the affective power of orality, where the spoken word is posited as possessing the power to bring fortune as well as misfortune, to bring not only rain and bountiful harvests, but blight and blindness, for "speaking ill," and for "speaking ill of love" in particular. It reinforces Socrates' ongoing critique of the affective power of rhetoric, and his fear of being struck blind for "speaking ill of Love" in particular. His critique of Homer here, as one struck blind by the affective power of the word, reinscribes his critique of the affective power of epic myth, poetry, ceremonial rhetoric, and sophistic discourse. Socrates' entire elenchus throughout his speaking/

teaching career was geared toward unveiling and mitigating just this: the affective power of the Word on the Athenian citizenry and its particular ability to manipulate opinion by corrupting reason: whether under the sign of the epic, poetic, epideictic, or forensic Word.

For Socrates, "speaking ill of Love" must have seemed blasphemous indeed, to the point of tempting the Fates. Hence the urgent imperative for atonement, which further evidences that, in contradistinction to the state's accusation, he practiced dialectics, not with impunity but with piety. The conviction that he has "sinned against the god" is evidenced by the violence of his shame, guilt, and fear. These comprise the dark undercurrent of the *Phaedrus*, not just for Plato's Socrates but for Plato. Profanation of the philosophic ideal, and the guilt, shame, and fear associated with it, is a deep fount of the *Phaedrus'* signifying complexity. The poem of atonement not only evidences Socrates' pagan piety, but reverses the roles of accuser and accused in the *Apology*. This role reversal between the accuser and accused is evidenced when Socrates observes that Lysias' speech "was foolish and somewhat impious. What could be more dreadful than that?"

The respective fates of Homer and Stesichorus (blindness and the cure of blindness) also evidence the affective power of orality, which prompts Socrates' life-long elenchus. Speaking ill of Love results in blindness for both. Words of atonement for this sin result in the restoration of Stesichorus' sight. Homer's fate reinforces the alliteration between speaking ill and figurative blindness that Socrates associates with sophistry, and particularly the extent to which reason is blinded by the affective power of sophistic oratory. The blind Homer then is a metonym for the Athenian masses blinded by the affective Word of sophistry, as if by a drug, or "pharmakon," as Derrida asserts in *Dissemination*.

In Socrates' view, the greatest impediment and danger to reason is the pharmakon (or drug) of oratory, which Athenians "loved to their ruin." He dedicated his life and his death to correcting the "errors" of these signifying ways, and here bares his head and mouths his atonement to avoid a similar fate for a similar sin, by way of "wash[ing] out the brine from my ears with the water of sweet discourse" (243d).

THE IMPLICATIONS OF SOCRATIC SHAME

> Just consider, my good Phaedrus, how shameless the two speeches were, both this of mine and the one you read out of the book.
> —Socrates (243c)

Socrates' ritual of atonement attests to the violence of his shame—for having profaned the philosophic ideal by speaking in sophistic tongues, and by "speaking ill of Love," in particular. He abruptly ends his first speech, vowing to quit the scene rather than continue speaking in a sophistic vein: "I shall cross this stream and go away before you put some further compulsion upon me" (242a). The sudden rupture in Socrates' sophistic discourse occurs at the precise moment he is cataloguing the faults of the lover, speaking the greatest ill about the very thing he has dedicated his life to, philosophic Eros. With respect to the beloved, the lover is

> faithless, irritable, jealous and disagreeable, harmful to his property, harmful to his physical condition, *and most harmful by far to the cultivation of his soul* . . . the fondness of the lover is not a matter of good will, but of appetite which he wishes to satisfy. Just as the wolf loves the lamb, so the lover adores his beloved. (241c–d, my emphasis)

At this point, Socrates stops speaking—like an actor who falls out of character and is no longer able to keep up the pretense of his role, conscious of having "committed a sin against the deity"—by having "spoken ill" of Love. The phrase, "most harmful by far to the cultivation of his soul," leaves perhaps a particularly bitter taste on his lips. For this is precisely what motivates his educative impulse toward Phaedrus, not as a non-lover but as a lover. Thus, in speaking ill of Love, he is speaking ill of himself—betraying his own inmost soul. This is the price his elenchus exacts on his soul: he must recant his most deeply held beliefs to enact his dialectic elenchus. This is the cruel irony at the heart of his shame: he must renounce himself (temporarily) to edify both Self and Other. The mutual affirmation of self and other through philosophy is preceded by the mutual negation of self and other, as an affect of sophistry. No wonder Socrates feels like a Judas to his cause, struggling to reconcile the roles of exemplar and betrayer of the exemplar. His guilt for having profaned the philosophic ideal within himself is the crown of thorns he wears (along with the hood) and the cross of self-crucifixion he bears. Thus, the poem of atonement, by virtue of the violent shame that prompts it, evidences Socrates' masochistic tendencies, even as his elenchus evidences his sadistic impulses toward the sophistic Other. It may evidence as well the projection of Platonic shame, fueled not only by masochistic and sadistic, but parricidal, tendencies (themes I will develop at greater length in the Chapter 7).

The rupture, like that between the hood and his sophistic words at the start of this speech, similarly opens up the "dilatory space" of analytical recantation. Into this deliberate breach of recantation, Phaedrus is drawn. These two moments signify the birth of Phaedrus' critical faculty, even as they herald the turn from sophistic to philosophic discourse. Just as significantly, they evidence the generative violence of Socrates' shame, which inaugurates the series of transformative recantations. Socrates' sophistic speech is framed by two ruptures which put the "lie" to his sophistic words. Each recants a sophistic thesis that "speaks ill of Love:" the very foundation of Socrates' elenchus, insofar as the path to philosophic knowledge leads inevitably to and through Eros.

Immediately after profaning Love with a litany of the lover's monstrosities climaxed by the figure of the wolf in lamb's clothing, Socrates abruptly drops the guise of the sophistic non-lover, leaving Phaedrus to wonder "why did you stop?"

Why, indeed?

The answer is twofold. He pauses in order to purify the self of the effects of profanation and to edify the other by initiating the shift from rhetoric to rhetorical analysis with a ritual discourse of recantation that is concomitantly a critique of sophistry. I want to further explicate the eruptive force of a repressed shame that cuts short Socrates' sophistic speech on the "ill[s] of Love." Socrates' poem of atonement deeply informs the psychological origins of his pedagogy of recantation, even as it evidences the violence of his shame, guilt, and fear. To continue, he would have had to sing the praises of the non-lover, which struck him as perhaps even more shameful than enumerating the monstrosities of the lover. His poem of atonement announces a temporary truce in the war of discourses between sophistry and philosophy, in which the combatant pauses to cleanse his soul of the violent effects of this rhetorical warfare, seeking expiation for the sins committed thus far. His soul cleansed, he returns to the combat with blood on his lips.

Into the breach of this rupture between sophistic and philosophic discourse floods not only Socrates' dialectic recantation of sophistry, but his shamefaced recantation of his recantation of philosophy. Before he can recant sophistry, he must recant his recantation of philosophy. The fear of punishment in the form of Homeric blindness evidences the violence of his shame for having abandoned and profaned his philosophic ideal. The poem of atonement enables Socrates to "take back his word."

The effect of this shame is to produce a kind of madness—dramatizing yet again the affective power of the Word, for better or "ill." This madness affects his speech—as if sophistry itself is a kind of rhetorical madness, uttered by a madman, and to speak in sophistic tongues is to risk being maddened by it: "did you not notice, my friend, that I am already speaking in hexameters, not mere dithyrambics, even though I am finding fault with the lover?" (241e). It is not blindness he suffers, but a kind of rhetorical impediment, which for someone like Socrates was perhaps even more frightening, given the centrality of orality to his elenchus, given the extent to which his entire identity was bound up in that elenchus. His rhetorical madness is the first effect of his profanation of the philosophic ideal, for having "spoken ill of Love," which he worships above anything "in heaven or on earth," asserting that "there neither is nor ever will be anything of higher importance in truth" because it leads to the "cultivation of [the] soul" (241e).

The series of "higher," "truth," "heaven," and "soul" comprises a chain of signification that alliterates with the sign of "deity" by virtue of their mutual association with Love. These signs establish as well a dramatic juxtaposition with the signs of "madness," "crime," "error," "possessed," and "nymphs": a signifying chain associated with the sophistic non-lover, by whose signifying practices his soul has been tainted. Socrates feels keenly the painful effects of this shameful betrayal (revealing his masochistic tendencies) and now must pay the piper of his "stoops to conquer" rhetorical strategy of mimicry and meta-drama. Ironically, it is meta-drama that comes to his rescue in the first redemptive moment of his recantation: through the ritual of purification he performs to mitigate the violent effects of his profane apostasy.

Such is the violence of Socrates' shame that he even renounces ownership of his sophistic speech, assigning authorship instead to Phaedrus: "the speech that was spoken by you through my mouth," which was "bewitched" into speaking in sophistic tongues (242e). This claim and the signs associated with it ("bewitched") further underscore the affective power of the Word, even as they recuperate a measure of generative agency for Phaedrus-as-interlocutor. This recuperated agency reinforces the protean agency he enjoys as the beautiful beloved, whose violent effects on Socrates are evidenced by his repeated avowals of love, by his flattery of Phaedrus, and by the erotic flow of figuration incited by Phaedrus' beauty—all evidencing the powerful effect of the sublime on Socrates and his particular susceptibility to Beauty, whether in the form of beautiful discourse, a beautiful youth, or a beautiful youth mouthing beautiful discourse. Thus, the agency of the dialectic is indeed mutual, in contradistinction to the claims of many critics, who, by focusing merely on the disproportionate speech of master and pupil, are misled into assigning a disproportionate agency between them, to the exclusion of other elements that evidence the mutual agency of the master-pupil, self-other dyad, here evidenced by Socrates' assertion that Phaedrus was speaking through him in sophistic tongues.

This recantation of his own words is significant, for it underscores a recurring pattern in the *Phaedrus,* which it here reverses: in which Socrates speaks through the mouth of Lysias, even as Plato speaks through the mouth of Socrates. Here, it is the mouth of Socrates that has been usurped by the sophistic other (Phaedrus) in a reversal of roles between the signifying systems of philosophy and sophistry. But instead of producing "truth" or the "cultivation" of the soul, this usurpation of discourse by sophistry only generates madness and shame. Socrates succumbs not only to the affective power of Phaedrus' youthful beauty, but to the affective power of his sophistic discourse, evidencing the violent effects of this sublime conjunction of beauty and rhetoric, which posits as much agency for the pupil as for the master. Socrates is thrown off balance, put out of sort by the one-two punch of Phaedrus' beauty and his own shame, evidencing the dual nature of the sublime's effects on the beholder: its ability to both terrify and enthrall. His poem of atonement is prompted by his desire to work off the self-negating effects of a sublime that frightens.

This madness and shame create a sudden rupture in the tissue of the narrative—though like the expulsion of Adam and Eve from the garden as a consequence of sin, its violence is generative and liberatory, insofar as it gives birth to analysis, heralding the redemptive (re)turn to philosophy. Psychologically, the wound of profanation also evidences Socrates and Plato's kinship with a particular kind of artist (the artiste manqué), who creates out of his or her suffering, as a means of mitigating or objectifying its effects. In his poem of atonement, Socrates signifies out of a wound of shame, mitigating its violent, potentially self-destructive effects by objectifying it in the symbolic realm of word and ritual. For the artiste manqué, invention functions in a similar manner: as an objectification of a morbid suffering that debilitates but whose debilitating effects are mitigated by invention. Socrates' multiple inventions throughout his polemic (figuration, role-playing, mimicry, ritual) all attest to the operation of an ancient vitalism, thus far under-theorized by criticism. Socrates' poem of atonement dramatizes the objectification of his shame in the realm of the symbolic, through its alliteration with the myth of Stesichorus and the uncovering of his head—which mirrors and reverses the ritual hooding of his head at the start of his speech, as if to shield himself from the shameful effects of it.

The violent effects of Socrates' shame that necessitate the rite of purification are further evidenced when he confides that "all along while I was speaking my discourse, something troubled me, and 'I was distressed,' as Ibycus says, 'lest I be buying honor among men by sinning against the gods" (242c–d). His shame is due to the fact that by speaking against Love, which "is a god or something divine" (242d), he has indeed sinned against the god. His shame is due to the fact that he now sees the grievous "error" he has committed: "so now I understand my error." Thus, his poem of atonement is truly a recantation insofar as it is a "confession of error" (Webster, 612): "But now I have seen my error" (242d). Indeed, the entire palinode will be dedicated to the necessity of getting Phaedrus to see the "errors" of sophistic signifying practices: that it errs against the beautiful and the ethical.

The magnitude of Socrates' profanation is evidenced by the fact that his personal daemon (a reinscription of the pagan spirit-helper) suddenly appears to warn him of its effects: "it always holds me back from something I am about to do." This daemon acts as a moral compass, if you will, is figured under the sign of Ethos. Its dramatic appearance in the *Phaedrus* ("when I was about to cross the stream, the *spirit and the sign that usually comes to me came*") reinscribes Socrates' invocation of his personal daemon in the *Apology:* "I have a divine or *spiritual sign*. . . . it is a *voice* and whenever it speaks it *turns me away from something I am about to do*" (31d, my emphasis). In the *Phaedrus,* Socrates continues: "I thought I heard a voice from it which forbade my going away *before clearing my conscience,* as if I had committed some sin against the deity" (242c–d, my emphasis).

The chain of mutual signifiers ("spirit," "sign," "voice," "holds me back," "turns me away," "from something I am about to do") underscores the extent to which these two moments in the *Apology* and *Phaedrus* not only inform one another, but reinforce the alliteration between piety and philosophy, wherein piety acts to "correct" the "errors" of an over-corrective philosophic inquiry, purging it of its sophistic tendencies and its rhetorical excesses (megalegoria, mimicry, deception, profanation), and the effects associated with those tendencies, by *re-cultivating* his soul, as it were. In sum, these two rituals of recantation deeply inform the meaning of the protrepticus, even as they prefigure the dialectic recantation of sophistry which commences in earnest immediately after the poem of atonement. Finally, they evidence the rhetorical complexity of the *Phaedrus* and the vitalism associated with its rich signifying systems and with the symbiosis of its symbolic and material realms.

THE DIALECTICS OF RECANTATION

Socrates voices his desire to recant the sophistry espoused by Lysias before it is too late to reverse its idolatrous effects upon Phaedrus, whom he hopes to "hold back" or "turn away" "from something he is about to do," who is about to "accept a non-lover before we can stop him." Socrates shifts Phaedrus' gaze from idolatry of rhetoric to rhetorical analysis by "challeng[ing] Phaedrus' estimation of the speech on Phaedrus' own level" (Griswold, 52). Yet his own "criticisms are, in fact fairly superficial, touching only on the formal, the technical, or what he calls the 'rhetorical'(235a)" (52), including the deficiencies of its arrangement. Yet the superficial nature of Socrates' initial analysis of Lysias' text is itself efficacious, fundamental to his edifying process.

Socrates commences his rhetorical analysis, in other words, by modeling an analysis with training wheels, as it were, which is tailored to Phaedrus' limited cognitive abilities. As Griswold observes, "the turn to analysis of techne in the second half of the *Phaedrus*" underscores the ubiquity of analysis in Socrates' discourse, in his effort to educate the untutored mind of his pupil, to move his cognition from a state of unreflective idolatry of discourse to an informed analysis of it. This calls into question the grounds for Ferrari's defense of Lysias' speech. Socrates' focus on its superficial errors was simply further evidence of his "kairic" awareness, which prompts him to customize his critique to his pupil's superficial cognitive abilities. The extent to which eros is replaced by analysis as the higher rungs of the cognitive ladder are reached is evidenced by the focus of Socrates' discourse on "the problem of rhetoric (259e–262c); division, collection, and the paradigms of rhetoric (262c–266c); and the manuals, the masters of the techne, and the five descriptions of the method of knowing . . . (266c–274b)" (165). Griswold continues:

Socrates' first speech played the role of intermediary between the other two. Consequently, its emphasis on orderly, rule-governed thinking occupied an intermediate position between the self-interested calculations of Lysias' speech, and the reasonable madness of the palinode. So too now, the techne of thinking is pedagogically useful because it is inferior to philosophic rhetoric but superior to merely popular rhetoric. (162–163)

The discourse during this second conversion is a "reflection on procedure, method, and language," on the abstract scientific concepts of analysis, privileging the interpretative act (197). It models a "Techne [that] is a rule governed, precise, comprehensive, and a rigorous method of analysis that is teachable . . . " (199). These intermediate speeches function like rungs on the ladder of cognitive development. As Griswold observes, "the enthusiastic and erotic idiom of the first half seems replaced by a detached and analytic idiom" (157), as part of a developmental cognitive process, as the focus shifts from eros to rhetorical analysis, including analysis of rhetoric itself. Griswold continues: "the use of the method of analysis Socrates goes on to delineate demands the self conscious awareness that in order to reach a given goal one must take a determinate series of steps" (163).

Freirean praxis similarly grounds a series of developmental stages in which "investigation of the generative themes . . . initiate[s] the first stage" (102). The "second stage" involves the "codification" of the "complex of contradictions" discovered in the "situations" being "examined" (106). The "third stage" involves the eternal return of the Word to the World, at the site of investigation to "initiate decoding dialogues in thematic investigation circles" (110) at the point of contact between a problematic reality and those affected by it. The "last stage" involves a "systematic interdisciplinary study of the findings," which are then "codified" for dissemination according to the "best channel of communication for each theme and its representation" (114). Each radical pedagogy embodies a developmental process of cognition relative to a problematic reality. At every stage, dialogic communication is the medium of edification, from the "unveiling" of a problematic reality through analysis to the application of that analysis to the problematic reality in order to mitigate its dehumanizing effects, whether associated with the excesses of sophistry or colonialism. With respect to Socrates' radical pedagogy, a scientific emphasis on superficial codes that decodes the limitations, flaws, and weaknesses of Lysias' text (its want of complexity, unity, and arrangement) is in turn followed by an intermediary stage of analysis, which in turn prepares the way for more complex criteria of analysis, in a rhetorical analysis that scales a "ladder" of cognition.

The increasing dialogic nature of the discourse evidences Phaedrus' rising cognition and ability to participate in the analysis: "Phaedrus seems to have progressed a bit" (158), to the point that he questions Lysias' status as the "ablest writer of the day. . . (228a)" (Griswold 158). The techne of division and classification, as Griswold observes, is another mechanism of the retrospective wisdom that characterizes the *Phaedrus,* insofar as the order and unity it imposes are an a posteriori phenomenon relative to knowledge. It does not unveil knowledge; it merely organizes it, imposes an analytical order upon it, underscoring the primacy of the assumption that wisdom in Plato is retrospective. As Griswold observes, "the techne is not a way of *discovering* new knowledge; it is a way of *organizing* something one already knows. . . . that is to say, the techne is retrospective" (185, my emphasis). This observation calls into question the alleged tyranny of a Platonic sign that is always and already transcendent and a priori.

The *Phaedrus* dramatizes the deep alliteration between discourse and analysis of discourse. As Griswold observes, it "not only *shows* dialectic at work; it indirectly supplies . . . a commentary *about* the dialectic" (219). In this, too, it prefigures Freirean praxis, in which students "reach a perception of their previous perception" (108). This constant fluctuation between rhetoric and analysis of rhetoric is not only a strategy of dialectic edification, but of artistic production: it is as central to Socrates' elenchus as it is to Plato's art. For the artist, as Rank observes, escapes domination by his or her art by escaping from art into analysis of it, forever fluctuating between creative and critical impulses, between invention and the codification of it. Socrates is as gifted as an orator as he is as a critic of oratory. Plato's *Phaedrus* reflects a similar paradox: as a work of art deeply informed by the art of analysis. As Griswold observes, "*Phaedrus* is much more explicitly devoted to reflection on discourse about eros than is *The Symposium* and so manifests a curious detachment . . . ," even as the artist detaches his soul from the totalizing effects of art by retreating into analysis of it, developing a science of art that embodies his/her aesthetic ideology—even as Socrates performs his science of dialectical analysis, enumerating the criteria that define his notion of beautiful discourse.

If there is a radical evangelicalism to Socrates' own rhetoric, it is because he foresees the dangers of a rhetoric of persuasion when it is allowed to circulate uncritically through the masses. The counter-discourse he advocates is intended to prevent the subjugation of the Athenian subject by the power of persuasion, by arming that individual with a means of defending himself or herself from the dangerous conjunction of power and persuasion. Though aimed immediately at the edification of the individual Other, the ultimate objective of Socrates' radical praxis is the edification of the Athenian citizenry. The edifying discourse of dialectical analysis operates through the individual to subvert the collectivizing effects of sophistic rhetoric and the traditional discourses it enshrines: epic myth, dramatic poetry, epideictic speech, and forensic rhetoric. Phaedrus is Socrates' dialectic guinea pig: a human metonym for the Athenian subject in Socrates' project of social engineering toward the creation of an ideal human type.

112 *The Radical Pedagogies of Socrates and Freire*

Dialectics is by nature a dissident critique of power and of the state apparatuses and discourses through which that power circulates. Socrates thus concentrates his praxis on the youth, on the pupil, in an effort to facilitate "the triumph of energy and youth against the resistances of age, tradition, and hierarchy" (Brooks 64)—which is precisely why the state tried him for "corrupting the youth of Athens." Socrates' critique of discourse evidences the degree to which the power of the state depends on the power of persuasion—and on the concomitant suppression of resistant, critical discourses, toward a univocal discourse that privileges sameness by demonizing difference, that cultivates an economy of discourses, as Foucault observes, and fears the carnivalesque insurrection of heteroglossic signifying practices, as Bakhtin asserts. Figuration, as well as mimicry, myth, and meta-dramatic discourse, reinforces this dialectic project.

THE IMMORTAL FLUTTER OF EROTIC FIGURATION

Through dialectic discourse that speaks well and highly of Love in its relation to logos, Socrates sets about in earnest to "cultivate the soul" of Phaedrus. He begins by refuting Lysias' claim that the madness of the lover is a curse, arguing by contrast that it is "the greatest of blessings"—and the surest proof of authentic love. He then models his analytical hermeneutic, subdividing madness into four kinds (the madness of the prophet, the priest-healer, the artist, and the lover), all of which are divinely inspired. He trumps this analysis with an analysis of the nature of the soul, deploying the trope of the winged chariot. He demonstrates that, in contradistinction to the profane eros of Lysias' non-lover, the sacred Eros of the philosophic lover is evidenced in its lofty intent and effects (on both lover and beloved, Self and Other): in the mutual edification that flows from it. For instead of thinking of the beloved as a mere object of his own sexual desires, the philosophic lover "reveres the beautiful one as a god" and "would offer sacrifice to his beloved as to an idol or a god."

The violent effects of the beloved's beauty upon the lover underscore the authenticity of his love, reinforcing the thesis that "madness" is the "greatest of all blessings." Here, Socrates' polemic rises to new affective heights through the flight of figuration and a rhetoric of erotic innuendo, surpassing anything found in Lysias' text—and perhaps anything in western literary canon, save perhaps Albertine's erotic discourse on the "ices" in Proust (*La Prisonnière*). Socrates offers this madness as a proof, perhaps the surest proof, of the lover's love, with a figurative litany of the effects of Beauty, which figuratively give wings to his soul, bringing the metaphor of the winged chariot to life, in a passage worth quoting in its entirety:

> And as he looks upon him, a reaction from his *shuddering* comes over him, with *sweat* and unwonted heat; for as the *effluence* of beauty

enters him through the eyes, he is warmed; the effluence *moistens* the germ of the feathers, and as he grows warm, the parts from which the feathers grow, which were before *hard and choked* . . . become *soft*, and as the nourishment *streams* upon him, the *quills* of the feathers *swell* and begin to *grow*, from the roots over all the form of the soul, for it was once all feathered. (251a–c, my emphasis)

The significance of the passage for the recantation of sophistry, and its claims regarding the non-lover, are difficult to understate and they invite further scrutiny. The signifying chain of "shuddering," "sweat," "effluence," "enters him," "moistens," "hard and choked," "soft," "quills," "swell," and "grow" evidences the degree to which philosophic Eros, instead of recanting erotic love, assimilates it. Additionally, as a dramatic figuration of the effects of the erotic sublime, Plato's passage ranks with the most memorable ever penned, including those penned by Wordsworth, Ruskin, and Proust, whose aesthetic ideologies (and the works that embodied them) were nothing if not monuments to theories of the sublime.

What is perhaps most significant in this passage, however, is its dramatization of the mutual edification of the dialectic dyad, which here dramatizes the "cultivation" of Socrates' soul within the context of cultivating Phaedrus' soul—which dramatizes the mutual edification of master and pupil through the mutual cultivation of their souls. If Phaedrus' soul is cultivated by the beauty of dialectic discourse, Socrates' soul is cultivated by the transformative effects of Phaedrus' beauty, embodied in his looks and in his love of beautiful discourse. It underscores the mutual agency of the dialogic educative process, in which the cultivation of Socrates' soul is compelled by Phaedrus' beauty, even as he was compelled by Phaedrus to give a sophistic speech, like many before him. The agency Phaedrus enjoys in this mutual process, by virtue of the compelling effects of his beauty and of his ability to compel others to give beautiful speeches, refutes the notion that he is a mere passive interlocutor, a "straw dog" to Socrates' dialectic agenda.

If mimicry and meta-drama were used to enact the apostasy from philosophy, to establish a false other-other resemblance under the sign of sophistry, then by contrast erotic figuration is dramatically used in the palinode to recant Lysias' thesis regarding the "evil" of Love, to demonstrate its goodness, beauty, and efficacy as a path to mutual edification, establishing a genuine self-self alliteration under the sign of philosophic love. Figuration and dialectic analysis are the dual modes by which sophistry is recanted in favor of philosophy. To the extent it serves the dialectic polemic, figuration replicates the vitalizing roles of myth, meta-drama, and poetry, further evidencing the *Phaedrus'* rhetorical complexity.

Socrates' figuration works in consort with a rhetoric of erotic innuendo to recant the thesis of an "evil" Love, reinforcing the thesis of a philosophic Love, operating within the process of mutual edification:

> Now in this process the whole soul *throbs and palpitates*, and as in those who are *cutting teeth* there is an *irritation and discomfort* in the gums when the teeth begin to grow, just so the *soul suffers* when the *growth of the feathers* begins. . . . then when it gazes upon the beauty of the [beloved] and receives the particles which *flow* thence to it . . . it is *moistened and warmed*, ceases from its pain and is *filled* with joy. (252c–d, my emphasis)

Socrates' observations dramatize the dual effects of the sublime. If it is capable of inciting pleasure on the one hand, it is also capable of inducing pain, as evidenced by the signifying chain of "cutting teeth," "irritation," "discomfort," and "soul suffers." These things reveal the inherent suffering associated with the sublime, and with philosophic love in particular, which by virtue of its dialogic imperative is dependent on an Other, whose beauty and/or beautiful discourse exercises a power over the soul of the Self, subverting its agency and independence: a suffering which also betrays the masochistic tendencies of Socratic inquiry, which punishes the Self in its self-reflexive, corrective examinations as much as the Other in its corrective interrogations. To the extent this suffering becomes an impetus to art, to the extent it agitates the creative impulse, it also establishes the kinship of Plato and Plato's Socrates with the artiste manqué, or suffering artist.

Socrates further unveils the masochistic suffering associated with philosophic love:

> But when it is *alone*. . . . shut in with the *yearning* . . . so that the whole soul, *stung in every part, rages with pain* . . . is *greatly troubled* by its *strange condition*, it is *perplexed* and *maddened,* and in its madness it *cannot sleep* at night *or stay in one place* by day, but is filled with *longing* and *hastens* wherever it hopes to see the beautiful one. . . . Therefore, the soul will not, if it can help it, be left alone by the beautiful one . . . and *despising all customs* and properties in which it formerly took pride, it is ready to be a *slave* and to sleep wherever it is allowed, as near as possible to the beloved, for it not only reveres him who possesses beauty, but finds in him the *only healer* of its greatest woes. Now this condition, fair boy, about which I am speaking is called *Love.* . . . " The Winged One, because he must needs grow wings." (251d–e, my emphasis)

Thus, the soul grows its wings through the sublime effects of love, both beautiful and terrifying. In fact, what Socrates here portrays is a portrait of the Sublime that prefigures by 2,000 years the depiction of its violent effects by "its eighteenth century originators" (Gray, Wordsworth, et al.), its nineteenth century interpreters (Ruskin) and its twentieth century modernists (Proust, Joyce et al.)—whose "theories of the [S]ublime" deeply inform aesthetic ideology (Landow 185), and particularly the aesthetics of the *Phaedrus:*

> The notion of reaction is at the center of theories of the sublime: the spectator upon encountering sublimity in art or nature [or love], reacts emotionally . . . theories of sublimity, which were frequently concerned with *violent emotional reactions*, made the intensity of the aesthetic experience a matter of concern. (70–71, my emphasis)

—as Joyce does in *Portrait*, with Stephen's reaction to the terrors of the religious Sublime; as Proust does in *A la recherche*, with Marcel's violent response to the Sublime in "art or nature" (the hawthorns, the "little phrase," the steeples of Martinville, etc.), and as Plato does in the *Phaedrus*, with the violence of Socrates' reaction to Beauty, incarnated in Phaedrus and discourse—in which the "external qualities of the object [excite] the psychological experiences of the beholder" (93). What Plato dramatizes in the *Phaedrus* is the experience of the beloved sublime upon the loving beholder. Further, the edifying effects of sublimity are no less transformative and redemptive for Plato's Socrates than they are for Joyce's Stephen or Proust's Marcel. The transformative shock of the sublime redeems Socrates, Dedalus, and Marcel through philosophic eros and art respectively.

Socrates' figurative eruption recants the claim of Lysias' low thesis regarding the "evils" the lover perpetrates upon the beloved, by showing that as a consequence of the violent effects of love, the lover does violence, not to the beloved but to the Self—compounding the masochistic impulses of the dialectic examination, confident that under the lash of these growing pangs, the soul's wings will grow. Similarly, the suffering it necessarily inflicts on the beloved through the destruction of the pupil's dangerous infatuation with sophistry will "cultivate" the growth of the wings in the beloved's soul: through heightened powers of cognition and the effects of a mutual eros grounded in mutual edification—through the mirroring effect of eros and edification. "So the stream of beauty," as Socrates asserts, "passes back into the beautiful one through the eyes, the natural inlet to the soul, where it reanimates the passages of the feathers, waters them and makes the feathers begin to grow, filling the soul of the loved one with love" (251a–c).

Socrates' figuration of the effects of the sublime evidence the *mutual* edification of self and other, dramatizing an educative process that is genuinely dialogic. In Socrates' discourse on the "feathers" of the soul, under the influence of beauty, the erotic is never figured as an end in itself, distinct from the philosophic, as in Lysias' text, but as intimately linked to the soul's edification, as are feathers to a bird's flight. Thus, the profane eros of Lysias' sophistic discourse is absorbed into the sacred, philosophic Eros of Socrates' polemic.

Thus, erotic figuration becomes yet another effective signifying stratagem of the dialectic polemic, further evidencing the *Phaedrus*' rhetorical complexity, reinforcing the rich signification of irony, allegory, satire, history, myth, mimicry, meta-drama, dialectics, and sophistic signification, which are all part of the complex rhetorical weave of the dialogue. In contradistinction to the explicit eroticism of Lysias' thesis (it is better to grant "favors" to the non-lover than the lover), Socrates' erotic innuendo reinforces his overall rhetorical strategy, revealing the extent to which the erotic impulse is necessarily assimilated into the edifying impulse, not as part of a either-or binary between eroticism and philosophy, but as part of a continuum under the sign of philosophic love. Sexual "favors" are not granted as part of an educative quid pro quo; instead, the erotic is figured as a natural, if animalistic, force of the soul to be assimilated into its higher, reasoning, edifying impulses, evidencing the hierarchical tension between the "unruly horse" and "the charioteer," the sexual and the philosophic. As Socrates observes,

> He desires to see his friend, to touch him, kiss him, and lie down by him. . . . now as they lie together, the unruly horse of the lover [the sex impulse] has something to say to the charioteer, and demands a little enjoyment in return for his many troubles . . . but the other horse and the charioteer *oppose all this with modesty and reason.* (256a, my emphasis)

That Socrates literally gives the last word to "reason" is significant, for it dramatizes the extent to which the profane impulses of the divided soul are to be tamed and assimilated by the sacred impulses of mutual edification, the extent to which the sexual is mastered by the intellectual, and the profane eros of Lysias' text is recanted by the sacred eros of Socrates' palinode.

Socrates' erotic figuration heightens the "vitalism" of Platonic inscription, evidences the extent to which the cognitive and creative are conjoined in the rhetorical. The passage underscores the efficacy of figuration in a polemical context, insofar as it further recants Lysias' thesis of a profane eros, even as it figuratively dramatizes the origins, performs the nature of Socrates' divided soul, by evidencing the developmental effects of the sublime on that soul, as figured in the imagery of the "feathers," "quills," "teething gums," whose growth in the presence of the sublime culminates in the soul's maturation, as evidenced by the flight of the "winged chariot."

Further, the chain of figuration here prefigures Freire's use of figuration to reinforce his pedagogical polemic, as evidenced by the efficacy of his "banking" metaphor to describe the subjugating effects of colonialism, and of colonial education in particular, in which the master's knowledge is "deposited" in the subject—as if the subject is nothing more than a "repository" for the master's wealth, including his wealth of "knowledge" (58). Freire's polemic on colonialism, no less than Socrates' critique of sophistry, is reinforced through figuration. Metaphors of disease reinforce the violence of colonialism upon the subject, which acts like a "pathology" (60) through "narration sickness" (57) to "anesthetize"

(146) and "inoculate" (147) the colonized, as a form of "castration" that reduces individuals to "living corpses," to "shadows" confined to a "blind alley" (100).

In both radical pedagogies, figuration recants the logic of power and the power of persuasion through which it circulates. Yet, as Hawk rightly observes, these strategies of invention are a largely under-theorized aspect of rhetoric and composition, as is the broader category of "vitalism," despite their "relevance to pedagogies of invention" (4) to a vision of rhetoric that recuperates its lost complexity. These tropes of the creative reinforce the logic of the cognitive, are generative with respect to its meanings—and thus, to the "vitalism" of a text. Platonic inquiry is heightened by Platonic invention: by the effective use of the figurative, meta-dramatic, poetic, and epic. Hawk underscores the centrality of "vitalism" to classical rhetoric, "tracing vitalism's beginning with Plato's pupil, Aristotle" (9), by way of mitigating its marginalized status in contemporary composition studies. As a species of creative thought, "vitalism" has been marginalized by a "rhetoric of exclusion" (11), which reinscribes the master-slave hierarchical binary of cognitive/creative, in which the scientific is privileged over the artistic, the analytical over the inventive. This historical suppression of the creative in the history of rhetoric, however, heightens the efficacy of theorizing it from a Derridean perspective, by "enact[ing] the ancient practice of dissoi logoi, making the weaker argument the stronger" (10). I want to apply Hawk's theory of "vitalism" as a dissoi logoi to Plato's *Phaedrus*, in an effort to further trace the origins of vitalism beyond Aristotle, to his mentor, Plato, toward the recuperation of its efficacy as a strategy of argumentation and as a signifying practice that is particularly effective by virtue of its ability to not only generate meanings, but heighten the affective power of polemic discourse through its appeals to logos and pathos.

The creative, throughout Phaedrus, sets up the scientific; the figurative prefigures the analytical. Socrates' figurative incantation on the generative effects of the sublime on the beholder's soul reinforces and foreshadows the dialectical recantation. Its ritualized rhetoric not only reinscribes the rituals of the hood and the poem of atonement, but heralds the return to reason. In the wake of these rhetorical rites, the art of rhetoric gives way to the science of rhetorical analysis, which comprises the foundation of Socrates' critical pedagogy. As Griswold observes, Plato is not only modeling the efficacy of division and classification to analytical thinking, but also modeling a critique of the *limitations* of division and classification, in order to further develop Phaedrus' faculty for critical thought, upon which the desire for dialectic edification depends for its fulfillment. Socrates' rhetorical analysis of his own speech is, as Griswold asserts,

> intended by Plato to tell us something about the limitations of the method, [not only] in the great palinode (Socrates' second speech), but in the *jarring transition* from [it] to the discussion of method

[which is similarly] designed to teach us about the limitations of the palinode. (11)

Socrates' critique of his own criteria of analysis (the limits of division and classification) is tantamount to yet another recantation. As such, Socrates' critical pedagogy is a precursor of models in use today, where the strengths, limits, assumptions, and implications of a given argument are assessed as part of a rhetorical analysis across disciplines, their diverse "feasibilities" "tested" retrospectively.

Instead of modeling these elements of analysis concomitantly, however, Plato's Socrates models them sequentially: first offering a sophistic argument as an example of persuasive discourse, only to recant it with a critique of its limitations, developing a model of analysis that moves from simplicity to ever increasing levels of complexity—that scales a ladder of analytical thinking. As Griswold observes, "Plato's pedagogy in these cases relies heavily on *irony; views are initially advanced* with great seriousness, but in a context relative to which they can be seen to *undermine themselves*" (11, my emphasis) as self-deconstructing texts. Words enact meanings, which in retrospect are supplanted by fresh, if contradictory, meanings—in a dialectics of meaning-making that is not only Platonic but Proustian, and perhaps here evidences its influence on Proust, whose narrative similarly relies on a strategy of retrospective recantation in its development of meaning, in which the real recants the ideal, only so that both are recuperated in the remembered. (For a more detailed discussion of this signifying "search engine" in Proust, see Brown's *The Gardens of Desire: Marcel Proust and the Fugitive Sublime,* 2004) The original meaning of any purported position is trumped by a higher purpose and a hidden agenda: to foster critical thought, as the art of persuasion is trumped by the art of analysis, reinscribing the hierarchical relationship between rhetoric and philosophy, persuasion and analysis. Under this retrospective analytical gaze, strengths are revealed to be weaknesses, beauty is exposed as counterfeit, truths are discovered to be opinions, and "signs [mis]taken for wonders" (Bhabha 159). As in Proust, meaning dwells in a contradictory flux until stabilized through a retrospective gaze, which recants previous meanings that are absorbed into a harmonizing and transformative signification—under the signs of philosophic eros and art respectively.

This drama of recantation becomes the vehicle for the edification of the beloved Other, operating through rhetorical analysis, figuration, myth, meta-drama, and a host of signifying practices, each of which develops the polemic through a strategy of systematic deconstruction. A text of sophistic persuasion becomes a mere (pre)text for dialectical analysis, which in turn becomes the (pre)text for further analysis, as the sophistic sign of persuasion yields to the sophisticated sign of dialectic analysis. This transformation is facilitated not only by the resemblance of Socrates' first speech to Lysias' text, but by the "peculiar intimacy" of sophistic and philosophic discourse. Sophistry is placed on a pedestal by Socrates because it has been placed there by his beloved pupil, only so that it might be toppled from its pedestal through a discourse of dialectic analysis, by which it is supplanted on the pedestal.

The challenge Socrates issues to the pupil, Phaedrus, is akin to the challenge Plato issues to the reader: "to look deeper" at a text for its hidden, unstated meanings (Griswold 12), to be reflective toward it, skeptical of its purported meanings, inquisitive of its embedded meanings, curious not only about what its says, but what it omits—examining its unstated aims, implications, and problematic effects. His methodology has significant implications for the first-year writing workshop, by virtue of its emphasis on rhetorical analysis, close textual readings, the interpretive act, and argumentative strategies, within an interactive learning environment. Socrates models the very act of critical interpretation he is trying to instill, as if to assert that it is only through interpretation that a text's meanings can be apprehended: implying that meaning is made as much through the act of interpretation as through the act of authorship, by the reader as well as by the writer. Thus, meaning is negotiated between the aggressions of the text's effect upon the reader and the interpretative aggressions of the reader toward the text—is itself the result of a kind of rhetorical combat between speaker/writer and reader/critic, waged through and over signification.

Throughout *Phaedrus,* Socrates models the aggressions of interpretation, while deconstructing the aggressive affective power of sophistic signification, reinscribing his aggressive deconstruction of the legal writs brought against him in the *Apology* by Meletus and Antyus. Thus, ironically the *Phaedrus* dramatizes the mutual aggressions of a text's affective power and interpretation of it, in a lethal combat over signification, its meanings, and its effects, which is in effect a war waged by other means. The *Phaedrus* reinscribes on a symbolic plane the combative violence of the rhetorical war waged between sophistry and philosophy in the courtroom, the agora, and the marketplace. Analysis disarms the affective force of rhetoric in order to unveil its deeper grammar, as if defusing a ticking bomb. For Socrates, a sense of urgency attends his rhetorical analysis of Lysias' text, if he is to reverse the effects of Phaedrus' idolatry: the most immediate of which is the "granting of favors to a non-lover," but the most enduring of which is a cognitive naïveté that leaves the citizen susceptible to the self-interested manipulations of sophistry.

As with Freire's discourse, one of the most dramatic and transformative effects of Socrates' dialectic elenchus is its violent unmasking of the incestuous dyad of power and the power of persuasion. To apprehend a text's deeper grammar, the veil of its affective power must first be unveiled, its seeming strengths revealed as weaknesses, its seeming "beauty" exposed as counterfeit. As Griswold notes, "the speeches of the first half of the dialogue are used as examples of artful and artless rhetoric," to hold a mirror up to their limitations. Each speech is a successive rung on the ladder of critical thinking, in which Socrates models the strengths of a speech as a precondition for exposing its limitations in a subsequent analysis, in order to develop the faculty of critical thought. Everything in Socrates' discourse is self-reflexive, including irony itself, which as Griswold asserts "is designed to be understood as dissimulation" (13). Throughout the *Phaedrus,* recantation is central to this process of critical edification: a dialectic polemic that is reinforced by a web of signifying practices (irony, satire, and allegory; myth, meta-drama, and figuration) that evidence not only its rhetorical complexity, but its enduring "vitalism."

6 The Error of His Ways
Getting It Wrong to Get It Write

> The "dialatory space" of narrative . . . the space of retard, postponement, *error, and partial revelation*—is the place of *transformation:* where the problems posed to and by initiatory desire are worked out and worked through.
>
> —Brooks (92, my emphasis)

Socrates' critique of sophistry is very much a *trial by error*, insofar as he puts the errors of Lysias' text on trial. But it is also a polemic that proceeds by *trial and error*, exposing the errors of its own ways in order to sharpen Phaedrus' critical faculties relative to the beauty of discourse. The deliberate errors of Socrates' method provide Phaedrus' "teething" intellect something to "cut its teeth" on. Thus, Socrates' dialectic is at once predatory and edifying, insofar as it teaches the pupil how to think critically relative to a text, in the same way a cheetah instructs a cub how to hunt: through a "live-action," trial-and-error demonstration of intellectual hunting that insists upon the pupil's participation, that implicates the pupil in the process of thinking critically.

The edifying process is facilitated not only by the errors Socrates exposes in Lysias' discourse, but by those he "seeds" in his own. These errors give master and pupil alike something to "feed" upon, to sharpen their dialectic claws upon. Socrates' mimicry of sophistic discourse is akin to providing Phaedrus with a captive mouse, whose parts are given "life" through performance, to awaken the pupil's critical hunger. To enhance the development of Phaedrus' cognitive powers, Socrates needs a "live" (as opposed to a "dead") discourse. So, instead of just letting Lysias' words lie passively on the page, he brings them to life through his own performance of them. This performative, "live-action" approach to critical thinking is but one source of the "vitalism" that attends Socratic inquiry. Thus, he teaches Phaedrus how to think critically relative to a text as a cheetah teaches its cub how to hunt, using a "live" prey to quicken cognitive instincts, somewhat as a cat toys with a mouse. Socrates' trial-by-error and trial-and-error method grounds the making of errors in the making of knowledge. In each case, the would-be knower gets it wrong before he gets it write.

Further, is not this the essence of the writing process and the teaching of it? Free-writing, rewriting, and drafting all ground the luxury, indeed the necessity, of getting it wrong to get it right, of a trial-and-error approach that lies at the very heart of Socratic inquiry. Errors, those very flaws of a finished text, are the virtuous enablers of its creation: are generative, protean—each a source of its dynamic vitalism. They subvert control, but this too is a "fortunate fall." For it is the loss of control that engenders error, which in turn engenders words worthy of being controlled. In other words, to discover words worthy of being controlled, we must first surrender control of the process—to error, to trial and error, giving free reign to the error of our ways in order to get it write. Writing that ends by being ordered begins in chaos. We make a mess of words to make meaning of them—and by them. What matter the mess we make of a kitchen, if the plate is well presented? Error is the essential ingredient of the transformation from sophistry to philosophy, in a journey that begins by getting it wrong in order to get it right.

As a meaning-making process, the *Phaedrus* dramatizes and enshrines an epistemology of error. Socrates exposes the errors of sophistry to expose the error of Phaedrus' idolatry of it. He then exposes the errors of his putative philosophic discourse to unveil a genuinely beautiful discourse of philosophic Eros. He further exposes the errors of writing relative to orality, as earlier he exposes the errors of epic myth relative to the blindness of Homer and the seduction of Oreithyia—all as preamble to Plato's exposing the errors of Socrates' megalegoria and sophistry.

These errors open a "dilatory space" between a given sign and what it signifies that invites critical thinking. Mutual edification occurs in the "dilatory space" Socrates opens between sophistry and philosophy through a series of recantations, exposing putative strengths as weaknesses and virtues as "errors." Socrates' meaning-making process operates in this mode of "error and partial revelation" (much the same as Proust's explication of any given sign), where the meaning of any given speech is partially revealed initially, only to be supplemented, if not contradicted, retrospectively, by fresh meanings—which are in turn recanted and supplanted, in a chain of signification that proceeds from errors to correctness, from mistaken wonders to authentic wisdom.

Further, this methodology of meaning-making, in contradistinction to the evolution of the Proustian sign, is inherently social insofar as it is dialogic. With respect to Socratic inquiry and Freirean praxis, the meaning of a given sign is developed dialogically through explication of its errors and contradictions, which are dialogically decoded to enable the discovery of fresh meanings. This dialogic process wrests the authorship of meaning relative to a given sign away from its originator (whether sophist or colonial), conferring that agency instead upon those formerly objectified by the sign.

Thus, Plato's dramatic dialogue is akin to Shakespeare's *Much Ado About Nothing*, a "dramedy" of errors whose serial mis-notings culminate in the ultimate recognition of authentic knowledge. The ontological and epistemological engine of this meaning-making privileges the generative role of error and contradiction, upon which cognition feeds to sate its hunger for knowledge. Further, this retrospective explication of signs is transformative for both teacher and pupil insofar as it converts self-negation into self-affirmation relative to reality: gives the self a liberatory means of asserting itself in reality, through signs, whose possession is first and foremost a means of self-possession.

THEORIZING A RETROSPECTIVE EPISTEMOLOGY OF ERRORS

The "errors" of Socrates' first three speeches are generative of the associative wisdom inherent in the retrospective gaze: "the place of transformation"—for Socrates and Phaedrus, as well as for Freire's peasant and Proust's narrator. As Brooks observes, "it is at the end—for Barthes as for Aristotle—that recognition brings its illumination, which then can shed retrospective light" (92). Thus, Socratic wisdom is inherently corrective and retrospective. It is further, a-temporal, inasmuch as it is sedimented neither in the past, present, or future, as meanings are recanted retrospectively in favor of fresh meanings, which in turn look to a future by which they will be recanted. Yet, it is principally through the sign's retrospective explication that meaning is made, in Plato as in Proust. Deleuze succinctly describes this Plato-Proust genealogy with respect to the retrospective explication of signs: "[T]here is a certain Platonism in Proust . . . and the disjunct use of the faculties in their involuntary exercise has . . . its model in Plato's education of a sensibility open to the violence of signs" (160). It is similarly through the retrospective gaze that the historical signs of colonialism are explicated in Freirean praxis. Indeed, is it precisely this mutual explication of the "violence of signs" that evidences the epistemological genealogy of Plato, Proust, and Freire, even as it underscores the tragic origins of each "educative" model. If ideas "come before," it is only so that they may be altered, recanted, and supplanted by ideas that "come after." The initial "violence of signs" is mitigated by fresh meanings, generated retrospectively. The violence is mitigated as well by its transposition from the realms of the real and the historical to the realms of the symbolic—the more so if this transposition is effected dialogically, through the solidarity of self and other.

The operation of this retrospective explication throughout the *Phaedrus* recants Plato's assumption of "forms" that "come before" language, of a "Truth" that transcends signification, of an "Idea that is always 'before,' always presupposed, even when it is discovered only afterwards" (Deleuze 97). Thus, the retrospective explication of errors is central to the meaning-making process of Socratic inquiry, even as Invention in both Socratic and Platonic discourse is a function of error, a by-product of it. Error in the *Phaedrus* is thus central to both the invention of meaning and its recantation, both commences and culminates the meaning-making process: is central to both the art and the science of the *Phaedrus*, to its creation and its dialectics.

Due to error, the explication of any text or sign's meaning is only partial and is subject to alteration, addition, or contradiction by future explications that often recant previous meanings. Thus, meaning in never fixed, never singular, but is endowed with a fluid multiplicity, as evidenced by its retrospective, temporal unfolding. The drama of the *Phaedrus* is, consequently, the drama of "postponement and error," of disillusionment and misperception, which creates the "dilatory space" where meaning is made. In this gap between belief and knowledge, persuasion and analysis, resemblance and reality, the sign and signification, meaning is created by Plato's Socrates—and its creation is transformative, for teacher and pupil alike, whose lives henceforth are to be lived, not on sophistic but on philosophic terms: in pursuit of the Beautiful informed by the Ethical. Thus, if the origins of Socratic inquiry and Platonic Invention are selectively *tragic*, insofar as they are rooted in historical-political wounds, the educative method each enshrines may be likened to a *comedy of errors*.

The retrospective edifications of the *Phaedrus* are driven by serial recantations, in which Socrates takes "previously generated speeches as material with which to illustrate the method" (199). He models rhetoric in order to model rhetorical analysis, as a means to the edification of Self and Other. Socrates' strategy of ironic resemblance and recantation underscores the transformative agency of the retrospective gaze. This method of "temporally unfolding" meaning privileges the retrospective gaze, in which "only the end can finally determine meaning" (Brooks 22). Meaning appears, disappears, then reappears as something altogether different. As Brooks observes, this is "the very nature of narrative plot, consuming itself as it projects itself forward, retracting as it extends [as Socrates retracts each successive speech], calling for its end from its beginning" (53).

In this, the predatory aggression of Socrates' elenchus acts like a "Trojan horse" to destroy sophistry from within its own signifying practices, replicating its own deceptions. In his trial, he deploys this "Trojan horse" defense to kill sophistry within the walls of its own authority: the courtroom. He similarly approaches Phaedrus "bearing the gift" of seeming idolatry of sophistry, mimicking not only sophistry but Phaedrus' idolatry of it. Rhetorical disguise is Socrates' weapon par excellence, the "lamb's clothing" that conceals the "wolf," as it imitates Lysias to destroy his argument and to mitigate the most immediate effect of it: his beloved pupil's seduction by a rhetorical and political rival.

Brooks underscores the significance of the retrospective gaze to the meaning-making process modeled in the *Phaedrus* and in Socrates' elenchus, which tends "toward a finality that offers retrospective illumination of the whole. . . . in which only the end can finally determine meaning"(22). Meaning, in the *Phaedrus* is never fixed, but fluid; it is not sedimented in a given position but develops over time and is a function of interpretative perspective and cognitive capacity. Phaedrus' cognitive abilities develop as meanings are unfolded by Socrates, making possible the unveiling of additional meanings that further develop cognition. Socrates' radical praxis underscores the primacy of the retrospective gaze to all narrative, which, "as a system of meaning, must conceive itself as essentially retrospective" (Brooks 301).

Each of Socrates' successive speeches is metaphorical, insofar as it is "same-but-different" (91). As Brooks asserts, "plot . . . *must use* metaphor as the trope of its achieved interrelations" (91). Thus, the wisdom of *Phaedrus* is associative inasmuch as one speech's meaning is only developed through its associations with another.

Throughout Socrates' elenchus, the acts of interpretation, analysis, and revision are privileged in what comprises a process-friendly precursor of today's composition workshop, where texts are not posited as fixed, univocal artifacts, but as works-in-progress whose meaning evolves dialogically: in consort with a reader's interpretative gaze; through a series of recursive drafts; or within the context of a feedback-loop between self and other, student and peers, or student and instructor. Similarly, the *Phaedrus* dramatizes the *process*, as opposed to the product, of dialectic edification. Phaedrus never becomes the master, the philosophical lover, but is always and already a pupil, whose relationship to philosophic Eros is one of *becoming*. Socrates, the putative master, is still very much the pupil, who comes seeking knowledge of the beautiful and of the self from the pupil, as part of a process of mutual edification.

The process of meaning-making that Brooks describes reinforces the relevance of Freire's "problem-posing" pedagogy, "where the problems posed to and by an initiatory desire are worked and worked through" (22). Post-Freudian theory further underscores the genealogy between the radical pedagogies of Socrates and Freire, insofar as it grounds the retrospective nature of the meaning-making process, in which the problematics of the "buried, yet living past" are posed to the intellect for further decoding, in an effort to free the subject from their injurious effects, from the "violence of signs": whether it is the manipulative effects of sophistic discourse upon Phaedrus or the subjugating effect of colonial discourse upon the colonized. The avowal and recantation of partial, sophistic meanings in favor of fuller philosophic meanings evidences the centrality of "detour" and "digression" to Socrates' meaning-making process. His elenchus commences with a necessary detour into sophistic discourse, which is followed by interruptive digressions into religious confession, a rhetoric of erotic innuendo, or the mythic or historic past, but which always ends with the eternal return of dialectic analysis.

Further, this retrospective gaze is not only revelatory but redemptive for Plato's Socrates, as it is for Phaedrus. The transformative effects on the "knower" are the final and greatest of the edifying effects of the protrepticus, evidencing its genuinely dialogic nature—an end that can only "be achieved through detour" (Brooks). The process is recursive, insofar as it dramatizes the eternal return to a point of origin: a preceding text. This repetitive impulse of narrative is yet another effect of the desire to "assert an active mastery" (Brooks 98). Further, "*repetition by three* constitutes the minimal repetition to the *perception series*," as evidenced in the three speeches of Socrates, in the three moments of Socrates' discourse: the false sophistic position, which is recanted in favor of a more genuinely philosophic position, which in turn is recanted as a necessary intermediate text, in favor of a mature philosophical text.

Repetition through discourse is a primary means by which the self asserts itself—asserts mastery, control, or domination of its surroundings. It is as well a primary ordering principle of narrative, of artistic discourse across genres, including the genre of dramatic dialogue. The repetitive impulse is also protean insofar as it agitates the creative urge, inciting the desire to escape from the endless bind of reiteration. Thus, repetition and escape from the closed circle of repetition dwell in a generative tension, whose principal effect is thrown off in the symbolic realm in the form of "theme and variation," or of "thesis and development" in academic discourse, in which a text repeatedly returns to its point of origins, which it continually reworks to diverse ends. It is not merely the repetition, the "perpetual recurrence of the same thing," but a transformative, if not redemptive, liberation from the repetitive bind that dialectics, like psychoanalysis, seeks.

Dialectical philosophy transcends the feedback-loop with sophistry upon which it depends. Its transcendent edification arises from its eternal return to sophistry—indeed like Vygotsky's "gyre" of critical cognition. Dialectic discourse for Socrates performs the same function as Freud's "talking cure" in psychoanalysis: freeing the knower from the repetitive bind of discourse and its effects.

The repetition, return, and recursivity of Socrates' discourse relative to sophistry feeds its transformative appetite. Socrates' discourse not only consumes the discourse of the Other, but cannibalizes its own discourse to nourish, transform, and disseminate itself, as a means of transforming the Other. Perhaps more than any work in the annals of the western literary tradition, Plato's *Phaedrus* dramatizes the aggressions of the Self toward the Other (Lysias and Phaedrus): aggressions that culminate in the edifying transformation of Self and Other. As Brooks succinctly observes, "an event gains meaning by its repetition" (99), even in a text where a series of dramatic discourses comprise the primary "events." Similarly, the "repetition of traumatic events," such as the persecution, prosecution, and execution of the beloved ideal, Socrates, "can be seen to have the function of seeking retrospectively to master the flood of stimuli, to perform a mastery" of the traumatic event—to heal the wound, as it were, with the winding shroud of writing—by staging the eternal return of philosophy to sophistry, and by re-staging the trial of the exemplar as a "problem" to be "worked out and worked through."

Plato's writing functions as a "talking cure" to mitigate the effects of a traumatic past (the trial and execution of Socrates), which it "works out and works through" by objectifying it in the realm of the symbolic. Similarly, Socrates' dialectic elenchus in the *Phaedrus* functions like a "talking cure" for self and other, insofar as it mitigates the wounds of Eros (so eloquently figured in the discourse on the feathers), and whose dagger-thrust is given a fresh twist by the jealousy incited by the immediate specter of the beloved's seduction by a rhetorical and political rival. His discourse also functions like a "talking cure" for Phaedrus, insofar as it remedies the affective power of sophistic signification, evidenced in the idolatry it induces in the beloved pupil.

Socrates reworks the problem of sophistry through repetition, through the eternal return of philosophic discourse to sophistic rhetoric, whose problematic effects are reworked to escape their repetitive bind: to heal the wound by opening up a "dilatory space" between idolatry and analysis, sophistry and philosophy, past and present that is transformative to the extent it is edifying and/or healing. Repetition and return comprise a primary organizing principle of the dialogue, on both the macro and micro, metaphoric and metonymic levels, in which the fragment reflects the whole. *Phaedrus* returns to the critique of sophistry that commences in the *Apology*, even as it returns to the forensic theme of the *Phaedrus* ("it is better to love a non-lover") in a series of speeches.

Return, repetition, and recantation are each essential to the dramatic progression of Socrates' narrative. To the extent Socrates' dialectics of recantation relies on detour it is a deviant discourse, grounded in a series of dramatic deceptions, in which multiple masks enable its continual unveilings of itself and sophistry, in textual counterpoint. Brooks further explicates the psychological implications of the narrative strategies of error and correction, of detour, deferral, and repetition: "That plot should prove to be deviance and error is fully consonant with Freud's model in 'Beyond the Pleasure Principle,' where the narratable life of the organism is seen as detour" (139). Plato's meaning-making process in *Phaedrus* anticipates by two-and-a-half millennia the relative nature of meaning in modern and post-modern texts, which similarly posit the social and temporal nature by which meaning in constructed: as a negotiation between self and other, writer and reader, the affective power of texts and the interpretative aggressions of their reception, and finally between temporal perspectives (past, present, future)—in which additional, often contradictory, meanings are excavated retrospectively.

Similarly, Socrates' discourse commences with a detour into sophistry, proceeds through a second detour into a discourse of pseudo dialectics, before culminating in a discourse that is genuinely dialectic. Consequently, Plato's dialogue in *Phaedrus,* "represents the opposite of the straight line: it is the longest possible line between two points, or rather, the maintenance of the greatest possible deviance and detour between beginning and end, depending on the play of retardation, repetition, and return in the postponement and progressive unveiling of the end" (155–156). These detours are necessary to create the ruptures between discourses, which foster the "dilatory space" where critical thought is born. Socrates' detour into the debased realms of sophistic discourse is necessary in order to approach his genuine destination: a life dedicated to philosophic eros.

As Socrates leads Phaedrus, so does Plato artfully lead the reader "through an elaborate dilatory space that is always full of signs to be read, but always menaced with misreading until the very end" (156). Socrates mouths signs that willfully mislead as a necessary [pre]text for his re-reading of the same signs, by way of leading Phaedrus from an uncritical idolatry of sophistic discourse to a critical appreciation of its "errors," limits, contradictions, and want of ethos relative to dialectics. Thus, Socrates' pedagogical model is predicated on three dialectical moments: the artful construction of a flawed, sophistic discourse, the willful deconstruction or contradiction of that discourse, followed by the construction of a discourse more truly beautiful because dialectic. As Brooks notes, such a narrative is "a layered text that offers different versions of the same story [speech]" (277). Socrates' discourse habitually "doubles back on itself," calling into question its origin, "suggest[ing] another kind of referentiality," in which a discourse is invented to trump a discourse, only to be unmasked as a debased form of discourse itself, as Socrates models the dialectic meaning-making process, where signs taken for wisdoms are interrogated for the meanings they conceal—and by which they are contradicted. Thus, the act of interpreting signs over time is privileged as the means to knowledge and transformation, to art and immortality.

Socrates, as Brooks avers, functions as a "fictive reader" embedded in the text whose purpose is to "stage efforts at decipherment and interpretation." Almost the entire text of the *Phaedrus* is given over to the decipherment of given signs: to interpreting the signs of Lysias' speech, then the signs of Socrates' successive speeches, as well as the signs of various myths and images. Each text is an artifact of temporal interpretation, dramatizing the dialectical search for meaning through signs whose meanings are given, then recanted, then recuperated in revelations that synthesize their prior contradictions. Further, the edifying effect on master and pupil is as *transformative* for Socrates and Phaedrus as it is for Proust's Marcel and Freire's peasants. Recall that the final stage of Freirean praxis involves the linguistic codification of the contradictions unveiled in a problematic local context, that is "read" critically as if it was not only a text but a (pre)text for transforming the relationship between subject and material context. For the Socratic dyad, the transformation extends from the here to the hereafter, insofar as it involves not only the mutual edification, but the mutual immortality of their souls. To the extent Socratic inquiry models interpretation as "decipherment," it resonates with Freire's "decodings" of material realities and the dialogic medium of those decodings.

THE RANKIAN GAZE: INVENTION VERSUS ANALYSIS

The final revelation of meaning in the retrospective moment is not meaningful in and of itself, but only insofar as it provides the impetus for the transformation of the self: from a passive object of signification to a knowing, signifying subject. In his role as "fictive reader," deciphering the signs of discourse, interpreting the signifying practices of sophistry, Socrates prefigures the role (and art) of criticism—performing the interpretative act by which criticism is defined, splitting the dialectic gaze between invention of discourse and interpretation of it. He also heralds the Freirean educator, who dialogically "reads" local contexts critically.

This too is a necessary survival strategy by which the Self escapes the repetitive bind of Invention and the destructive effects associated with it (morbid fatigue, servitude, repetition): substituting for discourse, analysis of it—even as the artist mitigates the destructive effects of the creative impulse by substituting for art, analysis of it. The critical, interpretative impulse rescues the Self from the totalizing effects of the creative impulse. As Rank observes,

> [T]he artist type, with his tendency to totality of experience, has an instinct to flee from life into art, since there to a certain extent he can be sure of matters remaining under his own control; but this *totality tendency itself . . . in the end takes hold of creation also, and this totality of creation then threatens to master the creative artist* as effectually as the totality of experience. . . . Here the conflict of the artist versus art becomes a struggle against his own creation . . . which forces him to complete surrender in his work. How the artist escapes this new danger is one of the obscurest and most interesting problems of the creative artist. (385, my emphasis).

How indeed does the artist, and Plato in particular, escape this bind between the imperative to create and the imperatives of creation? The solution he develops further evidences the authenticity of his "evil genius." Socrates' radical shift from rhetoric to rhetorical analysis evidences this generative tension between art and analysis of it, which was perhaps projected onto Socrates by Plato, in an effort to mitigate the effects of servitude to either philosophy or art—by shifting the focus from philosophy to criticism of it, from invention to analysis. Socrates' codifications of the art of dialectic rhetoric evidence the extent to which Plato mitigates the self-negating effects of his art through analysis of it. These dual rhetorics of art and analysis evidence the eternal tension between artist and critic in the souls of Plato and Plato's Socrates: a conflict embodied in the trope of the winged chariot and its combative steeds.

Rank's theories of the origins of the creative impulse, particularly as they inform the career of the artiste manqué, further illumine the radical shift from the art of rhetoric to the science of rhetorical analysis in the *Phaedrus*: "this is the diversion of creation into knowledge, of shaping art into science." Rank continues:

> [The individual] passes suddenly from the formative artist into the scientist, who wishes . . . to establish psychological laws of creation or aesthetic effect. This diversion of artistic creation from a formative into a cognitive process seems to me to be another of the artist's protections against complete exhaustion in the creative process. (387)

The artist mitigates the effects of servitude to creation by escaping from art into analysis of art, combating the artistic with the scientific, creativity with criticism. If in the early stages of the *Phaedrus,* the artist in Socrates predominates, as evidenced by his inventive use of figuration and myth, mimicry and meta-dramatic discourse, than from the moment the art of rhetoric shifts to rhetorical analysis in the second speech and the palinode, the artist is superseded by the scientist, who "wishes to establish . . . laws" defining the nature of "beautiful" discourse, as the creative is diverted into the cognitive, and "creation into knowledge." The relevance of Rank's aesthetic theory is further evidenced by the representation of the educative impulse in ancient Greece as essentially an artistic impulse, to give living shape to a new type of individual, in Socrates' case under the sign of philosophic Eros. Unfortunately, criticism and pedagogy has focused on the analytical, scientific codifications of the Phaedrus to the detriment of its rhetorical complexity, emphasizing the centrality of unity, definition, division and classification to the exclusion of its rhetorical Invention and "vitalism," valorizing a genre of writing that is a reductive caricature of its ancient source, that emphasizes forms over complexity of content and signifying practices, logic over invention, the science of rhetoric over the artistry of it.

In this shift from art to science in the *Phaedrus* we see Plato working off the effects of his long servitude to creation. We see it as well in his subversive break from the aesthetic ideology and philosophic ideals of the master, Socrates. The rupture between the artist and the scientist in Socrates' discourse is not absolute, however. For in Socrates' "hymn to love," which heightens the beauty and effect of the palinode, the artist returns, giving form to meaning with a flow of erotic figuration as original as any in the annals of western literature, evidencing the eternal interplay between invention and dialectics in the *Phaedrus*.

Invention returns to illumine through figuration the scientific laws of the polemic. As Rank notes, "conscious reflection about creativity and its conditions and about all the aesthetic laws of artistic effect [ensures] the survival of the ego amidst the all absorbing domination of creation" (385). In Socrates' critique of dramatic poetry, lyric poetry, and epic myth, which interrogates their affective power upon the masses, we see evidence of this "conscious reflection about creativity and its conditions and . . . the aesthetic laws of artistic effect."

This raises a profound question: is Plato's critique of writing an attempt to work off the self-negating effects of writing, to leverage a "dilatory space" for a soul constrained by its servitude to art, and the art of the dramatic dialogue in particular? I will address this issue in greater detail in the next chapter. The *Phaedrus* continually dramatizes this enabling fluctuation of Socrates' discourse between invention and interpretation, even as the process paradigm of the contemporary composition workshop privileges the dialectic between invention and analysis, similarly placing an early emphasis on invention strategies (free-writing, journaling, webbing), which gives way to close textual analysis and formal arrangement as the process of textual production proceeds. The paradox for teacher and student alike is that a recursive process is used to produce a linear product: a text that will be read from left to right, top to bottom, beginning to end. Yet, the process by which we reach this end is one of detour and digression, as Socrates' radical pedagogy of recantation dramatizes.

Freire's praxis similarly emphasizes a critical recursivity, though with a fundamental difference. Whereas Socrates' radical pedagogy in the *Phaedrus* models the recursive return of the Word to the texts it constructs and then deconstructs, Freirean praxis grounds the eternal return of the Word to the World, which it similarly decodes. The recursivity of Socrates' dialectics of recantation deeply informs the process-oriented approach to written literacy, in which the same ground is re-worked, the same "text" re-written, its claims and syntax subject to a self-reflexive interrogation, its superficial analyses developed for depth and breadth, its rhetoric heightened through figuration, its counter-arguments refuted by opposite claims, supported by evidence, developed with analysis. Its fundamental assumptions (the flaws of the lover) are brought under radical attack; its appeals to ethos, pathos, and logos strengthened.

A text is read only to be re-read, to develop the pupil's ability to "read" critically—to develop his or her own "reading," or interpretation of the text, by applying several criteria of analysis: is its logic complete, selective, or contradictory? Do its assumptions and claims stand up to interrogation? Does the evidence and analyses support the claims and assumptions? Is the argument effectively arranged; does it define critical terms? Are the criteria of analysis effective and sufficient? Are its implications fully explicated? Does it effectively address and refute the counter-arguments? Does it make effective use of appeals to logos, pathos, and ethos? Does it possess rhetorical complexity, and is that complexity enriched with figuration? Is its thesis significant, does it bear on a problematic reality? To the extent Socrates' discourse models effective textual analysis, grounds the act of interpretation, in a polemic that is a model of rhetorical complexity, it is extremely relevant to contemporary composition studies. Further, to the degree its privileges analysis-as-action, Socratic inquiry may be viewed as a useful precursor of social-epistemic pedagogy. Socrates' critique of sophistry not only implies future actions, but is itself an action. As Cornel West asserts, "every opinion expresses an act of the will, of preparedness for action . . . an opinion is a deed . . . intended to guide other deeds" (38). Analysis of a problematic reality not only implies interventions upon that reality, but is already an intervention upon it insofar as it mitigates the violence of its signs upon the self, recuperates a measure of agency for the self relative to reality, through the mere act of "talking back" to it. Each act of naming this problematic reality to an Other is a further "deed," that proliferates in the deeds it "guides." In other words, the violence of signs is mitigated by the mere act of "naming" them. This is why analysis of problematic realities is a form of active learning, in which learning is action.

THE VYGOTSKIAN TURN: SOCRATES AND THE DIALOGIC CLASSROOM

The shift from rhetoric to rhetorical analysis, from the art of rhetoric to the science of dialectic analysis in Socrates' educative paradigm can be usefully informed by the cognitive developmental theories of Lev Vygotsky's *Thought and Language*. The relationship between language and knowledge is fundamental to both Plato and Vygotsky, whose texts mutually inform one another. The assumption that undergirds the educative model of each is that knowledge is a by-product of language, that cognitive development comes *after* not *before* language and is an a posteriori, not an a priori, phenomenon relative to language—that knowledge is socially constructed, given the dialogic nature of language.

This has profound implications for how we teach—for pedagogical methodology. It underscores, for example, the efficacy of an interactive, dialogic pedagogy, which by placing students in social situations that privileges the use of language and fosters the development of critical thought. How does this work?

Pedagogy, to be effective, should reflect the relationship between language and thought. As Vygotsky asserts, in contradistinction to Piaget, language is not the effect of thought, but the cause of it. This simple yet revolutionary thesis has profound implications for teaching, and particularly, for how we teach, to the extent it informs pedagogical assumptions and methods. If it is true that language shapes thought, if this is the fundamental assumption from which pedagogy proceeds, then theoretically, by placing students in situations where they can speak to one another (or an Other), we are developing their thought processes. Further, if language shapes thought, and language is social, then thought is developed socially—through dialogic interaction with an Other. Hence, the theoretic foundation for the student-centered, interactive, dialogic writing workshop, with its emphasis on collective interpretation of texts and small feedback groups, on macro and micro interactions relative to the production and analysis of critical texts.

The strongest point of alliteration between the educative models of Plato's Socrates and Vygotsky is the social nature of each, which foregrounds the master-pupil dyad insofar as it privileges discourse as the medium for the making of knowledge and the development of critical cognitive abilities. Cognitive edification occurs in the *Phaedrus* as it does in *Thought and Language* in a "zone of proximal development" between Self and Other, learner and teacher, dialectician and interlocutor. Vygotsky defines this interactive zone as "the place at which a child's . . . spontaneous concepts meets the *systematicity and logic* of adult reasoning" (xxxv, my emphasis). Here, the child's "spontaneous concepts" might serve as a stand-in for Phaedrus' idolatry of sophistry.

The master-pupil dyad of Socrates-Phaedrus dramatizes precisely this educative dynamic, to the extent that Phaedrus' "spontaneous," uncritical idolatry of Lysias' sophistic speech "meets" the systematic rhetorical analysis of Socrates' "adult reasoning," with its emphasis on definition, division, classification, arrangement, peroration, and so forth. Vygotsky continues, asserting that these scientific concepts originate in "the classroom [and] impose on the child logically defined concepts," which finds its parallel in the *Phaedrus* in Socrates' insistence on definition ("love," "madness," "rhetoric," "dialectics") as a necessary precondition of his rhetorical analysis (xxxiii).

The Platonic master-pupil dyad alliterates even further with Vygotsky's model of cognitive development, insofar as the child/learner's spontaneous concepts "in working their way *upward* to the more abstract clear a path for the scientific concepts in their *downward* development toward greater correctness" (xxxiv, my emphasis). Hence, the aptness of Vygotsky's metaphor of the "gyre" to capture this dialectic interaction between spontaneous and scientific thoughts, in which the upward movement of the child's uncritical thought meets the downward movement of the adult's scientific, analytical, abstract concepts. There is, thus, in Socrates' radical pedagogy a dual "stoops to conquer" strategy, in which he stoops to conquer sophistry by imitating it, and stoops to Phaedrus' level of spontaneous "thinking" in order to conquer it with dialectic analysis. He first lowers his own thinking to Phaedrus' level, in order to raise the pupil to his own level of cognitive analysis, much as a child's edification develops through discourse with an adult.

There is, in the *Phaedrus,* a similar downward-upward movement between sophistic rhetoric and philosophic analysis (which is underscored by the imagery of ascent: "Olympus," the "Divine Banquet," the "winged chariot" of the soul, etc.), dramatizing the upward movement from idolatry to analysis, concrete to abstract thought, eroticism to philosophic Eros, and sophistic to philosophic discourse. Socrates' pedagogy commences at his student's current level of cognitive development, which is governed by an uncritical idolatry of what it perceives to be beautiful discourse. Phaedrus may thus be posited as a surrogate for the first-year composition student, whose cognitive abilities at the outset often evidence a similar want of critical reflection.

Yet a further alliteration exists between the cognitive developmental models of Plato and Vygotsky, as figured in the *Phaedrus* and *Thought and Language*. This is evidenced in the dominant images each uses to represent the upward movement of cognitive thought. Whereas Vygotsky deploys the metaphor of the "gyre" to capture the upward movement of the child's spontaneous thoughts in conjunction with the downward movement of the adult's scientific concepts, Stanley Fish alludes to the "Platonic ladder" to capture the upward mobility of Phaedrus' cognition: "the value of any point in it is that it gets you . . . to the next point in logical-demonstrative terms. As a level of insight . . . each rung, as it is negotiated, is kicked away" (13). Sallis notes the ubiquity of other images of cognitive ascent. Phaedrus' promise, for example, to erect a statue in Socrates' honor, "wrought in gold beside the offering of the Cyspelids at Olympia . . . if Socrates should succeed in bettering Lysias, [for] he would then have succeeded in that ascent to the abode of Zeus" (122). The statue imagery is significant not only as an emblem of cognitive development, but also as a dual emblem of immortality by virtue of its being "wrought in gold" and placed at the "abode of Zeus."

The upward movement away from a debased sophistic rhetoric to an honorific philosophic discourse is reinforced by additional images of ascent. As Sallis notes, "the third kind of movement of the soul . . . is the movement up to the divine banquet. When they go to their feasts and banquets, the gods make the *steep ascent up to 'the summit'*" (143, my emphasis). This upward movement of the soul is enervated by "the sight of the truth, which nourishes those very wings by which the soul is enabled to ascend . . ." (147). Cornel West similarly underscores the edifying effects of philosophic Eros on the soul: "the struggle is grounded in human love and human wisdom—the two fundamental requisites for the genuine flowering of we featherless, two-legged, linguistically conscious creatures made in the image of God" (*Prophetic Thought*, x).

The statue, the divine banquet, and the ladder are not the only images that capture the ascent of cognition in the *Phaedrus*. The charioteer as an emblem of the soul's flight toward cognitive truth and immortality is perhaps the most dramatic image of this pattern: a flight achieved by the laborious reconciliation of the tensions between the profane and the sacred, the passions and the reason, the impulses and the will. Plato deploys each of these images to capture the upward movement of the pedagogical protrepticus from sophistry to philosophy, persuasion to dialectics, belief to knowledge, and love of the beautiful body to love of the beautiful idea. Hence, a dialogue that commences in the sensual realms of Eros culminates in the logical-spiritual realms of the soul, into which eros has been reabsorbed.

Socrates' pedagogical approach alliterates with Vygotsky's model of cognitive development in another important aspect. Instead of proffering at the outset a dialectical critique beyond Phaedrus' cognitive grasp, Socrates resorts to an intermediary device, beginning with something that Phaedrus can grasp: a sophistic speech akin to that of Lysias but one that is (like Lysias' discourse) fatally flawed. It is just these flaws ("errors") that invite his subsequent dialectical critique (second speech). In this first speech, Socrates emulates the practice of the farmer ("husbandman"), who first prepares the ground before sowing it with seeds, demonstrating his grasp of "kairos," of the extent to which effective rhetoric is shaped by situational context and the composition of a text is determined by its context. The metaphor of the "husbandman" sowing seeds of edification in the pupil precisely conveys the dual movement of edifying discourse in the *Phaedrus*, as Socrates first stoops to sow his seeds in the sophistic ground of Phaedrus' soul, in which will germinate and from which will sprout the upward reaching tree of dialectical knowledge. The downward-into-upward, ground-to-summit movement of the dialogue is perfectly captured by the imagery of the seed-sowing husbandman, with his kairic awareness of the ground and the season best suited to his edifying seed.

Socrates evidences the extent to which his discourse is shaped by kairic awareness of the Other (audience) when he initially refuses Phaedrus' request to give his critical assessment of Lysias' speech. This refusal is prompted by the realization that such a critique would be lost on Phaedrus, as a result of the pupil's want of cognitive development, as evidenced by his idolatry of a flawed sophistic speech. What is wanted is some intermediary mechanism of cognitive development. Hence, his first, flawed sophistic speech, which allows him to model a dialectic critique within a rhetorical context that Phaedrus can grasp. It is a speech with training wheels, as it were. Rhetorically speaking, these training wheels are his strategy of ironic deflation, as John Sallis observes:

> He ironically denies having even noticed whether the author of the speech has said what he ought to have said; this irony with respect to the content . . . serves to leave open the question in order that it might later be dealt with in a much more effective way than would be possible here. (118–119)

Unable to immediately bridge the gap in Phaedrus between the youth's love of sophistry and a more critical appreciation of its flaws (as well as the superiority of philosophic discourse), Socrates realizes he must first build a bridge, or construct a rhetorical ladder, for conveying Phaedrus from a mode of thought characterized by idolatry to a loftier cognition informed by reasoned analysis. His first speech dramatically fulfills this purpose. Consequently, Socrates' initial refusal to pass critical judgment on Lysias' speech reveals not only his "kairic" awareness of the Other, but his "pleasant bend of the Nile" mode of cognitive development, in which he turns Phaedrus by degrees from idolatry to critical consciousness. His rhetorical strategy relies heavily on such tropes as "kairos" (situational context), "prosopropea" (mask-wearing), and "aporea" (doubt) to foster in Phaedrus a measure of critical detachment from the sophistic words of Lysias and himself.

If the first speech is a ladder with which to reach the higher levels of cognitive development, the second speech kicks this ladder out from under Phaedrus by exposing its flaws through dialectic analysis. Thus, Socrates facilitates Phaedrus' cognitive development by situating his instruction slightly ahead of Phaedrus' cognitive ability, in a way that alliterates with Vygotsky's L + 1, or learning + 1, methodology. As Vygotsky observes, such instruction "marches ahead of development . . . aimed not so much at the ripe as at the *ripening* functions" (188, my emphasis). Socrates' developmental pedagogical model evidences the wisdom of Mike Rose's adage in *Lives on the Boundary*, that "students will float to the mark you set" (26), for Phaedrus rises to the successive levels of cognitive development that Socrates models in his first two speeches, through the sequential use of mimicry, meta-drama, myth, recantation, and analysis, in which the teacher first models a flawed sophistic speech as a (pre)text for modeling a dialectical critique of it.

Plato's emphasis on kairos throughout the *Phaedrus* further alliterates with Vygotsky's concept of "decentering": a process wherein the learner develops the ability to *think in terms of the Other,* which is the rhetorical counterpart to thinking/speaking with a refined sense of audience. As Rank asserts in "Beyond Psychology," "the psychology of the self is to be found in the Other." Plato's emphasis on kairos is reflected in many passages, but most particularly in Socrates' analysis of the various kinds of "souls" and the means by which each is most effectively persuaded. This emphasis on kairos in Plato and on the decentering process in Vygotsky's model of cognitive development resonate with fundamental post-modern assumptions regarding the relationship between thought and language, insofar as the "child's intellectual growth is contingent on his mastering the social means of thought," which occurs principally through language in a "zone of proximal development" with an Other (94).

To put it more succinctly: language is not a function of thought; thought is a by-product of language. Cognitive development, in other words, occurs in a social milieu, as a result of the learner's manipulation of sounds-as-symbols through interaction with the Other. Hence, cognitive development, whether in the Platonic or Vygotskian paradigm is "prompted not from within but from without, by the social milieu" (108).

As an educative model that focuses less on the outcomes of thought and language and more on the process of their formation, the *Phaedrus* is deeply alliterative with post-modern process-oriented pedagogies. Moreover, its radical project of developing analytical consciousness in the classroom as a critique of social injustice and political corruption is consistent with the social-political-ethical orientation of current social-epistemic approaches to pedagogy. The *Phaedrus* is nothing if not a dramatic discourse on the learning process and on the dialogical nature of that process with its "dependence on cooperation with adults and on instruction" (Vygotsky 189).

The social nature of cognitive development in Plato's *Phaedrus* and Vygotsky's *Thought and Language* is evidenced by the fact that the Other appears to be absolutely essential to the coming-into-critical-consciousness of the learning Self. By using language to model critical thinking (analysis, definition, division, and classification), Socrates is effectively teaching Phaedrus how to think critically for himself. Platonic invention, with respect to both its origins and outcomes, is social in nature. It is not only deeply rooted in a desire to avenge social injustices, and the execution of Socrates in particular, but is inspired by the primacy for Plato of the Self-Other, master-pupil dyad, as a vehicle for love and edification, revenge and immortality. As Brooks asserts, "meaning is thus dialogic in nature . . . born of the relationship between tellers and listeners" (26). Griswold concurs: "the effort to know oneself cannot be severed from discourse and rhetoric" (198–199). The critical role that language plays in this transformative process "foreshadows again the importance of rhetoric in the effort to control the soul" (134), the centrality of which was also acknowledged by Freud, insofar as this "talking cure" formed the foundation of his therapy.

To the extent it foregrounds language in the making of meaning, as well as the political ends of the knowledge-making process, Socrates' radical praxis is inherently post-modern. Both the means by which knowledge is constructed in Socrates' radical pedagogy, as well as the ends it serves, are social—which is why it stands as an ancient precursor of post-modern praxis, whose assumptions, methods, and ends similarly privilege the ethical, the social, and the political. Whether in the classical or post-modern moment, rhetoric is essential to the quest for logos insofar as it makes knowledge visible, apprehensible, in the realm of the symbolic—which is why knowledge of artful and ethical rhetoric is essential to the practice of philosophy. Rhetoric is as essential to the agenda of the sophists as it is to the aims of the philosopher, is as necessary for the construction of public opinion as it is for the discovery of philosophic self-knowledge. Rhetoric is used to opposite ends by sophist and philosopher: to manufacture belief and to analyze the means by which it does so, in their diverse quests for consent and cognition.

The path to knowledge, as Ferrari observes, requires an Other: "without the right companions . . . he lacks the means for coming to know himself" (25). Griswold agrees: "if there is a way of preventing a confusion between a false opinion and a true opinion of something . . . it ultimately resides in dialogue . . ." (185). The question thus arises: is Socratic inquiry truly dialogic or merely a wolf in lamb's clothing that reinscribes a master-slave dialectic, in which the pupil's voice is subsumed by the dialectician's? Further, is the dialogic wisdom it dramatizes an a priori or a posteriori sign, one that comes before or after language? If Socrates' radical pedagogy is a genuine genealogical forebearer to Freire's pedagogy, does this genealogy extend from its goals, assumptions, and methods to its view of knowledge and how it is made? Is Socrates' radical pedagogy an epistemological as well as an ontological precursor of Freirean praxis?

7 Plato and the Tyranny of the Transcendent
A Radical Re-Reading

> For it is above all against sophists that this diatribe against writing is directed: it can be inscribed *within the interminable trial* instituted by Plato, under the name of philosophy, against the sophists.
>
> —Derrida (106, my emphasis)

The trope of the "trial" is central to the *Phaedrus*. Platonic Invention, and the *Phaedrus* in particular, ground the trial of Socrates, insofar as they restage the trial as an "interminable trial" of sophistry, perhaps to mitigate the violent effects of a "buried, yet living past," of a political wound that passes from master to pupil. Even more significantly, this "trial" proceeds by trial and error, positing a succession of "texts" as examples of the Beautiful, only to recant them, supplanting them with texts that more closely approach the ideal of Beauty in discourse, signified by the conjunction of Eros, Ethos, and Logos. In this chapter I want to theorize two additional "trials" of the *Phaedrus:* the trial of writing by Plato's Socrates and the trial of philosophy by Plato.

To what extent, then, does the *Phaedrus* recant not only sophistry and writing, but philosophy? As a dramatic dialogue, the *Phaedrus* may be viewed as a series of conflicts waged successively between philosophy and sophistry, and between Socrates and Lysias in particular, between the higher and lower impulses of Socrates' soul, between the impulses toward philosophical love and mutual edification on the one hand, and the impulses toward erotic love and vengeance on the other; and finally between orality and writing. In this chapter I want to focus on the last conflict, commencing the inquiry with a central question: to what extent does Socrates' attack on writing evidence a deeper conflict between Philosophy and Art, master and pupil, the science of dialectic inquiry and the art of the dramatic dialogue? To what extent does Socrates' recantation of writing evidence Plato's recantation of philosophy in favor of art: and the art of the dramatic dialogue in particular?

Socrates' pedagogy of recantation in the *Phaedrus* has profound implications for the meaning-making process, for the relationship between thought and language, for the master-pupil dyad, for the ethics of Socrates' elenchus and Plato's art, for the origins of the creative impulse, and finally for its relevance to social-epistemic praxis. Further, the ubiquity of its retrospective wisdom calls into question perhaps the most fundamental postmodern criticism of Plato: the assumption of an Intelligence that always and already "comes before" language and the signifying subject, that underscores the tyranny of a transcendent Truth: that comprises, in effect, an ancient ancestor of Intelligent Design. In this chapter I want to theorize the implications of the meaning-making process as it is presented in the *Phaedrus,* particularly as it bears on social-epistemic praxis and postmodern criticism of Plato. Finally, I want to theorize the protean rift between philosophy and art, master and pupil from a post-Freudian, Rankian perspective, insofar as the tensions of the educative dyad between master and pupil deeply inform the origins of the creative impulse.

In *Dissemination,* Derrida collapses the voices of Socrates and Plato in his critique of the recantation of writing ("instituted by Plato, under the name of philosophy"). This "trial" of writing brings the trial of sophistic signifying practices that Socrates has staged throughout to a fitting climax—as the last in a series of dramatic recantations. Underscoring the catastrophic implications of Plato's critique of writing, Jasper Neel observes that "Plato lays a curse on rhetoric and writing . . . by claiming that truth, by definition, cannot occur in writing" (202–203). Like Derrida, Neel conflates the voices of Plato and Socrates, assuming one speaks for the other. I want to open a "dilatory space" between master and pupil, philosopher and artist, oralist and writer that radically "re-reads" the implications of the trial of writing.

Continuing his trial of writing, Plato's Socrates asserts, speaking in the voice of the god-king, Thamus, "no written discourse, whether in meter or in prose, deserves to be treated very seriously" (277e). By contrast, only philosophic words, "written in a soul . . . *for the sake of instruction . . .* should be considered the speaker's own legitimate offspring" (278a, my emphasis). Thus, writing has only metaphorical value, as words "written in a soul," and its only metaphorical purpose is pedagogical, "for the sake of instruction." It has no raison d'être outside the dialectic elenchus. By virtue of its eruptive, insubordinate potential relative to its author, writing is to be kept on this short pedagogical leash. Socrates' censorship of writing evidences his fear of it, as it subverts authorial control of the dialectic. In the absence of the author, it invites the Other into the meaning-making process, as an interpreter of the written text—as, in effect, its co-author. What Plato's Socrates fears with respect to writing is the loss of control over the meaning-making process, on which he has a virtual monopoly as the foremost practitioner of his dialectic elenchus. To the extent writing wrests control of this process from his hands, it is tantamount to suddenly having a "dark steed" on the other end of his chariot reigns. Rather than surrender control of the meaning-making process to writing, he would destroy it.

His critique of writing reinforces the ancient Greek hierarchy, the collective aesthetic ideology, that sets the educative impulse above the creative—that indeed not only saw education as the art of arts, but the artistic urge as arising from the educative impulse. In other words, writing is profaned by the creative impulse; its only fitting purpose is in servitude to the educative elenchus, and even then only metaphorically, as words "written" on the soul for the purpose of edification. The question thus arises: if Platonic Invention began as an effort to enlist writing in the project of dialectic edification, did there come a point when writing took over the process, became an end in itself—became, in essence, its own master, in a radical departure from the oral elenchus, which it dares to critique, as part of a liberatory apostasy from philosophy to art, whose object of deification was not the dialectic elenchus but the dramatic dialogue as the medium for the soul's immortal objectification? Is Socratic inquiry then liberatory in a dual sense: insofar as it seeks not just the liberation of the signifying subject from the chains of sophistic signification, but enacts this liberatory impulse within a dramatic dialogue that signifies the liberation of art from philosophy, pupil from master, and writing from orality?

In radically re-reading this critique of writing, I want to offer a different thesis: that it signifies, not Plato's renunciation of writing- but his recantation of the master and philosophy in favor of art, writing, and the art of the written dramatic dialogue. Derrida and Neel are unsparing in their critique of Plato and Plato's Socrates, making no distinction between the two in this attack on writing. Neel underscores the hypocrisy of Plato's position: "in order to attack writing and sophistry, *Plato* becomes a writer and a sophist" (23, my emphasis). Neel continues:

> This is disingenuous. But *Plato* is playing for much higher stakes than dominance of mid-fourth century Athens. He has set out to *define thought for humanity*, and his strategy is more than disingenuousness; it is *vicious,* for he uses rhetoric and writing to define and then occupy the moral high ground, and then tries to destroy the means he has used *so that no one else can use that means again* ... Plato wants to use writing, rhetoric, and sophistry to destroy themselves. What he must leave behind, however, is writing. (23, my emphasis)

Plato's critique of writing thus calls into question the ethos of his own discourse—which relentlessly interrogates the ethos of sophistic rhetoric throughout the *Phaedrus*. As Neel observes, "if there was a marker on *Phaedrus,* it would say, '*Plato* lies here' in both senses of the verb, for he must become a sophist to destroy sophistry, and he must become a writer to destroy writing" (28, my emphasis). In purporting to use dialectical "truths" to disarm sophistic lies, Plato himself "lies" about his own sophistry, as well as the efficacy of his sophistry.

I want to liberate Plato from the accusations of Derrida and Neel, gain his "acquittal" as it were on appeal, by re-staging the *trial of Plato* by Derrida and Neel, in which Plato is found guilty by association with Socrates, as if the two were one. The thesis I will argue is that Plato's critique of writing evidences not his hypocrisy relative to writing, but his renunciation of

Socratic philosophy in favor of his own art. Derrida and Neel convict the wrong individual, convict Plato along with Plato's Socrates as if there was no distinction between them, no possibility for difference in their aesthetic ideologies relative to writing and oral dialectics. Artist and philosophical persona are alike guilty by association. Thus, in the writ Derrida and Neel bring against Plato, for every mention of Plato's name I would substitute the name of Plato's Socrates.

Now, some may well argue this is a difference without a distinction, insofar as Plato's Socrates is always and already Plato, because most of what we know of the historical Socrates is filtered through Plato's fictional projection of "Socrates." Yet, to the extent the persona of Socrates in the dialogues, and particularly in the *Phaedrus,* may logically be posited as a blend of fact and fiction (he was tried, he did martyr himself, he did mentor Alcibiades, Critias, and Charmides, he was Plato's teacher, etc.), we can argue that there is a difference between Plato and *his* Socrates—that the philosopher is not an absolute cipher for the dramatist and therefore does not speak absolutely, or perhaps even authoritatively, for him. For to assume he does is to argue that any and every character in a play speaks definitively for Shakespeare, that the anti-Semitism of *Merchant* is his own, that the subversive portrait of monarchy in *Hamlet* is wholly his own. This is not to argue that these may not be projections of the artist's own beliefs, but to argue that they are absolute projections of his beliefs, as Derrida and Neel do in the conflation of Plato and Plato's Socrates relative to the critique of writing, is to admit no possibility of difference between them: between an artist and his inventions. Finally, the fact Plato writes may be seen as a recantation of the critique of writing mouthed by his fictional philosopher, which leverages a "dilatory space" between master and pupil conflated by Derrida and Neel. This is the dilatory space of Invention relative to dialectics and reinscribes the carnivalesque disruptions and interruptions of Platonic Invention throughout the *Phaedrus,* relative to the dialectic elenchus. The verdict of Socrates' trial of writing is effectively and eternally reversed by the fact that in the end Plato is left writing, in a final twist that leaves the last word, not to Socratic inquiry but to Platonic Invention, to the dramatic dialogue by which the elenchus is subsumed. Thus, the Phaedrus dramatizes not only the movement away from sophistry toward philosophy ("where do you come from Phaedrus and where are you going?") but also the equally liberatory movement of the pupil away from the master, of Plato away from Socrates, of writing away from orality, and of art away from philosophy, into its own free-standing, signifying realm. In this, Socratic inquiry and Platonic Invention further evidence their pedagogical kinship to Freirean praxis, which similarly depicts the liberatory impulse not merely of the subject relative to his or her colonial master, but of the student relative to the teacher. The critique of writing signifies not the eternal devotion of the pupil to the master, but Plato's liberatory differentiation from the master, by virtue of his refusal to recant writing, evidenced by the silent if eternal proclamation voiced by the dramatic dialogues: I am an artist. I am a writer. I am a dramatic dialogist.

PLATO AND THE POSTMODERN GAZE: RE-READING A LOGOS THAT "COMES AFTER"

Before theorizing the subversive implications of Plato's art relative to Socrates' philosophy, I want to explicate the implications of Socrates' recantation of writing within the broader strategy of recantation that characterizes his dialectic elenchus. Socrates' pedagogical method reflects his complex, original, and presciently postmodern view of the meaning-making process. Meaning is not fixed but rather evolves through this retrospective gaze, as initial meanings are supplemented or contradicted by fresh meanings. Griswold's observations are instructive: "The *Phaedrus* offers us a palinode recanting the first two speeches of the *Phaedrus*; then a recantation . . . of this palinode; then a recantation (introduced by the Theuth/Thamus story) of this recantation; followed by Plato's recantation (visible in the deed of writing) of the critique of writing expressed by the personae in his text" (218–219). Griswold continues: "various points of view are presented as though they were final and are then purposefully undercut to reveal a further, unanticipated meaning" (218). Thus, "Socrates first speech is recanted by his second speech," even as it recants Lysias' speech. Plato's recantation of writing in the persona of Socrates is recanted by the fact of his writing the dramatic dialogue. Is Plato's art thus a dramatic recantation of the master's philosophy, even as dialectics is recanted by the dramatic dialogue that seemingly enshrines and immortalizes it?

The recantation of writing deconstructs itself—by the fact of its being written—as Derrida and Neel observe, though each fails to further develop the implications of this recantation within a recantation, to tease apart possible alternative "readings" of it: readings that suggest the attack is evidence not of the mutual hypocrisy of master and pupil, but of a growing rift between them, between philosophy and art, and between dialectics and invention. This rift, though under-theorized by criticism, not only evidences the usefulness of Rankian theory, but reinforces the cogency of Hawk's theory of classical "vitalism" (invention), which seeks to remedy its under-theorized status in rhetoric and composition.

This temporal, retrospective explication of a sign's meaning signifies a surprising alliteration between Platonic, modern, and postmodern signification: in which a meaning is assigned only to be contradicted or recanted, even as this contradictory meaning is itself supplanted, retrospectively by fresh meanings—in a chain of signification that is unstable, shifting, fluid, and contradictory until its "wisdom" is consecrated and consolidated, retrospectively, under the sign of philosophy, art, or memory, as "the point of view from which we come at last to regard the world" (Proust, *WBG* 168).

The "wisdom" of the philosophical sign is not a free-standing, a priori signified, but rather the product of a comparative analysis between sophistic and philosophic signifying practices, negotiated dialogically between self and other, master and pupil. In other words, "its wisdom," like the wisdom of the Proustian sign, is associative and retrospective; recuperative, transformative, and redemptive—insofar as the soul is not only edified but immortalized—its "sin" against the deity, master, or mother expatiated and redeemed under the sign of philosophic love and art, respectively.

In this retrospective pedagogy of recantation, the "errors" of a previous "wisdom," of "signs taken for wonders," are exposed by a corrective wisdom, whose "errors" are in turn corrected by a retrospective wisdom, in a chain of signification in which meaning is forever being made, lost, and recuperated. A sign's putative meaning is tentative, ephemeral, transitory—subject to explication over time, until developed retrospectively under the sign of philosophy, embodied in the sign of art. There is, however, no period affixed to this meaning-making process relative to a text, which invites further explication of its meaning by those who "come after" its production (critics, readers), who continue the work of retrospectively explicating its meanings. These meaning-makers who "come after" a text in effect usurp the author(ity) of the meaning-making process from the author: precisely as Plato's Socrates feared in his attack on writing. His fear is hypocritical, however, given his own adversarial "reading" of Lysias' text, as if he would indeed deny to all who "come after" him the same privilege of meaning-making. Thus, Socrates' critique of writing deconstructs his own elenchus, to the extent it exposes the inherent contradiction of his methodology, while cutting off the source of the discourse his elenchus feeds upon: the written texts of Lysias and Meletus, in the *Phaedrus* and *Apology* respectively. His dialectic elenchus enacts his theory regarding written texts: that they cannot defend themselves against those who "come after," who construct, deconstruct, or reconstruct their meanings—as Lysias' text could not defend itself against him.

Even Socrates' fear of the written word reinforces his assumption of a meaning that "comes after," that is subject to retrospective explication of a given sign. If meaning was a fixed, unalterable, a priori signified, he would not fear its usurpation, alternation, or transformation by meaning-makers who "come after" the text. Further, in his explication of Lysias' sophistic text, Socrates has committed the crime for which he accuses posterity relative to writing: re-authoring a written text's meaning. And for this, all should be grateful, for how impoverished its meanings would seem, and our appreciation of them, sans his retrospective explication of them. In other words, he has demonstrated the very efficacy of the thing he criticizes about writing: that it lends itself to the explication of meanings never intended by the writer. If this is wrong, then so, by definition, is his critique of Lysias' sophistic text. In order to cancel writing, he must cancel his entire elenchus.

The *Phaedrus'* dramatization of a retrospective meaning-making process is consistent not only with social-epistemic pedagogies but with expressivist pedagogy. As Peter Elbow asserts, "meaning is not what you start out with but what you end up with . . . writing is a way to end up thinking something you couldn't have started out thinking (15). Elbow's assertion contradicts the cognitive assumptions of Piaget that dominated American education (and particularly, theories and practices of cognitive development) for decades. "First you figure out your meaning, then you put it into language" (14). It also succinctly describes the cognitive process modeled in the *Phaedrus*.

This central assumption of a Logos that transcends signification would seem to be contradicted, or at least problematized, by the *Phaedrus*, whose dialogic process of meaning-making evidences that if a transcendent Logos exists, it is inaccessible sans dialogic discourse. At the very least, we are left with a deeply ambivalent Socratic "wisdom," which, as figured by Plato in the body of his work, is neither an entirely a priori nor exclusively a posteriori phenomenon. But even this view complicates criticism's assumption of a transcendent Logos that is itself never recanted, that is always and already an absolute a priori signified. Its seeming recantation in the *Phaedrus* by a logos that "comes after" language merely enriches the texture of contradictions that characterize the text—and that seemingly defy a critical gaze intent on "laying out its meaning" under a single sign, including the sign of an a priori logos.

Cornel West similarly problematizes the postmodern critique of an absolute truth on ethical and political grounds. West asserts that such a critique is counter-productive to counter-hegemonic struggles and therefore to postmodernism's own critique of power and ethical imperatives. By denying the existence of an Absolute Truth, postmodern critics deny the truth of an Evil capable of persisting in the form of racism, injustice, or violence, beyond the bounds of language. Yet, the persistence of Evil, the reality of historical tragedy, is a necessary evil for resistance to it. Thus, the absolute truth of historical injustice and perpetual violence is absolutely essential to their resistance, to the struggle against the evils of racism, injustice, and the violence associated with them. As West asserts, invoking the struggle of Josiah Royce, "he defends this vision of the absolute because he looks to the truth for aid in that struggle" (46). The evil in the world is tragic precisely because it exists independent of language, persists as a transcendent signified, necessitating perpetual struggle against it.

A historical evil that is contingent fosters the fatally complacent assumption that it will disappear of its own accord and die of natural causes. Freire's struggle against the violence of colonialism is predicated on the assumption that its truth is absolutely real, whether it is named or not. Naming it merely inaugurates the struggle against its absolute realities. As West attests, "such absolute reality and absolute truth are the most concrete and practical and familiar of matters" (47). West develops the significance for liberatory resistance of a truth about evil that is absolute: [R]eality and truth must in some way be absolute . . . because it is the last and only hope for giving meaning to the strenuous mind for justifying the worthwhileness of our struggle to endure" (47). If our view of tragic Truths is that they are historically transient and linguistically contingent, then the hope upon which all liberatory struggle feeds gutters like a flame for want of air. Perpetual awareness of the Truth of perpetual evil fosters the hope for perpetual struggle.

PLATO WRITES OFF SOCRATES: THEORIZING THE DYNAMICS OF THE MASTER-PUPIL DYAD

The question arises: is Socrates' rhetorical hypocrisy further evidence of a rift between master and pupil, in which the pupil's art recants both philosophy and its founding philosopher? If so, is Plato's recantation of Socrates an act of symbolic parricide that undoes the verdict of acquittal in the symbolic trials he repeatedly re-stages in his dialogues, in the eternal return of Platonic invention to the scene of a traumatic crime: Socrates' trial and execution? Is the *Phaedrus* evidence that if Platonic invention arises from a desire to recuperate and reify the exemplar, it ends in the recantation of both the exemplar and his dialectic elenchus, ends in the recantation of orality by writing, which deconstructs orality's recantation of writing?

Further, is this recantation of philosophy by art, of orality by writing, inevitable given the inherently rebellious and subversive nature of artistic genius relative to its exemplars? Is the overthrow of art by philosophy in the *Phaedrus* an inevitable sign of self-assertion, under the signs of Invention—an ultimate display of a generative *vitalism* that subsumes and subverts the philosophic sign that gave birth to it? Is Socrates' attack on writing, which is essentially an attack on art, evidence not only of the artist's recantation of the master, but of the extent to which the sign of philosophic Eros has been assimilated into the signs of Art, signified by Plato's refusal to recant the dramatic dialogue and by his willingness to recant philosophy? Does the *Phaedrus* not only dramatize the violent struggle in Socrates' divided soul between sophistry and philosophy, eroticism and philosophic eros, reason and passion, but the equally violent struggle in Plato's soul between his loyalty to philosophy and his calling to art—and particularly the art of the dramatic dialogue? Further, is dialectic's assimilation by Platonic invention a foregone conclusion, in which a soul torn between its divided loyalties to philosophy and art ultimately renounces the former in favor of the latter: a conflict not only harmonized on the symbolic level through art, which often harmonizes the conflicts that give birth to it, but resolved by the efficacy of an immortality conferred not by philosophy but by art?

Is philosophic Eros then the sacrificial lamb laid on the altar of Platonic invention—as evidenced in the *Phaedrus,* which is nothing if not a symbolic monument to an ideology of sacrifice, in which philosophy is partially sacrificed to sophistry in order that sophistry may be sacrificed to philosophy, to redeem and reverse the historical sacrifice of Socrates to sophistry, even as writing is sacrificed to orality, as a penultimate offering that prefigures the sacrifice of philosophy to Art? Is philosophic discourse then a cannibal that devours sophistry, only to be cannibalized in the end by Platonic invention, which always and already returns to feed on its own inventions, including the invention of Plato's Socrates?

Thus, the problem with Derrida and Neel's reading of the attack on writing is that it overlooks the possibility of alternative readings, and particularly the significance of a rift between master and pupil, dialectics and dramatic dialogue, philosophy and art, of which there is sufficient evidence in the dialogue to invite such an alternative reading, including the violation of virtually every rule of classical composition in its invention. By virtue of its ruptures, discontinuities, contradictions, and rhetorical complexity, the *Phaedrus* is a monument to Platonic Invention that contains within it a monument to Socrates' elenchus. This meta-monument to philosophy is presented to posterity, cracks and all, insofar as Socrates' desire for mutual edification in the pursuit of philosophic Eros and humanistic political reform is depicted alongside his eroticism, megalegoria, vengefulness, and sophistry. Thus, the *Phaedrus* is not just an homage to Socrates' elenchus, but an implicit critique of it. As such, it honestly dramatizes the abiding, painful, and generative ambivalence of the master-pupil educative/ artistic dyad, in which an imitative idolatry of the master ends, as it inevitably must, in the master's overthrow. Derrida and Neel's assumption of an undifferentiated Plato-Socrates dyad is itself problematic.

If, on the other hand, we assume a more differentiated dyad between master and pupil, philosopher and artist, fresh possibilities of meaning begin to "breathe" in this dilatory space between orality and writing, relative to orality's recantation of writing. Phaedrus' idolatry of sophistry may be understood as a projection of Plato's initial idolatry of Socrates, which inevitably tends toward his own becoming identity as an artist, and in particular, as a writer. The profound suffering he experiences for having thus recanted his exemplar in order to fulfill his own artistic destiny is evidenced in the guilt, shame, and fear that courses through the *Phaedrus* like a dark undercurrent and is repeatedly projected onto his fictive persona. In this, the *Phaedrus* not only replicates the cathartic effect of art that is induced by suffering, but stands as an early example of the relationship between suffering and art, prefiguring the career of the artiste manqué, dramatizing the violence associated with the master-pupil relationship—and with the recantation of the master by the pupil that is an unavoidable if protean feature of that dyad, as evidenced by the art, the codification of art, and the critique of the master that flows from this conflict.

The Socrates-Plato hybrid persona belies a rift at the deeper levels of signification. Plato's subversion of an a priori Logos that always and already "comes before" is part of a broader subversive departure from the philosophic Ideal and the teachings of the master/father/ philosopher/ lover. Further, these subversive elements, especially in Plato's later, mature dialogues, deeply inform the multiple dramas of recantation Plato stages in the *Phaedrus*, whose origins are rooted in the shameful effects of his profanation of the Ideal, of his apostasy from Socratic philosophy. Having devoted almost his entire writing career to re-staging the trial of Socrates, to winning his acquittal on appeal to posterity, Plato reverses course, penning a liberatory critique of Socratic philosophy, breaking free of the signifying chains of dialectic inquiry—and its imperatives toward orality, sophistic critique, and a transcendent Logos that "comes before."

What then are the other subversive elements of Platonic Invention, aside from his interrogation in the *Phaedrus* of an a priori "wisdom" that precedes and supersedes language? Secondarily, what is the relation between subversion, shame, and Plato's recurring drama of recantation? The developing rift between master and pupil is evidenced in a host of subversive elements, in the shame that is the inevitable consequence of Plato's subversive writing, and in the cunning artistry of his efforts to mitigate the effects of his subversive profanation of the philosophic Ideal—signifying the "evil genius" of Platonic Invention.

The shame associated with Plato's recantation of the philosophic Ideal (evidenced in his covering his head and in his ritual of purification before and after his first sophistic speech, and in his efforts to recant writing) underscore the widening rift between master and pupil, "shows he does not entirely agree with Socrates' position (as presented in the *Phaedrus*) on the matter" (Griswold 219)—that he possesses a more ambivalent attitude toward writing and the philosophic teachings of the master, which brings his loyalty to the master into direct conflict with the imperatives of his own genius.

The fact that Plato's dialogues "are not modeled along the lines touted by Socrates as definitive of a well-composed text" reinforces their status as emblems of profanation: "By writing, Plato signals a disagreement with Socrates' criticism [of writing]" (Griswold 219). The dialogues are, moreover, blasphemous departures from the Socratic ideals of composition, inasmuch as they "look like a buzzing confusion of ideas, arguments, images, myths, digressions, and interjections" designed to subvert at every turn the aesthetic ideals of unity, clarity, and organization touted by Socrates. Their rhetorical complexity is eruptive, messy, contradictory, and protean—again evidencing their inherent vitalism: a vitalism that is subversive relative to dialectic philosophy. Throughout the *Phaedrus*, invention subverts and complicates the dialectic project. Throughout, Plato is trying to serve two masters: Socrates and his own evil genius. The *Phaedrus'* project of redeeming and immortalizing the exemplar is preempted by the vitalism of its own inventions. If it commences as an homage to the Father of its birth, it ends by becoming the Mother of its own Invention. Thus, we are left with the simple observation that in the *Phaedrus*, dialectics is subsumed by vitalism.

All that was repressed in Socrates' dialectics erupts onto the empty Platonic page in a rebellious, if not riotous, artistic apostasy. Its efforts at systematic coherence are continually disrupted by its generic transgressions and its eruptive inventions. Even Plato's "anonymity" in the dialogues "is an indispensable element of . . . his response to Socrates' criticism" (220), and perhaps yet another means of coping with the effects of profanation, of mitigating the suffering associated with his apostasy from the philosophic ideal of oral dialectic—which made it impossible to mouth such heretical views in his own voice. We are left to wonder: is Socrates' attack on writing a self-reflexive critique of Plato by Plato—evidence of Plato working off the effects of shame for having profaned the philosophic ideal in writing, by writing? The turn from orality to the pen, from dialectic speech to dramatic dialogues is itself a liberatory artifice, insofar as it frees the pupil from strict adherence to the aesthetic and polemic ideologies of the master, and the Self from the chains of Socratic signification.

Plato gives a cunning twist to his subversion of the master's teaching by having Socrates speak in a manner that subverts his own teachings: the pupil speaks subversively through the voice of the teacher being subverted, and does it in the genre (writing) that the teacher condemns . . . and was condemned by at his trial: writing. Plato's mimicry of Socrates is no less *menacing* than Socrates' mimicry of Lysias—is a "Trojan horse" that recants philosophy as Socrates' mimicry recanted sophistry. The ironic insolence of Plato's insurrection against the Ideal of orality further attests to the cunning of his "evil genius."

Thus, Plato, by writing, is enacting the very subversive tendencies of the written word that Socrates feared. As the master asserts in the Myth of Theuth, written words are untrustworthy spokespersons when accosted by posterity or appropriated by one's enemies; they are like orphans in need of the absent father to defend them against those who would unscrupulously use and abuse them for their own ends:

> And every word, once it is written, is bandied about, alike among those who understand and those who have no interest in it, and it knows not to whom to speak or not to speak; when ill-treated or unjustly reviled it always needs its father to help it; for it has no power to protect or help itself. (275e)

As Griswold asserts, "once something is written, it floats about, getting into the hands of those who understand it, as well as those who do not" (208). The prospect of his written words getting into the wrong hands in posterity strikes a desperate terror into Socrates' soul—which may be a projection of an identical fear in Plato's soul relative to his own writing. By recanting orality for writing and dialectics for the dramatic dialogue, Plato in effect commits a patricide, replicating the verdict of Socrates' trial, condemning the father as he immortalizes him. Socrates' condemnation of writing is Plato's attempt to wash the blood from his hands, to expatiate a sin against the father—and concomitantly, an attempt to distance himself from the patriarchal discourse of philosophy, for the Mother of his own Inventions.

Perhaps this shift from philosophy to art evidences a shift from the influence of the masculine to the influence of the eternal feminine, and particularly from the teachings of the patriarch to those of the matriarch, from Socrates to Perictione, Plato's mother. A body of recent scholarship is recuperating the lost influence of the feminine in classical rhetoric, as evidenced by the works of Susan Jarratt, Cheryl Glenn, and Cara Minardi. In *Re-Membering Ancient Women,* Minardi underscores the influence of mothers in educating their sons, which was "the custom in classical Athens" (114). If indeed the case, then Perictione's influence on Plato would reinscribe the female and familial influence of the Pythagorean tradition, as evidenced by the career of Themistocles, "who was not just [Pythagorias'] teacher, but also his sister" (141). As Minardi observes, "the familial relationship was an important element of Pythagorean, and later, Neo-Platonist" education. As the sister of Critias, aunt of Charmides, mother of Plato (all students of Socrates), Perictione is perhaps the absent presence, the uncited influence, in the development of Plato's philosophic and aesthetic ideology and in the shift from dialectics-as-combat to dialectics-as-mutual edification, with its concomitant shift from an interlocutor-as-Other to an interlocutor-as-Self. Perictione's influence on Plato may also be seen in Plato's discourse on the nature of the soul, which is central to the thematics of the *Phaedrus,* and perhaps derivative of Perictione's "On the Harmony of Women," which similarly focuses on the nature of the soul. Thus might we map a genealogy acknowledging the influence on Plato not just of the patriarchal but the maternal, not just of the masculine but the feminine, not just of Socrates but Perictione, and not just as philosopher and teacher but as a writer: in this, replicating the influence of the feminine on Socrates: of Aspasia and Diotima, whose respective emphasis on dialectics and love may have merged in Socratic discourse under the sign of "philosophic Eros." Several of Socrates' teachers appear to have been women, evidencing the primacy of the feminine in classical education: a tradition informed by the Aspasia-Socrates, Diotima-Socrates, Themistocles-Pythagorus, and Perictione-Plato dyads.

Socrates' fear of writing, projected onto Thamus, evidences his agonistic view of dialectics and his militant, patriarchal view of rhetoric-as-combat whose purpose is "victory": an attitude toward rhetoric perhaps conditioned by the decades-long blood feud between oligarchs and democrats, philosopher and sophists, whose public discourse became a blood sport that claimed the lives of his prized pupils (Alcibiades, Critias, and Charmides), as it would his own. Perhaps sickened of the violence and the stain of vengeance associated with the agonistic combat between sophistry and Socratic inquiry, Plato, in his later career, charts a new course, reflecting the influence of mutual edification over victory, of the dramatic dialogue over dialectics, of Invention over Inquiry, of art over philosophy.

Thamus' critique of writing voices Socrates' fear of being left defenseless by the written word, even as it evidences the lethal politics of public discourse at the time, which demands "spoken words [that] can defend not only themselves but also the one who sowed them in the soul of the student" (211). An author's written words are like disobedient, if not patricidal, children who provide his enemies with a cunning means of destroying him, by his own hand as it were. Is Plato this orphaned, patricidal son who rises up to condemn the patriarch anew in writing, inciting the eternal return of Socrates' own words, in all their megalegoric, erotic, paranoid amplitude? As Derrida notes, "this misery is ... the distress of the orphan," which also masks "a desire for orphanhood and patricidal subversion" (77)— prompting the constant if futile vigilance of the author, whose relationship to his own words moves from a state of absolute control over them to the equally absolute surrender of that parental control. The rift between master and pupil evidences the inability of the signs of philosophy to control the sings of art, evidences the futile impotency of the signs of Socratic dialectics relative to the eruptive potency of the signs of Platonic Invention—and this is demonstrated from one end of the Phaedrus to the other, from its eruptive cornucopia of myth and erotic innuendo, meta-drama and mimicry, history and allegory, irony and satire, in a dramatic dialogue whose signifying practice veers violently from the persona of the philosopher to the inventions of the dramatist: as if signification in the *Phaedrus* were a violent struggle between the discourses of philosophy and art, in which the dialectic is ultimately absorbed by the artistic, and Socrates' recantation of writing assimilated into the pupil's writing.

Is Plato's insurrection an effort to assert his own mastery under the sign of art in liberatory counterpoint to the mastery of the philosophical sign, embodied in Socrates? To assert his mastery as an artist, Plato must renounce his mastery of philosophy, abdicate the role of philosopher for that of writer—where the imperatives of the two callings are incompatible. Platonic Invention signifies the death of Socrates' mastery of the philosophic sign, the loss of his authorial control over the dialectic narrative he would construct for all time, even as it signifies as well the pupil's death to philosophy and rebirth to art. Plato dramatizes this dramatic loss of authorial control over the philosophic sign in the violent if futile attack Socrates launches on writing, with the outraged vehemence of a patriarch damning the insubordinate, patricidal revolt of an heir. By putting this critique into the mouth of the master, Plato is perhaps working off his own "creative guilt feeling," revealing and objectifying the masochistic impulses underlying his attack on writing (which is also an attack on himself for his Judas-like betrayal of the martyred exemplar). He bares his back to the (tongue) lashes of the patriarch, as if flaying his own mortified flesh before a dialectical deity. As Derrida asserts, writing enacts the patricide that orality prohibits, with respect to the liberatory if not treasonous career that words enjoy once they escape control of the authoring pen, enacting meanings never intended, mouthed by others who conscript them for their own purposes, often at cross purposes to the author's intentions or interests—as Derrida does with Plato's text, reinscribing the violence Socrates does to Lysias' text—and the pupil does to the master's words.

The pupil fulfills the prophetic fears of the master, penning words that rise up to kill the master a second time—as part of the necessary and inevitable liberatory struggle of the artist to free himself from obedient servitude to the master philosopher, to cast off the yoke of mimicry for the winged chariot of his own immortal Inventions. Sophistic words set in the stone of writing become stones with which their victims are publicly stoned to death. But might they also be stones by which their author is stoned to death, after his death? As Brooks succinctly observes, "desire passes through what Lacan calls the 'defile of the signifier'; it enters the symbolic order, where it can be reordered, reread, rewritten"—which is precisely the problem Plato's Socrates has with writing (301).

The subversive if not patricidal implications of Plato's writing are also evidenced in the setting of Socrates' attack on writing, which is removed to an ancient Egypt and further removed to the realm of the dead. The Egyptian setting of the polemical myth is yet another form of liberatory "mask wearing," another means by which Plato disowns the spoken words of Socrates. For it enables Plato to displace his critique from the present to the past, from Greece to ancient Egypt, from the realm of the living to the kingdom of the dead. Not only does this removal to an ancient past effect the death of writing, as a discourse of the Dead, but it effects as well the death of philosophy by virtue of Socrates' evocation of a dead, antiquated discourse to effect his critique of writing. The ungrateful Dead pronounces the death of writing with the breath of dead discourses. Embedded in Socrates' attack is Plato's critique of Socrates, which hides within it like a "Trojan horse." As Neel observes, through the effective use of irony, myth, allegory, personification, and mask-wearing (prosopropea), Plato "has hidden himself more thoroughly . . . than any writer in history" (27).

The Egyptian setting is significant for another reason, for it performs the funeral of writing by reinforcing its association with death: as a dead discourse of a dead civilization devoted to the cult of the eternally dead. The fact that the condemnation of writing is delivered by the god-king, Thamus, gives it additional authority: the god perhaps being a displacement of Socrates, launching his attack on writing from his kingdom of immortality. The rejection of writing by Thamus reinscribes Socrates' rejection of Lysias' speech and, by implication, all sophistry. Yet, as an emblem of a dead discourse, arising from the kingdom of the dead, mouthed by the King of the Dead (Thamus), Socrates' critique of writing is, for Plato, *dead on arrival,* further evidencing his attempt to distance himself from the words of the master.

By virtue of his subversive critique of Socrates' critique of writing, Plato opens a "dilatory space" for debate with respect to writing that Socrates would shut down—even as the master's dialectic elenchus intended to shut down debate on sophistry (and sophistic signifying practices) as absolutely evil. The patricidal nature of writing, exposed by Socrates in the Myth of Theuth, tropes on Plato's broader subversion of the master's signifying practices. Plato's mature dialogues, and the *Phaedrus* in particular, are subversive of virtually every Socratic ideal of composition, as well as "the ideal of modern academic writing [with its emphasis on clarity, coherence, arrangement, and unity of purpose]" (Griswold 221). Plato's "waning philosophical attachment to [Socrates'] method" has also been observed by Beversluis:

> As his thought develops, he advances many innovative *epistemological,* metaphysical, political, and educational theories, some of them built on his Socratic foundations, others *without precedent* in Socratic thought, and on occasion, *incompatible* with it. (377, my emphasis)

What we discover is a "Plato on the threshold of a radical novel conception of philosophy and an equally novel educational theory destined to invert Socratic moral psychology by assigning much *less importance to Reason* and much more importance to *moral habituation"* (376, my emphasis). Plato's *Phaedrus* is subversive of Socrates' notion of an a priori Reason that "comes before" language, a "transcendent signified," insofar as it dramatizes reason as an a posteriori effect of language and supplants its status atop the philosophical chain of signification with Ethos (recall, that the subtitle of the *Phaedrus* is "On the Beautiful, Ethical." In determining its usefulness for a social-epistemic praxis, one must account for the deeply ambivalent nature of Platonic writing in the *Phaedrus*. For if it is unsuited for pedagogical emulation by virtue of its "want of clarity of argument, univocacy of meaning, and overt statement of author's intentions and theses," then by contrast it is eminently worthy of emulation by virtue of its ethical critique of signifying practices of domination, its "moral habituation," relative to the real, the good, and the possible, and the rhetorical complexity of its polemic.

Close textual analysis of Plato's dialogues in the early, middle, and late periods of his career reveals their increasingly subversive nature—and their subversive representation of the dynamics of the master-pupil, dialectician-interlocutor dyad in particular. Plato's dialogues dramatize a movement away from the combative, adversarial, agonistic relationship of the early and middle dialogues, in which the interlocutor is distinctly sophist and absolutely Other, to a relationship in the mature period in which the interlocutor is a pupil, is always and already an Other-who-is-Same, a variant of the ideal Self, in which the representation of Logos as staged combat is absorbed by the humanizing imperatives of Eros and Ethos—in which the either-or polemics of persuasion are absorbed into the both-and/two-in-one imperatives of mutual edification.

The dialogues of this mature period signify a subversive break with the philosophic Ideal of the master, in which orality trumps writing, Logos precedes language, and polemics supersedes eros, ethos, and edification. In this mature period, Plato seems to move away from the either-or binary polemic of Socratic inquiry, which was perhaps the inevitable effect of a war of discourses between sophistry and philosophy, democracy and oligarchy, in which the rhetorical and political were conjoined in adversarial combat for thirty years. In his later period, Plato, by contrast seems to be moving in a "more fully human," if not equally revolutionary and subversive, direction: toward a logos that serves not the ends of war but peace, not the purposes of persuasion but the goals of edification, not the spirit of violence between individuals, but the ethos of eros between humans—as dramatized in the two-in-one, philosophical solidarity of master and pupil in the *Phaedrus*—a movement evidenced in the final words: "Let us go"—as if in these words, Plato is leaving behind not only sophistry, but an overly agonistic philosophy.

As with Socrates' recantation of philosophy in his first sophistic speech, so too must Plato purge from his soul the effects of his recantation of philosophy in writing—by recanting writing. Though he perhaps knew the gesture was futile, it was nevertheless necessary—to purge from his soul the violent effects of his apostasy from philosophy, in order to redeem his soul for posterity. Ironically, it is not this ritual of purification that would redeem his soul for posterity, but rather the genius of his own Inventions, which would guarantee the immortality of his soul.

Thus, Plato's subversive insurrection against Philosophy is perhaps most tellingly evidenced in its replacement by Art. What the dialogues of the mature period signify more than anything is this movement from philosophy to art and the dramatic transcendence of the persona of the philosopher, which is shed for the inventions of the Artist—who was always and already an artiste manqué, creating out of the trauma of a past, "buried, yet living"—and from out of the suffering associated with that trauma (the trial and execution of a beloved mentor), and finally from out of the suffering associated with the profanation of this philosophic Ideal: in the art of writing and in the beauty of Platonic signification it enshrines.

This transformation of the dialectic dyad from an agonistic either-or binary into a harmonizing both-and solidarity, touting the primacy not of polemics but of mutual edification, signifies, as Beversluis rightly observes, a paradigm shift in the dynamics of the master-pupil relationship, even as it signifies a rupture on Plato's part from the orthodoxy of Socratic dialectics. As Beversluis concludes,

> views set forth in the transitional and middle dialogues should not be ascribed to the historical Socrates. The methodology also changes. The

Socratic elenchus, ubiquitously present in the early dialogues, is completely absent from most of those which follow. . . . One of the most common explanations is that, as the *death of Socrates receded into the past* and Plato *came of age as a philosopher,* his enthusiasm for writing philosophical Socratic dramas gradually waned; and he *embarked on philosophical investigations of his own*—investigations of increasing complexity. . . . [in which Plato] reserved his severest criticism not for the demolished, but for the instrument of demolition and those who indiscriminately wielded it. (378, 382, my emphasis)

—including Socrates. This recantation of the master exemplifies not only Plato's "com[ing] of age as a philosopher," but even more importantly his coming of age as an artist. Moreover, the tensions in the Socrates-Plato, master-pupil dyad deeply inform the creative impulse (as evidenced in the careers of many artists, of which Plato is an apt case study), which begins in mimesis of a recognized master, as part of a long apprenticeship to art, but ends of necessity in the overthrow of that master's teachings, prompted by the original dictates of the artist's own genius, which increasingly labors under the yoke of an Other's aesthetic ideology, with which its own developing aesthetic ideology comes into increasing conflict.

These philosophic and aesthetic tensions between master and pupil become yet a further impetus to art, which, by objectifying them, mitigates their painful effect on the soul. In *Art and Artist,* Otto Rank gives perhaps the most definitive description of this developmental paradigm, underscoring the centrality of the master-pupil dyad to the artistic bildung:

The first stage in the growth of an artist is that which we have described as his "nomination" and which marks the *subordination of the individual* to one of the prevailing art-ideologies, this usually showing itself in the *choice of some recognized master as the ideal* pattern . . . at first his individuality vanishes, until later, at the height of achievement, he strives once more to liberate his personality, now a mature personality, from the *bond of an ideology* which he has himself accepted and helped to form. This whole process of liberation from a personal or ideal identification is *particularly intense and therefore difficult for the artist.* . . . In this creative conflict it is not only the positive tendency to individual self-liberation from ideologies once accepted and now being overcome that plays a great part. There is also the *creative guilt-feeling,* and this opposes their abandonment and seeks to *tie down the individual in loyalty to his past.* This loyalty is again opposed by a demand for *loyalty to his own self-development.* (371–372, my emphasis)

Rank's observations not only underscore the centrality of the master-pupil dyad to the artistic bildung, but shed light on a possible source of Platonic Invention, and of his attack on writing in particular, which may have arisen from his own "creative guilt-feeling," for thus having profaned, subverted, and renounced the "recognized master" who was the living embodiment of his aesthetic ideal. Plato's critique of writing is an attempt to work off the effects of his guilt, as well as a futile effort to "tie down the individual in loyalty to his past." Seen in this light, the attack on writing becomes a farewell homage to a master whose teachings have been assimilated, then altered, and finally abandoned, prompted by "loyalty to his own self-development," to the imperatives of his own "evil genius."

Rank's observations are cogent in their significance—perhaps because they are deeply informed by his own conflicted experience with the master, Freud, whose disciple and protégé he was—and whose heretical offspring he became. Freud evidences the intensity of this conflict between master and pupil when he confides in a letter to Rank, "you are the dreaded David who with his *Trauma of Birth* succeeds in deprecating my work" (qtd. in Taft, 79). Ironic that Rank's liberation from the master/father Freud is signified by a book that heretically theorizes the traumatic effects of birth ("separation anxiety") with such liberatory genius that the book itself incites a new trauma, rooted in the "creative guilt feeling" associated with his rebellion against the master's teachings:

> The only tangible statement which Freud's theory could give us about the artistic process was that which asserted the impulse to artistic productivity originated in the sex impulse. . . . But psychology could not explain how from the sex impulse there was produced not the sex act, but the art work. (26)

A similar process of liberatory insurrection is at work in the dialogues of Plato's mature period, particularly the *Phaedrus,* and particularly in his attack on writing. As a consequence of his rift with the master, Rank was banished from the Vienna circle, driven into professional exile in Paris, his work censored by the disciples of Freudian orthodoxy, precipitating a morbid crisis of despair, whose feelings of guilt and betrayal inflict great violence upon his own soul, as evidenced by the suicidal thoughts recorded in his Tagebücher (diaries).

THE DILATORY SPACE OF SHAME

This rift between master and pupil, though essential for the development of the pupil's own genius, exacts a steep price: in the suffering associated with feelings of betrayal, guilt, and profanation of the beloved Ideal. Plato's critique of writing is his apologia for not only profaning, but critiquing, the master in writing—for daring to subvert Socrates' principles of philosophy, for which he was put to death. It is Plato's attempt to work off the effects of his recantation. He works off the shameful effects of writing in writing a critique of writing, displaced onto the persona of the recanted philosopher. The violence of those effects is evidenced in the multiple and recurring dramas of recantation Plato stages throughout the *Phaedrus,* whose "rigor," as indicated in his attack on writing, and as Derrida observes, is evidenced "from one end of the *Phaedrus* to the other."

Might Plato's attack on writing be an index of his shame for having profaned orality with writing—an attempt to work off the effects of shame so ubiquitously dramatized throughout the *Phaedrus* (Socrates' hooding and baring his head)? Unable to disparage his art in his own voice, does he come to see his craft through the judgmental eyes of his master—as if imagining what Socrates might have to say of his apostasy from orality to writing, philosophy to art, teaching to invention—from beyond the grave? The artist works off the effects of his apostasy to art by flagellating his art in the persona of the recanted master. Plato stages within the trial of writing, not only a trial of Socrates, but the trial of himself by Socrates—to mitigate the violent effect of betrayal: the guilt, shame, and fear (of damnation) associated with his apostasy to art.

Thus, the artist works off, on the plane of illusion, the violence associated with his recantation of the master, of the master's mode of discourse, of the megalegoric violence associated with the master's elenchus and its stain of sophistry, of the bind of servitude to the master and his elenchic and aesthetic ideology. Indeed, the carnivalesque inventions of the *Phaedrus* may be seen as an eruptive rebellion against the master's insistence on unity, arrangement, definition, division and classification, in a composition that (de)composes its own rules. The rhetorical festival of mimicry, meta-drama, myth, and erotic innuendo, of history, irony, satire, and allegory disrupts the very dialectic it reinforces: enacting the very conflict between philosophy and art at the heart of the *Phaedrus* in a dialectic whose polemic is forever being intruded upon by its own inventions. As if in the *Phaedrus,* Plato was channeling two discourses (philosophy and art) whose tensions could not be absolutely reconciled or completely harmonized, insofar as one posed a threat to the other. Writing not only escapes the control of the elenchic master, but implies the eclipse of orality. Plato's apostasy from Socrates' oral elenchus is the abandonment of a dying discourse for an emerging one: a discourse he helps birth, or into which he breathes fresh life; a discourse that proves far superior to oral dialectics for fulfilling the soul's loftiest desire—for immortality. Sans writing, a dialectician's soul lives on only as long as his pupils live.

However, the apostasy to art exacts a steep price on the former disciple of philosophy. The signs of his own Invention do violence not just to the philosophic Other, but to the creative Self: in the form of guilt, shame, betrayal, and fear, touching off a morbid crisis that ironically further fuels the creative impulse, providing it additional materials and themes (the critique of writing), whose objectification in the realms of the symbolic help the creative self objectify as well the violent effects of its apostasy from the master, which are thrown off in further creation.

In the *Phaedrus,* Invention is as eruptive as the "buried, yet living past," as the ghost of a martyred master that incites it. The *Phaedrus* bears dramatic witness to the eternal return of each: of Invention and of a traumatic past, and of their volatile synergy, in which Platonic Invention re-visits and re-works the violence of a "buried, yet living past," immortalizing both philosophy and the first philosopher by transposing both into Art. Further, Plato works off the violence of his apostasy to art in art, in the trial of writing. Thus, the wound of art becomes further material for art, mitigating the effects of the wound—even as art mitigates the effects of the original wound that gave rise to it: the unjust trial and murder of a beloved mentor.

Art heals the wounds that both life and art inflict on the Self.

Thus, Plato's attack on writing is conceived in the liberatory anguish of a pupil's recantation of a master—in writing: projected as the master's recantation of the pupil. Plato's recantation of writing is a projection of his guilt, recanting himself and writing, for having profaned the master's oral philosophy in writing, through art. The *Phaedrus* dramatizes, among so many things, the violence of betrayal, as evidenced by the violent effects of Socrates' temporary betrayal of Love and philosophic Eros—perhaps prompted by the violent effects of the beloved pupil's impending betrayal of philosophy for sophistry, which in turn perhaps comments on the real pupil's betrayal of the master's philosophy, which is supplanted by an idolatry of art.

Plato's attack on writing is his attempt to rhetorically "cover his head" to hide the shame he feels and to exorcise the fear of "being called a sophist" by posterity: for having turned from orality to writing and, in the course of writing, for having written like a sophist. Thus, the "shame" a hooded Socrates feels relative to his recantation of philosophic Eros informs and prefigures the shame Plato feels for having recanted orality in favor of writing, dialectics in favor of dramatic dialogues, and the master's teachings in favor of his own art. Thus, an alternative way to "read" Plato's attack on writing is to understand it as being prompted by his shame and guilt, relative to his renunciation of orality: a recantation he enacts through the persona of Socrates, as a means of working off the violent effects of his own shame, guilt, and fear—and particularly his fear of being remembered as a sophist, for having written sophistically. As Neel observes, "the disingenuousness of a writer demanding such structure from discourse while at the same time employing writing as a mode of attaining that structure cannot be overstated" (42). The hypocritical irony of Plato's polemic is that "in order to privilege philosophy, dialectic, truth, and speech, didn't Plato have to become a sophistical rhetorician . . ." (55)? In claiming the high moral ground for philosophy, Plato dons for all time, if not a hood, then the donkey ears of an unethical philosopher.

Derrida and Neel's polemic rests on the assumption that Plato's Socrates *is* Plato, is here speaking for Plato. But what if this critique of writing underscores not the pupil's solidarity with the master, but his subversion of the master? What if Plato's attack on writing evidences not his hypocrisy relative to sophistry and writing, but his recantation of philosophy?

Leveraging a "dilatory space" between Plato and Plato's Socrates, between artist and philosophical persona, between writer and dialectician "loosens up" fresh meanings relative to Plato's attack on writing and relationship to philosophy, signifying a growing and liberatory rift between the *philosophy* of one and the *art* of the Other—that problematizes, as well, the Socratic assumption of a Logos that always and already "comes before" language. Thus, Plato's attack on writing deeply and ironically informs Platonic invention—which has further implications for contemporary theories of "vitalism."

In his defense of Socrates, Plato ends up condemning him—his verdict doing an about-face, in the end siding with Socrates' accusers, not directly but indirectly—while assuming the persona of the accused mentor. He condemns as he immortalizes the master. Socrates' critique of writing is yet another example of his megalegoric discourse, of his rhetorical overkill, and of the agonistic soul of his elenchus. It is Plato "hanging him out to dry," leaving him to twist in the winds of posterity, as the author and advocate of an extreme argument, that depicts Socrates at his elenchic worst. It is Plato writing off the master, in writing that recants the master's penultimate thesis. Perhaps it is his immortalization of the martyred mentor that enables Plato to condemn and subvert his teaching—as if to say, "I who have given you immortality, who have rescued you from the grave and from oblivion, have the right to present you to posterity, warts and all—as a megalegoric, vengeful, victory-at-all-cost erotic madman, who practiced the sophistry he preached against—and who perhaps even, as a result of his hubris and megalegoria, deserved the fate he got."

This is perhaps the redemptive wisdom of Plato's subversion of the philosophic Ideal: it frees him from its ambivalent imperatives, from the yoke of mere mimicry of a master, enables him to truly turn the page and "come of age"—not merely as a philosopher, but as an artist: something he had desired since boyhood, when he first aspired to be a dramatic poet, à la Aristophanes—as if his detour into philosophy was itself a long apostasy from his true calling as an artist. What the *Phaedrus* thus signifies (and signifies immortally) is not merely an apostasy from philosophy, but an apostasy from an apostasy. If philosophy signified for Plato an apostasy from his true calling to art, then his apostasy from philosophy signifies a necessary and inevitable return to a genuine calling, as an artist. It is not a "turning away" but a "returning to" the Ideal, consecrated under the sign, not of Philosophy but of Art—and of the dramatic dialogue in particular. The recantation of philosophy in favor of Platonic Invention, emblematized in the final recantation of the recantation of writing by writing, evidences the eternal return of "vitalism": the final victory of Invention over a dialectics of victory-at-all-costs. Thus, the final "turn" of the *Phaedrus* signifies a turning away, not just from philosophy to art, but from vengeance to forgiveness, violence to Love: from the sword of dialectics to the plowshare of creation.

CONCLUSION

The meanings of the *Phaedrus* are deeply ambivalent, and deeply conflicted—and this epic conflict and ambiguity are compellingly captured in the dramatic emblem of the divided soul: the winged, horse-drawn chariot, whose light and dark steeds signify not only the violence of the struggle between sophistry and philosophy, between the profane and sacred impulses of the soul, but between the conflicting imperatives of philosophy and art, orality and writing. The ultimate irony, notwithstanding the attack on writing, is that although Plato is a philosopher, he is first and foremost a writer. He not only becomes something Socrates never became, but he becomes the Other-as-Writer. Further, the taint of writing is as problematic for his soul as the taint of sophistry is for the hooded Socrates. The effects of writing upon Plato's soul are deeply ambivalent: if on the one hand it mitigates the violence of the various conflicts that divide his soul, by objectifying them in art, while at the same time recuperating the immortality of his soul, then on the other it inflicts further suffering in the form of shame.

It is but one of many forms of conflict the artist experiences with his or her art—yet, as with all conflict, it is generative of further art, which may assume the form of other genres to escape the totalizing effects of creating in one genre, or which may assume the form of art-about-art, of writing-about-writing, wherein the artist turns into a critic of art within his own art—in what becomes, for the artiste manqué, an endless feedback loop between suffering and invention—where the suffering caused by Invention, becomes itself a further cause of Invention: as evidenced by Plato's attack on writing, by his shift from art to criticism, and by the primacy of the desire to write-about-writing: in a manner that recants everything that has "come before." There is indeed a double-edged sword in Plato's attack on writing—for it signifies as well the ultimate recantation of the master and the liberatory rift between master and pupil.

The question remains: whose attack is it—Plato's or Socrates'? The fact that Socrates delivers the attack and that Plato continues to write after the *Phaedrus* would seem to evidence his growing distance from the master (and his agonistic teachings)—if indeed, it does not imply a critique of Socrates' criticism, whose extreme views relative to writing are left to twist in the wind for posterity, perhaps as an example of his megalegoric hubris: of his intolerant, reductive, either-or, agonistic dialectic philosophy—as if Plato is saying "these are his words, not mine," by way of opening a liberatory space between philosophy and art, polemicist and artist, Socrates and himself. His depiction of the master's attack on writing may thus signify a further subversion of the master's authority, which, by virtue of the extreme position taken against writing, undermines the entire philosophic edifice: posits Socrates in the penultimate passages of the *Phaedrus*, not as the dialectical savior of the Athenian citizenry, but as a megalegoric madman with a dialectic death wish.

Thus, the steed-drawn, winged chariot of the Platonic soul allegorizes not only the conflict between the profane and sacred desires for eros and edification, but the conflict between master and pupil, philosopher and artist—and the soul's violently divided loyalties between its living god and the god of its genius. What Plato's subversion of Socratic orthodoxy indicates is the triumphant assertion of his own personal "daemon" (or "divine spirit") under the sign of artistic genius in subversive counter-point to Socrates' personal "daemon" of dialectic inquiry, which "attached me to the city" to rectify its dehumanizing excesses, as embodied in sophistic signifying practices. The conflict between master and pupil evidences the irreconcilable conflict between their respective "daemons," embodied in their respective callings to philosophy and art, to oral dialectics and writing. Art consumes philosophy to sate the appetite philosophy awakens in it, even as philosophy consumes sophistry, which similarly arouses the hunger of the discourse that feeds upon it. Platonic Invention is nourished by the philosophy it mouths, as a hunter is nourished by the flesh of the devoured stag. The *Phaedrus* dramatizes the serial cannibalization of discourses in the progression sophistry-philosophy-art, persuasion-dialectics-dramatic dialogue. What it depicts is the violent struggle for survival up the food chain of discourses, in which a bottom-feeding sophistry is consumed by philosophy, whose place atop the signifying food chain is supplanted by Invention. In the end, what remains is writing, is Platonic Invention. What we are left with at the end of the *Phaedrus* is the spectacle of a Socrates who has been "written off" by Plato, who lies immortally within Platonic inscription, perhaps as a sacrificial offering to his own immortal Inventions. Just as the mother and Marcel are conjoined immortally in the symbolic mausoleum of *A la recherche*, so too are Plato's Socrates and Plato forever embalmed in the immortal tomb of the *Phaedrus*.

If Plato indeed "writes off" Socrates, the suffering associated with the "creative guilt feeling" of such a rebellion would be mitigated by the immortality he confers on the master, as part of the contractual exchange for his subversive condemnation of the master. Thus, the master's recantation of writing signifies the pupil's condemnation of the master—and the final victory of art over philosophy in the divided soul of Plato. Socrates' condemnation of writing, by exorcising Plato's guilt for writing, frees the pupil to go on writing—allows him to step from the long shadow of the master's philosophy into the light of his own Invention.

Writing is for Plato a "sin against the deity" no less than Socrates' hooded sophistry. Writing may indeed be likened to the dark steed, by virtue of its illegitimate, profane, and eruptive force relative to the white horse of oral dialectics. In dramatic contradistinction to the profane desire for sex, which is tamed and absorbed by the desire for edification, the profane desires for vengeance and writing are appropriated by Plato's dark genius, into a desire to write with a vengeance against the sophists and in a spirit of insurrection against the Philosopher. Writing is thus twice subversive: inasmuch as it subverts sophistry and philosophy alike, it is truly a doubled-edged sword that critiques philosophy as well as sophistry, that wounds the Self as well as the Other.

Plato's recantation of writing is also a recantation of the sophistic purposes to which writing is put, not by sophistry but by philosophy, not just by Lysias but by himself: to avenge a martyred mentor. It is always and already a recantation of philosophy as practiced by the vengeful, megalegoric spirit of Socrates' daemon. He recants writing as practiced by sophistry and philosophy to redeem it under the sign of Art, as embodied in the dramatic dialogue.

In the end, the eruptive violence of the dark steed of Plato's genius prevails over the philosophic ideology of the master, as evidenced by the subordination of oral to written dialectics, by the assimilation of the Socratic elenchus into the dramatic dialogue, and by the transformation of the dialectic dyad from a model of mutual hostility to one of mutual edification. If Plato's mastery of oral dialectics and the teaching of it enact his fidelity to the master, his turn toward the written word, and the writing of dramatic dialogues in particular, signifies a liberatory rupture from the teachings of the Master—whose only mitigating effect may have been the knowledge that while thus profaning the master, he was at the same time avenging his murder and immortalizing his soul.

The attack on writing is an act of expiation directed to the absent master and an absent posterity, designed to mitigate the effects of recantation—precisely in accord with the dual ritual of purification enacted by Socrates to mitigate the effects of his sophistic speech (the myth of Stesichorus and the baring of his head). The fact that Plato continues to write after the *Phaedrus* signifies that he now not only serves a new master (his own genius) but recants the recantation of writing. Writing thus signifies that he has truly and fully become his own master—has literally become the Other-as-Artist.

Writing is both the cause and effect of his liberation from philosophy: it is the agent of the freedom it signifies. Even the price it exacts in suffering is yet a further impetus to itself. As a pharmakon, even its harmful effects are beneficial—if not essential—to the artist. Thus, its poison is always and already a cure—producing the anti-bodies of Invention that immunize the Self to its lethal effects. Thus may the artist of all humans drink the poisonous dram of sorrow to the dregs and live to tell (or write) the tale. Entombed in the *Phaedrus* are the souls of sophistry, philosophy, and art, of Lysias, Socrates, and Plato. There, the din and thunder of the ancient war between sophistry and philosophy is absorbed in the immortal flutter of Platonic Invention.

8 Love in a Time of War
The Ethos of Eros

> Underneath the various guises Socrates has assumed ... he is the *discursive erotician* par excellence.
> —Griswold (136, my emphasis)

> Dialogue cannot exist, however, in the absence of a profound love for the world and for men.
> —Freire (77)

What role does Love play in the radical pedagogies of Socrates and Freire? Are erotic and philosophic love mutually exclusive? Is the radical pedagogy of Socrates truly dialectic and genuinely ethical? Assessing these things is fundamental to establishing an educative genealogy between Socrates and Freire, as well as between ancient rhetoric and social-epistemic praxis. In calling into question the ethics and generic integrity of Socrates' dialectic elenchus, critics have focused on several problematic aspects: its seeming marginalization of the interlocutor; its vengeful tendencies; its putative eroticism; and its reinscription of sophistic signifying practices. I want to re-stage this "trial of dialectics" in order to address these criticisms and to assess the relevance of Socrates' radical elenchus to social-epistemic praxis, and to Freirean praxis in particular.

Central to this inquiry are a number of questions: is Socrates' radical pedagogy a teacher-centered discourse masquerading as an interactive dialogue, reinscribing a master-slave dialectic of domination that speaks to, rather than with, the pupil—in which the World is named for the pupil by the master? Do the tilted dynamics of this "dialectic" dyad call into question its ethics? Is there in Socrates' radical pedagogy a genuine alliteration between eros, logos, and ethos? Is a praxis that privileges the conjunction of eros and edification relevant to contemporary education and to social-epistemic approaches to literacy in particular? What role, if any, does love play in the pursuit of knowledge for the common good in the struggle to transform social and political reality "for individual rights and social justice" (Giroux xxvii).

To answer these critical questions, we must assess the nature of the dialectician-interlocutor, master-pupil, Socrates-Phaedrus relationship in the *Phaedrus*. The conjunction of the critical, the political, and the ethical defines social-epistemic praxis, insofar as the pursuit of knowledge is not posited as an end in itself, but as a means of serving the common good:

as an intervention against injustice, the excesses of power, or the inequities of domination. As Giroux observes, "at the very least, radical pedagogical work proposes that education is a form of political intervention in the world and is capable of creating the possibilities for social transformation" (xxvii). To the extent social-epistemic praxis works in solidarity with those who are the objects of domination, generating a greater sense of agency and self-determination (the hallmarks of a more fully human existence), it is inherently ethical. In literature and composition, its concern with issues of canonicity, race, class, and gender underscore this ethical orientation. In anthropology, its ethical orientation is similarly evidenced in its concern with knowledge-making practices that instead of exploiting the Other, work in solidarity with the Other, using the knowledge gained not just to enhance the career of the ethnographer but to transform the material conditions that impede a "more fully human" existence for the ethnographic subject. In history, this ethical concern is evidenced by the attempts to deconstruct a master narrative that privileges the perspective of domination, constructing in its place a more inclusive narrative, that allows those who have historically been put under erasure by historians to "name their world" by naming their history. This same ethical concern defines postmodern inquiry across disciplines.

Socratic inquiry and social-epistemic pedagogy, by virtue of their ethical focus, align with American pragmatism in its pioneering, cold-war, and postmodern moments. As West observes, this pedagogy of American pragmatism posits "this notion of truth as a species of the good . . . in relation to temporal consequences, meaning that the future has consequences. And actually, if there is a distinctive feature of pragmatism, it is precisely this notion. That the future has ethical significance" (41). Thus, the relevance of Socrates' radical pedagogy to social-epistemic praxis hinges not just on the centrality of Logos to his meaning-making process, but of Ethos as well—on the ends which knowledge serves.

Of the many discourses in Socrates' pedagogical tool kit (mythic, poetic, mimetic, meta-dramatic, ironic, satiric, allegoric, sophistic, and dialectic), none has incited more debate than his discourse of erotic innuendo, operating in dialectic counterpoint to Lysias' overtly erotic thesis ("it is better to grant favors to a non-lover than a lover"). Is Socrates' discourse of erotic edification similarly informed by motives of seduction? Are the "favors" sought by Lysias part of the contractual agreement of philosophic love as well? Is the discourse Socrates constructs emblematic of a master-slave dialectic, insofar as the dialectician plays an active part, while the interlocutor is relegated to a passive role—in this replicating Freire's "banking model" pedagogy of domination, in which the authority of the teacher's voice is predicated on the silence of the student's—in which "knowledge is a gift bestowed by those who consider themselves knowledgeable upon those whom they consider to know nothing" (58), in which the agency of the teacher is predicated on the passivity of the pupil, whose passivity is perhaps the most desired outcome of "education": an educative model, which has as its goal not social transformation, but social control? Is Socrates' praxis truly dialogic or, as some critics assert, "egoistic" and "manipulative," concerned not with edification, but "victory"—perhaps even vengeance?

The answer to these questions depends on the degree of agency enjoyed by the Other in Socrates' "elenchus," or critical inquiry. The final judgment on the ethics of Socrates' dialectic teaching depends on whether one believes he is practicing a "banking model" or a "dialogic" form of education, on whether one believes the pupil is a passive object or an active subject in the meaning-making process. I want to interrogate the ethical nature of Socratic praxis, and the relationship between Eros, Logos, and Ethos in particular, to determine if it is manipulative or dialogic, driven by self-interest or the desire for mutual edification, by love or self-love, by a desire "to make the lover a better person" or "to satisfy the carnal desires of the lover" (Bizzell and Herzberg 59). As previously, I want to argue my case within the context of a figurative "trial" of Socratic inquiry.

THE CRITICAL TRADITION:
THE CROSS-EXAMINATION OF SOCRATES

A body of criticism has called into question the dialogic integrity and ethical claims of Socrates' praxis (elenchus). Critics have argued that Socrates' dialectic praxis is inescapably egoistic, insofar as the beloved is never accepted as an "individual" without qualification, but is always and forever constructed in terms of the lover's ideal, with the Other's passive acquiescence. What is in the best interest of the Other is determined by the dialectic Self. The Other, these critics assert, is never given a say in setting the edifying agenda, though his complicity is perhaps an index of his approval. Griswold problematizes the altruistic assumptions of dialectics: "How can the lover [Socrates] be so sure that he is . . . not just compelling the beloved [Phaedrus] against his nature to fit the lover's mold?" (129). How can we be sure that what isn't being asserted here is not the desire for the edification of Self and Other but "the desire for mastery" (129)? The perception is compounded by the "heavy emphasis placed on the leader's formation of the follower" (129). As Ferrari observes, "But for all that this transaction displays a more even distribution of power between its partners, it is nevertheless wholly manipulative" (108). Ferrari continues: "[D]oes the older man take advantage of his greater 'clarity' and conviction in order to impose his ideas on the boy? Is the force of his inspired example, despite his genuine good will, nevertheless surreptitiously manipulative—saying in effect to the boy: 'you must become what I am?'" (182). These criticisms mirror the critique of radical pedagogy, whose teachers are similarly accused of imposing their world view on students—and, if true, underscore a negative genealogy between Socrates and Freire, whose radical pedagogies reinscribe a teacher-centered pedagogy of domination that marginalizes the status of the student/interlocutor. Vlastos' critique is a case in point:

> Depicting [Phaedrus] as an adorable cult-object, Plato seems barely conscious of that fact this "holy image" is himself a valuing subject, a center of private experience and individual preference, whose predilections and choice of ends are no reflex of the lover's and might well cross him at some point (1969, 1981, qtd. in Ferrari 32).

The point, as Ferrari asserts, is moot because the lover, in order to make the Other into an image of his Self ("become what I am)," would first have to possess that self-knowledge. Yet the very discovery of this self-knowledge comes to him through his dialogic relation with Phaedrus, through the experience of philosophic love, through the epic struggle Phaedrus incites in his soul, between its "shameful" and "beautiful" tendencies, and the desire to absorb the debased into the honorific, to master the "shameful" with the "beautiful"—as so dramatically figured in the image of the winged chariot with its dark and light steeds.

Instead of "become what I am," Socrates' pedagogical goal might more accurately be posited as follows: "cultivate my soul, and I will cultivate yours." This mutual cultivation lies at the heart not only of Socrates' radical pedagogy, but also Freire's. The goal is not the "inculcation" of the student with the teacher's world view, but the mutual edification of student and teacher, in which the teaches learns as much from the process as the student: as Freire succinctly observes, "[B]oth are simultaneously teachers *and* students" (59). This is evidence of the truly dialogic nature of the educative dyad in the radical pedagogies of Socrates and Freire. To the extent education inherently inculcates, it underscores the agency of the teacher. Yet this agency is asserted only so that it may be surrendered or transferred to the student, who becomes the agent of his or her own edification, once this agency is dialogically enabled. As Ferrari observes, there can be no "guarantee that between two persons of philosophic mien the progress of love [will] be smooth and free from manipulativeness" (183). In the final analysis, manipulative and edifying tendencies are not mutually exclusive. There is and can be no education entirely free of pedagogical initiative, inculcation, manipulation. Yet this initial impetus toward mutual edification provided by the teacher is ethical only if it is transferred to the student, as the agent of his/her own self-becoming. But to posit an educative process cleansed of pedagogical initiative, agency, manipulation, or inculcation is an exercise in pure altruism.

As with so many other elements of the *Phaedrus,* including the setting, myth, writing, Eros, and rhetoric itself, philosophical inquiry is itself subject to double explication as a "shameful" and a "beautiful," a manipulative and an edifying discourse—in a dramatic dialogue whose binary oppositions never devolve into an either-or distinction, but are always and already implicated in a "both-and" peculiar intimacy that subverts their hierarchical representation. The self-edifying elements of Socrates' praxis are inherently dialogic, as evidenced by his words. He asserts, for example, that rather than "sowing" his thoughts in ink, the dialectician would be better advised to "sow in a fitting soul intelligent words which are able to *help* themselves and *him who planted them*" (277a). The communal, interactive, dialogic nature of the mutual edification is echoed by Freire: "the teacher is no longer merely the-one-who-teaches, but one who is himself taught in dialogue with the students, who in turn while being taught, also teach. They become jointly responsible for a process in which all *grow*" (67, my emphasis). Freire's emphasis on the mutual growth that occurs in turn reinforces Socrates' educative metaphor of sowing seeds "in a fitting soul" to foster the growth of both students and "him who planted them." As Freire concludes, "no one teaches another, nor is anyone self-taught. Rather, teachers and students "teach each other, mediated by the world" (67). Socrates' elenchus is deeply mediated by the world, insofar as it repeatedly engages the problematic of power and its circulation through the power of persuasion, and in particular reads the local context of Athenian politics critically.

That this mutually edifying "process" is deeply yoked to the soul's quest for immortality is evidenced by Socrates' next observation that it is "capable of continuing . . . for ever . . . which make[s] their *possessor* happy, to the farthest possible limit of human happiness" (277b). The happiness of the possessor implies (and is dependent upon) an Other whose soul is cultivated as a vehicle of the self's own immortality ("continuing forever"). Thus, the master-pupil dyad becomes not only a surrogate for the father-son relationship, but also for the lover-beloved dyad, to the extent that it harbors the prospect of imorality and happiness "to the farthest possible limit."

Critics of Socrates' elenchus find further evidence of its tendency to reinscribe a master-slave discourse in Socrates' description of the dynamics of the master-pupil dyad, in which imagery seemingly reinforces the object-status and passive nature of the Other-as-beloved-pupil:

> What nature are we to attribute to this new kind of being? We reply that it is the *receptacle*, and in a manner the *nurse of all generation*. . . . she is the natural *recipient* of all impressions. . . . But the forms which *enter* into and go out of her are the *likeness of eternal realities* . . . modeled within her *after their patterns*. . . . For the present we only have to conceive of three natures: first, that which is in the process of *generation* [the edified pupil]; secondly, that *in which the generation takes place* [the un-edified pupil]; and thirdly, that of which the thing generated is a *resemblance* . . . [the master]. And we may liken the receiving principle to a mother, and the source or spring to a father, and the intermediate nature to a child, and may remark further that if the *model* is to *take every variety of form*, then the matter in which the *model is fashioned* will not be duly prepared unless it is *formless*

and free from the impress of any of those *shapes* which it is hereafter to receive from without.... (48e–51b)

Plato's imagery underscores the paradoxical nature of the dialectic dyad, in which the Other is not entirely passive or active but both, as evidenced by the dual images of the "receptacle" and the "nurse of all generation": the one merely an inanimate object into which the contents of the Self are poured; the Other a living being in which the Self is generated, and by implication, the new self of the teacher, as well. The imagery also underscores the formative nature of the educative process, which of all arts most resembles sculpture by virtue of its plasticity: of its desire to shape an Other in the image of the ancient Greek ideal of humanity, as evidenced by the signifying chain of "model" "take . . . form," "model is fashioned," "impress," and "shapes." The description of this educative process by Plato's Socrates evidences the extent to which it was bound up in a project of human engineering, oriented toward the creation of a new human type, shaped in the image of the ancient Greek ideal of humanity: defined under the signs of beauty, edification, and civic engagement.

This is not to presume an Other, however, who is always and already merely a passive object of the dialectic self. To assume as much would be a reductive misrepresentation of the dialectic dyad as articulated and practiced by Plato's Socrates—would require that we turn a blind eye to the mutual agency and mutual edification of self and other, master and pupil. For it is clear in the *Phaedrus* that Socrates is as shaped by the process as Phaedrus, is as edified by the effects of Phaedrus' beauty as the latter is by the beauty of the master's discourse. As a result of the great war touched off in Socrates' soul between its sacred and profane impulses by Phaedrus' beauty, he comes to know himself better: understands that he is a person who is able to master the baser impulses of his soul (for sex, vengeance) with reason, love, and edification; understands that he is a person for whom life is not worth living without either self-knowledge or the knowledge of love that is its precondition and that such knowledge can only come to him through an Other.

The violent effects of Phaedrus' beauty trigger the war between erotic desire and the desire to edify, between erotic and philosophic love. It prompts Socrates' entire discourse on philosophy, which he comes to truly know through language, by speaking it to a beloved Other, within the context of love. To the extent he defines himself throughout the *Phaedrus*, he comes to know himself—a knowledge that comes to him from Phaedrus: a self-knowledge, which is but one effect of the Other's luminous beauty. His discourse on "the beautiful, ethical" evidences its own beauty and ethos to the extent it is prompted by the love and practice of mutual edification.

Socrates' imagery underscores the ambivalent both-and nature of the dialectic dyad, in which the Other is simultaneously configured as an object and subject, in a praxis that reinscribes both "banking model" and "liberatory" signifying practices, to the extent it privileges the authority of the teacher and the agency of the student, patriarchal and dialogical tendencies. The master-pupil dialectic, for example, is viewed as a variation of the biological father-mother dyad, whose function is to propagate, not a physical but a spiritual, intellectual offspring, as a form of immortality. As Derrida asserts, dialectics like the pharmakon of "inscription is thus the production of the son" (161). Dialectics is driven by the "logic of the supplement," in which "B is both added to A and replaces A," where "B" is the dialectic self (Socrates) and "A" is the untutored and "formless" other, or Phaedrus (xiii). Thus, the Socrates-Plato, master-pupil dyad is also a father-son dyad, insofar as Socrates' discourse gave birth to Plato's, whose dramatic dialogues are a "supplement" to Socrates' dialectic elenchus, which they sustain, and to which they give a form of immortality. These same patriarchal, father-son tendencies are evident in the Socrates-Phaedrus dyad, in which the "son" as a dialogic offspring fulfills the same goal as a biologic offspring: the immortality of the father.

This passage is significant because it presents the dialectic process not merely as a vehicle by which the Other is transformed, but as a process of mutual edification, in which the Self is re-formed in the Other. Socrates is not simply interested in edifying the Other, but in re-fashioning the Self in the Other. The Other is a vehicle for the display of the Self, a medium for the re-fashioned self. Socrates' praxis is thus composed of altruistic and narcissistic tendencies—hence, its mutually edifying nature.

"Modeled" is an apt term for Phaedrus insofar as, like a fashion model, he is appareled in the intellectual designer wear of Socrates. Dialectics is a form of self-fashioning. The affective powers Socrates ascribes to the "pharmakon" of Lysias text may be ascribed as well to his own dialectics, which similarly acts upon Phaedrus like a "drug," which "already introduces itself into the body of the discourse with all its ambivalence: This charm, this spellbinding virtue, this power of fascination" (70). Derrida continues: "Operating through seduction, the pharmakon makes one stray from one's general, natural, habitual paths and laws . . . they take him out of himself and draw him onto a path that is properly an *exodus*" (70, my emphasis).

Is Derrida's indictment an accurate reflection of the dynamics of the master-pupil dyad in *Phaedrus?* Are there aspects, motives, and outcomes of this educative relationship that warrant a more appreciative interpretation of it? The *Phaedrus* inscribes a violent drama of possession for the soul of the beloved Other, waged between sophistry and philosophy—in which the dialectic Self seeks possession of the ideal Other as a means of "disseminating" the self in space and time, in the here and hereafter. Perhaps more effectively than any other critic, John Beversluis calls into question the purported ethos of Socratic dialectics, relative to its goals, methods, and outcomes, noting the extent to which it relies on "often unscrupulous dialectical tactics" and "dialectic aberrations," including "shame tactics" (14, 40, 46). Beversluis continues:

> [T]here is a dark, even ominous side to this alleged moral gadfly who claims to care for the souls of his fellows but does everything in his power (often by whatever means) to deprive them of whatever shared insight they possess, offering them nothing in return. . . . (15)

Beversluis characterizes Socrates' method as "refutation as annihilation," in which he often behaves "like a mob orator" (342), whose "announced goal is to care for the soul of his fellows," but whose goal in reality is "victory": is not the edification of the Other, but the aggrandizement of the Self at the expense of the sophistic Other. Beversluis concludes that Socrates' "elenchus is psychologically inefficacious [and] morally harmful" (379), constituting a form of mis-education, or "educational mistreatment" (380).

Critics suggest that Phaedrus, like many of Socrates' interlocutors, was merely a foil to the dialectician's discourse, lacking the agency that characterizes a genuine dialogic pedagogy. According to these critics, the dialogue reinscribes a master-slave dialectic in which the dialectician enjoys the full entitlements of an active, knowing, speaking subject-position, while the interlocutor is reduced to the status of a passive, uncritical, listening object, to be molded and shaped as mere putty in the hands of the teacher—in what is tantamount to an ancient inscription of Freire's "banking model" of education: where the pupil is the mere repository ("recipient") for the knowledge transmitted by the master. As Beversluis notes, these critics "are thoroughly dismissive of the interlocutors and reduce them to the status of mere mouthpieces for views which are hopelessly confused or demonstrably false" (ix). Beversluis continues:

> For centuries they have been berating the interlocutors. . . . The result is a time-honored reading which may be summed up as follows: . . . [Plato's interlocutors] are ignorant about moral matters—often the very matters about which they profess expertise. Unable to define their terms they so carelessly employ or to defend the assertions they so confidently advance, they are helpless in the face of Socratic interrogation . . . exposed as theoretically and morally bankrupt. Worse still they are not committed inquirers, as is evidenced . . . by their perverse tendency to return to the workaday world unchanged and ready to go about their business as if these confrontations had never taken place. (1–2)

These critics, as Beversluis observes, conclude their indictment of Plato's interlocutors, asserting that while "secure in their false conceit of knowledge, they neglect the care of their souls [and thus] serve as permanent witnesses to the folly of the unexamined life" (2). As Beversluis concludes, "this seductive picture . . . has never been seriously challenged" (2).

RE-CROSS: RECUPERATING THE DIALOGIC SUBLIME

Another body of recent criticism, spearheaded by Beversluis' own inquiry, has developed a more appreciative reading of Plato's interlocutors, particularly those of the early dialogues, calling into question the assumptions and findings of an earlier critical tradition. Yet even Beversluis does not include in his corrective, appreciative reading the interlocutors of the later, mature works, including Phaedrus, whom he characterizes as yet "passive, cooperative, and eminently persuadable auditors, who listen dutifully and nod in agreement" (378). Beversluis continues:

> In the process, they cease to be recognizable individuals with minds of their own and tend to be faceless straightmen who can be relied on to produce the desired response. Everyone remembers Euthyphro, Crito, Ion, Hippias, Callicles, and Thrasymachus. But who has vivid memories of . . . Phaedrus [?] (378)

I would like to offer a more corrective reading of Phaedrus' agency relative to Socrates: one that recuperates the genuinely dialogic nature of his elenchus relative to the "beautiful, ethical."

As Beversluis offers a corrective reading of the agency enjoyed by the interlocutors in the early dialogues, so would I like to offer a corrective reading of Beversluis' traditional reading of the "marginal contributions" and "perfunctory" role of Phaedrus, whose unappreciated agency similarly justifies the title that bears his name. An appreciation of Phaedrus' agency relative to Socrates alters our understanding of the dialogue, and of the dynamics of the master-pupil relationship in particular. This corrective reading of his role commences with an appreciation of the "kairic" awareness Phaedrus evidences toward Socrates, from which his agency flows.

Phaedrus evidences a kairic awareness equal to that of the master dialectician and is no less astute in using it to his advantage. The mutual edification of the dialectic relationship, as Griswold observes, suggests that the "boy's contribution is far more than merely to offer himself as suitable clay in which the lover can mould his preconceptions" (173). His sublime Beauty (inward as well as outward) is an active rather than a passive force, as evidenced by the profound, transformative effect it has upon Socrates—assigning the pupil an agency equal in its affective power to that of the master dialectician.

Indeed, Socrates' idolatry of Phaedrus' beauty and love of beautiful discourse mirrors Phaedrus' idolatry of Lysias' sophistic discourse, reinforcing the dialogic nature of the dyad through the dramatization of the mutual affective power of physical beauty and beautiful discourse. For Socrates, Phaedrus is an emblem of transformation, redemption, and immortality, as evidenced by the beholder's desire to "create in [the beloved] the closest possible likeness to [his] god'" (253a–b, qtd. in Griswold 173). Without the beloved ideal Other, the Self is denied the path to its own edification. Further, Phaedrus is aware of the cards he holds, of the affective power of his beauty and discourse upon Socrates, and uses it to his advantage, playing on Socrates' idolatry of beauty and beautiful discourse to coerce him into giving a sophistic speech, by threatening to withhold these "favors" from the dialectician. These are hardly the gestures or discourse of an interlocutor who lacks agency or awareness.

The mutuality of the transformative exchange is underscored by Ferrari, who observes that "the philosophic lover, even if he comes to the boy as a well-disposed adult, discovers through the boy that he is not, after all, whole. Indeed . . . only by taking an interest in the boy's personal development can he himself now develop as a philosopher" (162). A measure of agency flows to Phaedrus inasmuch as he completes the dialectician, as the ideal Other completes the self, reinscribing Aristophanes' notion that the other provides what the Self lacks: the missing half of its soul. The mutuality of the exchange is further evidenced by the assertion that the beholder loves "the boy by whose agency *he* has developed" (Griswold 173, my emphasis). "This then is the psychological process figured in the lover's finding himself a statue to sculpt" (174).

Further, the transformative effect Phaedrus' beauty has upon the old master recuperates a measure of agency lost to his seeming passivity. Phaedrus, as Griswold observes, is "manifestly Socrates inferior in all important respects" (18), save two: his youthful, if not ideal, beauty and his love of discourse. Yet the first is decisive in attracting Socrates and in arousing his desires, while the second establishes a deep and spontaneous alliteration between their souls. Phaedrus' status as the living fount of the sublime and of its violent transformative effects upon Socrates, is inconsistent with the inconsequential role assigned to him by an earlier critical tradition. For these two reasons (beauty and love of beautiful discourse), Phaedrus is for Socrates the living incarnation of the ideal Other. And yet, as Griswold rightly observes, the dialogue is named after the unreflective student. Why?

The fact that Plato names his dialogue after the beautiful pupil and not the master is significant for several reasons. First, it underscores the centrality of the Other to the happiness of the philosophical Self, reinforcing the dialogic nature of the philosophic life. Second, it accentuates the primacy of Beauty to the dialectical life, insofar as both Eros and Logos are defined in terms of Beauty, are the mediums by which the desire for Beauty is satisfied. The dialogue was, after all, subtitled "on the Beautiful, Ethical." The mutual agency of Self and Other is transformative for both master and pupil. By naming the dialogue after the pupil, Plato draws our attention to the centrality of the beautiful in awakening the transformative desires for edification, justice, love, and immortality, for beautiful discourse and the philosophical life.

Phaedrus represents the ideal and necessary starting point of the dialectical journey, as a beautiful but untutored pupil, whose conversion to dialectics is therefore all the more dramatic, in what is after all a "dramatic dialogue." As Griswold asserts, "Phaedrus' very shortcomings make him an ideal character for development of what I take to be the central theme of the dialogue . . . every thing about Phaedrus points to the necessity for self-knowledge" (18). His shortcomings, however, do not signify an absence of agency, a passivity that would undermine, if not negate, the dramatic progression of the dialogue.

For drama to exist (in the symbolic, as in the material world), genuine conflict is required: no conflict, no drama. Conflict connotes a mutual agency in the opposing forces. A dramatic double conflict lies at the heart of the *Phaedrus:* in which Phaedrus is the object of a violent tug of war between sophistry and philosophy (Lysias vs. Socrates), and in which his divided loyalties trope on Socrates' divided soul, and in the violent conflict waged between its sacred and profane, sophistic and philosophic tendencies. Thus, a deep conflict is embedded in the soul of master and pupil alike: a conflict that is, moreover, essential to their mutual edification and transformation.

Finally, their mutual transformation through self-knowledge tropes on the transformative possibilities of this knowledge relative to the broader reality, dominated by sophistic signifying practices. The power to choose between sophistry and philosophy is an index of the agency Phaedrus enjoys—as long as that choice is genuine, and not determined for him by Socrates. The goal of Socrates' radical praxis is to ensure that the choice, whichever it may be, is based not on idolatry but on critical reflection.

In a sense, Socrates is the more dependent of the two, insofar as Phaedrus is the exclusive source of the Beauty he requires for his own edification and immortality, whereas for Phaedrus, there are many sources of the beautiful discourse his idolatrous mind requires. This explains not only the desperation, but also the genius of Socrates' pedagogy, the two elements of his violent response to the threat of sophistry posed by Lysias. The difference in the relative agency enjoyed by master and pupil (to Phaedrus' advantage) is also evidenced by the fact that Phaedrus is a beloved courted by two lovers, whereas Socrates is but one of two lovers competing for Phaedrus' philosophic love. As a luxury he can afford, Phaedrus' seeming passivity is an index of the agency he enjoys, as the object of the rhetorical competition between Lysias and Socrates.

This brings us to a surprising, if not ironic conclusion: what appears at first to critics to be a want of agency in Phaedrus may in reality be a surfeit of it, relative to Socrates, which would again justify Plato's naming the dialogue after him.

Thus, the theme of idolatry, like every important theme in the dialogue, is doubly explicated: insofar as Phaedrus' idolatry of sophistry is doubled in Socrates' idolatry of Phaedrus. The theme of self-knowledge (or mutual edification) is similarly doubly explicated, as a presence and an absence in Socrates and Phaedrus, respectively. Likewise, the theme of Eros is doubly explicated as an emblem of the profane and the sacred, in the same manner that rhetoric is doubly explicated as either debased or honorific, as a means of persuasion or self-knowledge, as a drug or remedy. As Griswold observes, the dramatic "context is one in which we observe the emergence of self-knowledge," not just in the Other but in the Self, as a consequence of the transformative effect of Beauty, whether incarnated in the Other or in discourse. The obstacles encountered in the pursuit of self-knowledge, including the unreflective nature of the pupil, his idolatry of a rival's discourse, and the dialectician's own struggle with the profane impulses of his desire, merely heighten the drama of the dialogue as well as its dramatic turn from sophistry to philosophy.

The agency of Phaedrus' role is further underscored by the fact that it is he who "introduces the themes of eros, rhetoric, writing, remembering, the nonlover . . . who takes the discussion and Socrates into the countryside" (Griswold 18)—who is the initiator of the discourse, who makes the first move. He is the messenger and conduit of discourses, profane and sacred. Further, the fact that discourse has come embodied in the beautiful body of this pupil represents for Socrates a sublime commingling of his two most ardent loves: for beautiful discourse arising from a beautiful Other. Phaedrus signifies the initial advent of the two-in-one, and as such re-awakens Socrates' "merger hunger" tendencies, which are activated in tandem with his "ideal hunger" and "mirror hunger" desires by the alliteration of beauty and beautiful discourse in the Other (Kohut).

The "favors" that Socrates seeks are of a much higher order, including not just profane but sacred desires as well. If rhetoric takes the "low road" with Lysias' discourse, it takes a much loftier path in Socrates' discourse—though not without the advent of an epic struggle in the soul of the dialectician between his profane and sacred impulses. For Socrates, Phaedrus represents the promise of fulfilling all desires of the soul in one person, which explains the violent effects of his beauty and discourse upon the philosopher's soul.

Phaedrus, similarly, is aware of Socrates' erotic predilection for beautiful discourse, upon which he artfully plays to satisfy his own desire for beautiful discourse, even though his definition of Beautiful is defective, limited as it is to an idolatry of sophistry. Blind to the edifying potential of discourse, Phaedrus merely sees it as performance or display, blessed with the same spellbinding affective power of poetry, drama, or epic myth. He is emblematic of the Athenian citizens who "loved good oratory to their ruin"—and his idolatry of sophistry is Exhibit A in the trial Socrates mounts against the affective power of sophistic oratory. Phaedrus is the perfect "interlocutor," insofar as he possesses a well-earned reputation as being an "impresario" of discourse, an arranger or promoter of beautiful public discourse, acting as a medium for its dissemination. Ferrari argues that Phaedrus' uncritical idolatry of discourse suggests he is a mere intellectual dilettante, "pursuing intellectual life for its extrinsic goods alone (the company of clever people, the thrill of swimming in deep waters)" (104). Lysias craftily exploits this tendency, evidencing a kairic awareness of Phaedrus' nature that rivals that of Socrates.

Phaedrus has devised the perfect bait for Socrates: a beautiful discourse about love. The old dialectician rises to the bait, as he inevitably must, his desire awakened by the prospect of a beautiful discourse about love in the hands of a youth who is Beauty personified. The prospect of the two-in-one is similarly recognized by Griswold, who observes that "the themes of eros and rhetoric are already combined in the persona of Phaedrus.... he loves to talk about love" (18). This conjunction of discourse and the Other under the sign of the Eros represents a kind of "perfect storm" of desire for Socrates. How could Socrates resist, much less refuse, the invitation to discourse with such a "guide," whose double allure is evident in Socrates' willingness to be "led" beyond the city walls he loves so dearly. Does Phaedrus' idolatry inspire his own? Or does the spectacle of Phaedrus idolatry inspire his mimicry of it—by way of holding a mirror up to his pupil's defective cognition? Or is his affectation of idolatry intended to disguise his genuine idolatry of the beloved pupil? Phaedrus' agency calls into question the reality of who is leading whom—and it does this throughout the dialogue. As Socrates confides, such is the effect of Phaedrus' beauty and discourse upon him that he would "willing[ly] be led like an ass." At times, it is impossible to tease apart the philosopher from the personas he adopts.

Phaedrus' agency thus calls into question the assertions of a long critical tradition regarding his putative passivity, even as it underscores the dialogic nature of the educative dyad. Phaedrus' successful extortion of a sophistic speech from Socrates is a tribute not only to his idolatry of sophistry, but also to his kairic awareness of Socrates. Playing upon Socrates' love of beautiful discourse, he "tries bribery, promising Socrates nothing less than a golden statue of himself at Delphi if he will make good his criticism and compete with Lysias (235d–e)" (103). Indeed, it is to spark just such competition for his "favors" that he confronts Socrates with Lysias' speech, coyly concealing it to "lead" Socrates on: to arouse his desire for beautiful discourse, to awaken his competitive instincts, perhaps even his envy and jealousy of Lysias, as a rival rhetor and now a rival for Phaedrus' "favors." The only thing more likely to arouse Socrates' interest in beautiful discourse is a beautiful discourse about love.

The depths of Phaedrus' kairic awareness of Socrates' nature is evidenced as well by the efficacy of the tactics he uses to manipulate the master's behavior. As Ferrari notes, "from bribery, [Phaedrus] proceeds to the threat of force (236c–d)" (104). The extent to which Socrates' soul is governed by its love of beautiful discourse is evidenced when he succumbs to Phaedrus' threat to deny him this source of sustaining pleasure, by swearing "a solemn oath that he will never again perform or even report to Socrates any speeches or discussions that he hears in the future, *unless Socrates gives him what he wants* (236d–e)" (104, my emphasis). The use of flattery, bribery, and emotional blackmail all evidence the extent to which Phaedrus, like Socrates, is governed by the desire for beautiful discourse, further reinforcing the dialogic nature of the dyad. On Socrates' part, this addictive love of discourse is evidenced as well by his confessions that he is a "word-lover" (236e, qtd. in Ferrari 104).

Phaedrus' understanding of Socrates' nature in this regard is as "kairic" as Socrates' perception of a similar predisposition to erotic discourse in

Phaedrus. As Ferrari observes, Phaedrus is "struck at the outset of the dialogue by how especially 'appropriate' (prosekousa) Lysias' speech on love would be for the *notoriously 'erotic' Socrates* to hear (227c) . . . " (4, my emphasis). In *Phaedrus,* the erotic is always in play, as both a cause and effect of discourse. For it is never a question of whether Socrates is eschewing eroticism for dialectics, as it is a question of his forsaking a profane eroticism as an end in itself in favor of a sacred Eros (or philosophical love) that is both the means to dialectical ends and the consummation of those ends.

This reversal of roles, as Ferrari observes, occurs throughout the "course of the erotic liaison itself, in which *both partners are allowed their measure of manipulation*" (108, my emphasis), as each effectively plays upon the desires of the other. Phaedrus flaunts his way-with-words as a form of display to arouse Socrates' desire—"and bargains with this plenty in order to compel Socrates . . . to emulate Lysias." In other words, he manipulates Socrates into emulating Lysias to further sate his idolatry of sophistic discourse. The disgust Socrates ultimately expresses (covering his head, quitting in mid-sentence) is due not just to his coerced mimicry of a discourse he disdains, but also to his knowledge that he is allowing himself to be manipulated by his beloved into emulating a rival lover, so as to heighten the pleasure of his beloved. To the extent Phaedrus is rubbing Socrates' nose in his rival's discourse, Socrates' own desire is being profaned—and he knows it. His disgust is compounded by the guilt he feels for thus allowing himself to profane that which is sacred, his philosophic love for Phaedrus. He allows himself to be manipulated and his principles to be compromised as part of his "stoops to conquer" strategy, which by converting the Self into a sign of the Other deepens the alliteration between them, for the moment effacing the differences between them as a precondition for assimilating the Other into the Self, thus, fulfilling the merger hunger desires of the Self. Their mutual love of discourse is mutually manipulated to their mutual gratification—as if they have entered a pact of mutual aggression in pursuit of their mutual desires.

Phaedrus is much more than a passive foil to Socrates' agency: a role in which he has been miscast by criticism. The "hard" agency he enjoys in the beginning, evidenced by the transformative and redemptive force of his beauty upon Socrates' soul, gives way to a soft agency throughout the dialogue that arises in the gaps of Socrates' discourse and from his status of Other, without whose active participation the desires of the dialectic Self could never be realized. Phaedrus' status as a worthy, even ideal, object of Socrates' desires for eros and edification is evidenced by the fact that he "has caused an almost unparalleled number of speeches to be delivered, whether by delivering them himself or compelling others to do so (242c–d)" (Ferrari 21). Phaedrus then gives proof of this agency, of this ability to compel beautiful discourses from others, by compelling Socrates to do just that. Phaedrus' agency is subversive, inasmuch as it inverts a master-slave dialectic, reversing the roles of the dialectic, prompting the reader to ask: who is the master and who the slave, who is the student and who the teacher?

Socrates' challenge is to heighten Phaedrus' appreciation of what is truly beautiful in discourse. As Griswold asserts, "Phaedrus' love of speeches springs not from a love of the truth but from a love of their form, their shape, or appearance. He loves 'beautiful' or 'rhetorical' speeches ... and is very impressed with the power of rhetoric in assemblies (259e–260a)" (22). He is infatuated with the seductive power of rhetoric, which is what makes him the perfect foil for Lysias' sophistic argument, which would use discourse to obtain sexual favors from a lover of discourses. All three rhetors exhibit a kairic awareness of the Other, playing effectively on the Other's love of beautiful discourse. As Griswold observes, "Socrates and Phaedrus must feast on discourses" (34). The staples of dialectical discourse (rhetorical analysis, definition, division, and classification) are supplemented by the wine-like effect of myth, metaphor, and figuration, whose affective power enhances the nourishing effect of dialectical analysis: all as part of a master course in dialectic analysis that Socrates conducts beside the Illissus, in the sobering glare of the sun, by way of dramatizing the beauty of the philosophic life.

As evidenced by the agency Phaedrus enjoys throughout the dialogue, Socrates' discourse is not part of a manipulative, master-slave narrative that contradicts its purported ethical concerns. Rather, its manipulative, self-interested tendencies are inevitable within the context of a pedagogy of mutual edification—in fact, they are natural to it. The very mutuality of the educative model implies motives that are self-interested, if not egoistic and manipulative of those ends. Though inevitable, these are not incompatible with the edification of the Other, in a praxis where altruistic and egoistic interests co-exist. Further, the mutual nature of manipulation in the *Phaedrus* belies the presumption of an active-passive relationship in the master-pupil dyad.

The ethical nature of Socrates' praxis is further evidenced by the epic conflict that the *Phaedrus* dramatizes: not only between the debased, "shameful" rhetoric of sophistry and the honorific, "beautiful" discourse of philosophy, but also between the profane and sacred impulses of Socrates' divided soul. Like so many elements of the *Phaedrus*, the ethical nature of Socrates' dialectical praxis must also be doubly explicated, insofar as it fulfills not only the sacred desires of the soul for the edification and immortality of Self and Other, but its profane desires as well, for revenge and erotic pleasure—so dramatically figured in the image of the winged chariot and in the opposed forces of its dark and light steeds. As Griswold asserts, "the charioteer represents reason, the black horse sexual desire" (96), and the conflict between these sacred and profane impulses evidences "the hierarchy within the soul" (99).

The shared values of master and pupil further mitigate the accusation of manipulations on the part of Socrates. As Ferrari observes, "the boy already shares as a matter of individual preference the values on which the lover wants them to build together" (184). His best interests are always and already the interests Socrates would define as his best. The effect of Socrates' discourse is not the manipulation of an Other's interests to suit his own but is the fulfillment of the mutual desires of Self and Other, of "lover and beloved [who] come to mesh in their aspirations" (184).

Phaedrus loves beautiful discourse, but he lacks the powers of rhetorical analysis to understand or appreciate what is beautiful or ugly about it, to the point even of mistaking ugliness for beauty in discourse—whereas for Socrates, the ethical and the beautiful in discourse are inseparable. Discourse is beautiful *because* it is good—which is to say, ethical. Sans ethics, it can make no claim to beauty. Sans ethics, the sacred must be forever incompatible with discourse, which devolves into mere rhetoric, in Socrates' view. What makes discourse beautiful is not merely its ability to generate knowledge as opposed to mere belief (through the use of analysis, definition, division and classification, arrangement, etc.) but its edifying effects upon Self and Other, its ability to serve both the individual and the common good.

Thus, part of Socrates' quest is to educate Phaedrus as to the nature of beauty, by defining it in terms of the ethical, of the good: the implication being that Lysias' discourse is "shameful" because it is unethical—its goal being not edification but seduction. Socrates' quest is to rescue discourse from the shameful ends it serves in Lysias' speech (and by implication, in all sophistic discourse), recuperating the beauty Lysias has profaned by elevating discourse to the philosophical realm—though in his own quest for victory and vengeance, Socrates will himself profane the sacred, as if catching the disease of profanation from his rival.

To the extent Socrates' elenchus mitigates the manipulative effects of sophistic signification on Phaedrus, it is ethical and entirely consistent with the focus of Freirean praxis. Manipulation of the subject through discourses of domination is, as Freire observes, "an instrument of conquest ... in which dominant elites try to conform the masses to their objectives" (144). Phaedrus' idolatry of sophistry evidences the extent to which he has already been manipulated by sophistic discourse. He is a metonym not only for the Athenian citizen of fourth century BC Athens, but also for the contemporary citizen subjugated by discourses of domination. As Freire observes, "manipulation ... attempts to anesthetize people so they will not think" (146). Phaedrus' unthinking idolatry of sophistry evidences the extent to which he has already been anesthetized by the state discourse of sophistry. Thus, the dialectic dyad of the *Phaedrus* is manipulative in a dialogic way, insofar as the manipulations of master and pupil are mutual and insofar as it mitigates the anti-dialogic manipulations of sophistry.

The ethical nature of discourse becomes the focus of Socrates' inquiry in the second half of the dialogue: "when is a discourse composed shamefully and when beautifully (258d)" (160). As Bizzell and Herzberg observe, "the teacher who is raising the student toward transcendence plants seeds in the students' soul that will eventually flower in turn, reproduce themselves in other souls. This kind of reproduction is superior to mere physical reproduction because it propagates only transcendent knowledge" (60). The series "plants," "flowers," "propagates," and "transcendent" reinforces the view that this dialectical process is deeply yoked to the desire for immortality.

With respect to the *Phaedrus*, then, this is why Beauty must be the starting point of the protrepticus, embodied in the false beauty of Lysias' text and in the genuine beauty of Phaedrus' looks and his love of beautiful discourse—this false and genuine Beauty acting with equal force on Socrates to incite his critique and his courtship (of Lysias and Phaedrus respectively), to awaken both the destructive and constructive, debased and honorific, dark and light impulses of his soul, embodied respectively in the dark and light steeds: inciting in his soul the epic struggle whose outcome defines who he is and establishes the primacy of the philosophic over the sophistic, the sacred over the profane, and Eros over mere eroticism. The *Phaedrus*, as Bizzell and Herzberg observe, dramatizes the movement from eroticism toward philosophic Eros. If "the motion toward transcendence must begin with carnality, with the physical attraction between two people," (59) and with Lysias' attempt to gain the "favors" of Phaedrus, it culminates in the mutual edification of Self and Other. As Ferrari observes, "the force of the boy's beauty is transmuted by the lover into passionate good will towards the boy . . ." (184). The ethical nature of Socrates' praxis derives from this "passionate good will."

The consensual and mutually beneficial nature of this contractual relationship is the exculpatory evidence against the accusation of unethical self-interest or egoistic manipulation. While it is true that the dramatic dialogue is the ideal genre for fulfilling the multiple desires that give rise to it, insofar as it "implicates" the Other as lover, interlocutor, and participant, its nature is nevertheless reciprocal and contractual, as Brooks observes. More than any other genre, the dramatic dialogue enlists the participation of the desired Other, "by soliciting the entry of a listener [interlocutor] into relation with the [self]" (283), far more explicitly than a narration directed toward an implied listener. The interlocutor is embedded in the "ambitus" of the dialectician, the Other conscripted into a "peculiar intimacy" and dramatic alliteration with the assertive self.

Socrates' project of self-assertion relies exclusively on discourse, creating the "need for an interlocutor, a listener who enters into the narrative exchange" (Brooks 216). The contractual nature of this dyad obviates against the accusation of manipulation, underscoring its genuinely dialogic nature. Brooks continues: "it asks for something in return for what it supplies. The contract can take many forms, from the seductive . . . to the 'meta-seductive' . . . to keep desire alive, to prolong and renew the intersubjective and interlocutionary relation" (216).

LOVE IN A TIME OF WAR: EROS AND THE SOCIAL-EPISTEMIC TURN

Are Eros and Ethos in an educational setting incompatible? Is there room for love in the search for knowledge? Is the centrality of Eros to Socrates' dialectic inquiry compatible with contemporary social-epistemic praxis? By nature, the philosophic life Socrates advocates is dialogic and erotic, is predicated on the conjunction of Eros, Logos, and Ethos, as evidenced by Griswold's definition of dialectics, which is "understood as the 'erotic art' of conversation (276e)" (6–7). We tend to see the pursuit of love and knowledge as separate endeavors, whereas to the philosophic lover of Socrates' era, the pursuit of Eros and Logos were inseparable. The path to self-knowledge led inevitably through love. Further, this search for self-knowledge both commences and culminates with Eros, which is both the cause and the effect of logos. Before we categorically dismiss love as irrelevant to the search for knowledge, we must assess the extent to which whatever knowledge we have gained of ourselves and our experience of life have been taught to us by love. In further assessing the relevance of love to social-epistemic praxis we must also account for love, not just in the romantic sense but as love of humanity, love of social justice—as an individual's love for the collective well being of the Other. In this sense, how could meaningful learning occur without love?

I would argue that, even leaving Eros aside, Socrates' praxis might yet deeply inform our own, given its emphasis on analysis and the civic actions that spring from it. Yet I would argue further that even Socrates' emphasis on Eros is compatible with contemporary liberatory praxis—that indeed the search for knowledge is always and already not only an act of freedom, but an act of love. The centrality of Love to Socratic inquiry underscores its affinity with American pragmatism. Again, West's observations are instructive: "Dewey . . . captures this best when he says that philosophy is a form of desire, an effort or action of love" (40). Similarly, "the Agapish of Peirce is all about an evolutionary love" (53). Philosophic Eros in Socratic inquiry is similarly "evolutionary," insofar as it embodies the evolution of the subject toward a "more fully human" Ideal and, in the *Phaedrus*, facilitates the cognitive evolution of the pupil from idolatry to critical consciousness, relative to the Beauty of discourse.

If in ancient Greece, Eros and Logos were always and already conjoined, then in the western educational tradition that has arisen out it, Eros and Logos have traveled separate paths, insofar as love of knowledge neither springs from nor culminates in Eros but is posited and pursued as an edifying end in itself, which when enlisted for the common good becomes a deeply ethical pursuit as well. Yet this seeming disjunction in contemporary education between eros, on the one hand, and logos and ethos on the other, masks an enduring synergy between them. In this, we discover yet another abiding affinity between the radical praxis of Socrates and Freire. As Freire observes,

> The naming of the world, which is an act of creation and re-creation, is not possible if it is not infused with *love*. *Love* is at the same time the foundation of dialogue and dialogue itself. It is thus necessarily the task of responsible Subjects. (77–78, my emphasis)

What radical Socratic and social-epistemic praxis seek to do is invest the pupil with the ability to "name the world" as a means of transforming it, is to foster an agency relative to reality rooted in a critical literacy whose most durable sign of edification is a "world creation in words" (Rank, *Art*)—that frees the human object from subjugation by reality into a naming subjectivity—that objectifies a reality that would objectify him or her, through a liberatory signification that displaces objectification into the realm of the symbolic—that keeps it at arms length, with a signifying firewall that ensures a "dilatory space" between knower and known.

In the *Phaedrus*, perhaps more than in the earlier dialogues, Socrates' dialogic inquiry is pursued in the spirit of love, seeking the mutual edification of Self and Other through a deep and enduring communion, where knowledge might transform not only the knowers, but also the world as they know it. Love is inseparable from the pursuit of transformative knowledge, for Socrates as it is for Freire—for it is rooted in the quest for knowledge, as evidenced by its status as a root-word in "philo-sophy." Freire continues:

> Because love is an act of courage, not of fear, love is commitment to other men. No matter where the oppressed are found, the act of love is commitment to their cause—the cause of liberation. And this commitment, because it is loving, is dialogical . . . as an act of freedom, it must not serve as a *pretext for manipulation*. It must generate other acts of freedom; otherwise it is not love. Only by abolishing the situation of oppression is it possible to restore the love which the situation made impossible. If I do not love the world—if I do not love life—if I do not love men—I cannot enter into dialogue. (78, my emphasis)

Thus, two-and-a-half thousand years after Socrates, Freire crafts a liberatory praxis that conjoins eros, logos, and ethos, that conflates love, knowledge, and ethical action for the common good. Insofar as Socrates' praxis frees Phaedrus from the dehumanizing affective power of sophistry, which would reduce him to an object, gaining his "favors" through the manipulation of his beliefs, it is a liberatory act of love. To the extent Socrates' praxis is devoted to this "cause of liberation," it is also an "act of freedom." As such, it is inherently ethical and political: by implication, an act of liberatory love for the common good of all, whose collective freedom is enhanced to the extent the subject is liberated from the manipulative chains of sophistic signification. The love that characterizes this dialogic praxis is rooted in its liberatory impulses and humanistic goals, which are inherently ethical because inescapably political—insofar as the end they seek is a "more fully human" being-in-the-world. Thus, even in the importance it assigns to Eros, Socrates' educative model is deeply consistent with social-epistemic praxis, and with Freire's liberatory pedagogy in particular, given its similar emphasis on "the pursuit of full humanity," whose "inquiry must be directed towards humanization" (73) and whose "efforts must coincide with those of the students to engage in critical thinking and the quest for mutual humanization" (62).

Further, the love associated with this liberatory praxis is not merely political and social, but personal. Love, for the desiring dialectician, springs from a human wound: the wound of the Self's differentiation from the Other inflicted at birth: a wound that can only be healed through union with an Other-as-Self. As Aristophanes asserts, "Zeus . . . cut each pair in half, and asked Apollo to heal the wound and to turn the face of each to the side of the wound 'in order that everyone might be made more orderly by the sight of the knife's work upon him'" (190e, qtd. in Santas 19). The phrase, "in order that everyone might be made more orderly," is significant, for it underscores the extent to which Eros humanizes the subject by taming its aggressions, toward a "more fully human" existence. Love also serves to mitigate the affective power of sophistic rhetoric on the masses to the extent it unites Self and Other in dialectic communion, privileging the progression of love/knowledge/action. Further, to the extent love fosters consciousness of the self's wound, "of the knife's work" upon the self, its self-reflexivity results in self-knowledge. Further, it evidences the extent to which Socratic inquiry and social-epistemic praxis are rooted in the collective wound of domination, which is healed dialogically in the winding shroud of words, spoken wound-to-wound between teacher and student, to mitigate the violence of a shared, tragic history.

Thus, the radical pedagogies of Socrates and Freire are rooted not merely in the political wounds of domination, but also in the wound of Love. Socrates' philosophic love for Phaedrus is an emblem of his love for the Athenian citizenry, whose collective subject he similarly hopes to free from the manipulative effects of power and the power of persuasion through which it circulates. To the extent his elenchus acts on this love, it too is an act of freedom. Freirean praxis is similarly an act of freedom rooted in love, manifested in his solidarity with the Other.

The *Phaedrus* also reinforces the concept of "grafting" that lies at the heart of dialectics, in which a dialectic text is "grafted" onto a sophistic text and in which Self and Other are "grafted" together, wound-to-wound, to facilitate the "dissemination" of Self and Other in space and time: in the material realm of the here and now and in the immortal realm of the hereafter—which is precisely what occurs in the "grafting" of Plato and Socrates, to the point that the real Socrates and Plato's Socrates are indistinguishable. At the heart of the impulse to love is a desire for the two-in-one: rooted in the soul's merger hunger tendencies, often operating in tandem with its ideal-hunger impulses. Dialectic inquiry thus becomes the medium par excellence for fulfilling the imperatives of Eros, which are both a cause and an effect of the dialectic bond. As Hesiod observes,

> They would fling their arms about each other and in mutual yearning to be *grafted* together. . . . On the death of a half, the other half would seek and embrace any half that would match the original pair. . . . These unions *were not sexual* since they sought to rejoin each other, *wound to*

wound. Thus, anciently, is mutual love ingrained in mankind, resembling our earlier estate and *endeavoring to combine two in one and heal the human sore.* (Hesiod, qtd. in Santas 19, my emphasis)

To the extent they "heal the human sore" through the wound-to-wound touching of teacher and student, the radical pedagogies of Socrates and Freire deeply inform one another, even as they evidence their profoundly ethical orientation. *The Symposium* further dramatizes the ethical relationship between eros and logos. As Santas observes, "Socrates introduces the wise woman Diotima as having taught him all he knows about eros: he explains how she practiced the very same cross-examination on him and how she introduced him into Plato's famous Ladder of Love, which elevates eros from desire for a beautiful body to love of Beauty itself" (25). Socrates crystallizes the relationship between eros and logos in his definition of philosophic love: set on the virtue of the soul rather than the transitory beauty of the body, "this love is constant and abiding, superior to popular love in the benefits it bestows on lover and beloved alike ..." (184c–185b). The passage is significant for it underscores the relationship between Logos, Ethos, and Eros, wherein Eros is both the cause and the effect of the search for knowledge, its origin and destination, totalizing every desire of the soul: for sex, edification, immortality, and social justice.

The reciprocity of the exchange, dramatized throughout the *Phaedrus,* argues in favor of its dialogic nature—in what is essentially a mutual exchange of Beauty, flowing between Socrates and Phaedrus, which propels them up the Ladder of Beauty, from the purely physical to the metaphysical. As evidenced by Socrates' discourse, the "something in return," the "favors" sought, are much more diverse, holistic, and honorific than the mere sexual favors Lysias seeks to obtain through discourse. The "favors" Socrates seeks are emotional, intellectual, spiritual, and physical in nature. The erotic, while never divorced from discourse, is not the sole aim of it, as is the case with Lysias' sophistic discourse. It is merely one of two steeds, which together represent the profane and sacred impulses of the soul. It is worth noting that, as evidenced in the image of the charioteer and steeds, the profane impulse is far more eruptive than the quieter desires embodied in the rational pursuit of love, wisdom, and immortality.

"Relations of promise, conversion," as Brooks observes, are all involved in the "contractual" situation between dialectician and interlocutor, master and pupil, Self and Other. Further, in exchange for the wisdom he imparts to the pupil, the master gains a form of immortality, to the extent his soul lives on in the teachings of the pupil, as Socrates does in the writings of Plato and as Plato does in the words of Aristotle, as if he had begotten a son. This too is part of the "contractual" exchange (233).

This contractual exchange occurs, moreover, in the realm of the symbolic, insofar as it is enshrined in discourse, in the art of dialectics and the dramatic dialogue. Desires that commence in the material realms of the flesh are consummated in the realms of the symbolic. As Brooks avers, "their interaction takes place in a special '[art]ificial' medium . . . those of the symbolic order—yet vitally engaged with the histories and intentions of desire" (235). The wound of desire, born of the "dilatory space" between Self and Other, master and pupil, dialectician and interlocutor, wish and fulfillment, subjugation and freedom, is eternally stitched in the realm of the symbolic, in the dialectic sign, both spoken and written. Brooks continues:

> there can be a range of reasons for telling a story [or engaging in dialectic discourse] from the self-interested to the altruistic. Seduction appears as a dominant motive, be it specifically erotic and oriented toward the capture of the other . . . [or] exhibitionistic, asking for admiration and attention. (236)

Yet, as a medium of self-assertion, the bounds between the ethical and unethical in discourse are easily blurred, as Brooks avers: "Yet perhaps aggression is nearly as common . . . often inextricably linked to the erotic: a forcing of attention, a violation of the listener" (236), as evidenced in the aggressive tendencies of Lysias' discourse toward Phaedrus, of Socrates' attacks on Lysias' speech, and of Socrates' discourse toward Phaedrus. The assertion of the self through self-knowledge requires that the Self act upon the Other in the mutual interest of both, in a manner that facilitates the self-assertion of each. Anything less than this would be tantamount to the practice of a purely self-interested and therefore unethical discourse.

Phaedrus, as an interlocutor, is necessarily "implicated in the thrust" of Socrates' desire. Each provides what the other lacks. The pupil provides the transformative impetus of beauty, as well as the transformative experience of mutual love, including both the edifying and wounding, self-enhancing and self-negating effects of Beauty. The wounds inflicted on the soul by erotic desire (madness), possessive desire (jealousy), and the desire for edification (the struggle to tame profane impulses) trigger the assertion of the self after threatening the negation of the self. Sans the wounds of Eros and Logos, the search for wisdom would devolve into a mere academic exercise, and the desire for edification would never evolve beyond the realms of wishful thinking. Experience in general, and the experience of Eros in particular, is the only true master who can instruct the soul.

In this, Socrates' radical praxis also demonstrates its enduring relevance to current best-practices in education: by privileging the generative connection between learning and lived reality, through a dialectical analysis always and already transgressing the walls between them. Logos is the offspring of Eros. Socrates is utterly dependent on an ideal Other for the realization of his ideal Self, not just because the Other provides the dialogue without which meaning cannot be made, but because it provides the experience of love, whose wounds not only incite the struggle between profane and sacred impulses in the soul, but also prompt the healing transformations of knowledge, discourse, and invention, which signify the birth of the ideal self. This ideal, philosophic self is the real "love child" of the merger of Self and Other.

CONCLUSION

What then are the implications for the western intellectual tradition, and for social-epistemic praxis in particular, of Socrates' radical pedagogy of philosophic love? If the question is whether Socrates' praxis is ethical or unethical, then the answer is that it is both—for its edifying goals, methods, and outcomes are profaned by its own sophistic tendencies toward the erotic and the vengeful, the sexual and sadistic. Yet Socrates' self-interested motives for self-knowledge, immorality, love, and "victory" over the sophists are not incompatible with the mutually edifying motives of his discourse. To the extent his "elenchus" shapes the Other and the world toward a "more fully human" ideal, it is ethical. The self-serving, even "shameful," elements of his praxis do not negate its ethical concerns; if anything, they humanize the philosopher, whose soul is not exclusively saint-like but a paradoxical, and entirely human, compendium of the sacred and profane, expressed respectively in signifying practices that are by turn "shameful" and "honorific."

The epic struggle between reason and passion, logos and eros, is ultimately a question of ethos. If the beautiful is configured by Lysias in terms of the profane, it is defined by Socrates in terms of the sacred *and* profane, of the hierarchical relation between them, and of the edifying absorption of the profane by the sacred. As Griswold concludes, speaking on behalf of Socrates, "What I 'really' want is to be satisfied as a whole, and this will include *not* allowing myself to be directed solely to satisfying what a lower part of me naturally wants (hence the need to tame the dark horse)" (99). The mutual edification of the dialectic progression is what elevates it above the mere gratification of carnal desires, which is the aim of Lysias' sophistic discourse. Socrates' goal is not purely selfish, insofar as he not only seeks to edify himself, but also to help the Other help himself. Ferrari notes that "in his mythic hymn, Socrates will transcend the manipulative strategy that has marked both relationships" (109). In the end, logos is absorbed into eros, and both are absorbed into ethos. Socrates' dialectic inquiry begins and ends in love, in an eroticized logic that transforms not only Self and Other but also their world in ways that make all three "more fully human."

A critical question thus presents itself: in deleting Eros from the pursuit of knowledge, has the western educative tradition reduced the pursuit of knowledge to a mere academic exercise—severing its symbiosis with the material, divorcing it from its origins in Beauty, violating the first premise of the ancient Greek educative paradigm that it purports to emulate: *if one would know, one must love*. Has the western educative tradition reduced edification from a holistic enterprise that engaged the entire being in the process (mind, body, and soul) to a purely cognitive project as part of a sequestered discourse with but an intermittent connection to experience, to the real—resulting in the Self's alienation from the world, the other, and itself, as a result of the alienation of eros and logos: by divorcing love from the love of knowledge and/or the love of humankind? Is alienation then the inevitable by-product of western education, the price paid for edification in the western intellectual tradition: which we might more properly see as a bastard offspring of Socratic inquiry? Finally, is the recent turn toward dialogic, interactive learning in reality an effort to recuperate Socrates' radical praxis, prompted not by the teacher's self-love but by a genuine "love" for the edification of the pupil and for the personal, social, and political implications of that "love"—in a praxis that conjoins the edifying effects of eros, logos, and ethos, that posits education as an act of freedom grounded in love? Further, is this recent dialogic turn driven by a similar recognition that language shapes thought (for better or worse, for either edifying or manipulative ends): that cognitive development through language and social control through rhetorics of persuasion are alike dependent on the development of signifying practices?

The dialogic edification that Plato's Socrates first modeled has political as well as personal and philosophical implications, insofar as such a radical praxis serves a dual purpose: the cognitive development of the citizen-pupil through the practice and analysis of language. Socrates models his critical pedagogy by practicing and then analyzing sophistic discourse to simultaneously heighten critical thinking and mitigate the dangerous effects of a manipulative, if not shameful, rhetoric of persuasion—in the process serving both the individual and the common good. Given the *Phaedrus'* deep ethical orientation, given the extent to which eros is absorbed into logos and both are absorbed into ethos, the radical praxis it models is richly consistent with social-epistemic praxis and a postmodern pragmatism, whose promise one discovers in its prophetic pedagogy.

9 Radical Pedagogy Reconfigured
Toward a Neo-Humanist Pragmatism

> The concentration of wealth begins by being inevitable, and ends by being fatal.... No lasting justice can be established for men, since the strong or clever will twist to their advantage any laws that are made.... The indifference of the public is the ruin of the state.
> —Durant (112, 117)

> For if we bestow the faculty of eloquence on persons destitute of ... probity and eminent judgment ... we shall not make them orators, but give arms to madmen.
> —Cicero (III, xiv, qtd. in Covino 43)

> Educators ... protect the State against its internal and external enemies.
> —Cairns (xxii)

I want to "test the feasibility" of radical pedagogy by theorizing a neo-humanist pragmatism informed by the radical pedagogies of Plato's Socrates and Paulo Freire. Building on the work of Cornel West, I want to craft a neo-humanist praxis that weds the liberatory pedagogy of Freire and the pragmatism of Peirce, James, and Dewey. Building on the work of Byron Hawk in *A Counter-History of Composition,* I want to craft a radical praxis that weds this neo-humanist pragmatism to a webbed, networked pragmatism that privileges the digital to engage the political, that mobilizes virtual mediums to engage material realities. Finally, I want to posit a neo-humanist pragmatism that emphasizes the under-theorized aspects of Freire's praxis to move it beyond the narrow limitations of "teaching resistance" into a broader pedagogical landscape, under the signs of "dialogic learning," "problem-posing analysis," and "civic engagement." Having mapped a genealogy of origins, goals, assumptions, methods, and "program content" in the radical pedagogies of Socrates and Freire, I now want to extend the pedagogic ground of this genealogy into the realms of contemporary social-epistemic praxis, by situation radical pedagogy at the protean intersection of postmodern pragmatism and post "flash-crash" America.

A nexus of questions prompt this "feasibility test." What would constitute the "program content" of such a radical praxis? What methodologies would characterize it? What theorists would inform its pedagogy? To what extent might it ground the classical rhetorical tradition and the radical pedagogy of Plato's Socrates in particular? To what extent would this neo-humanist pragmatism ameliorate the radical critique of radical pedagogy? To what extent might it meld the diverse methodologies of expressivism, social-epistemic praxis, and an ancient rhetorical tradition in the search for pedagogical complexity—for a methodology no less edifying for being diversified? As I have attempted to show in this comparative analysis of Socrates and Freire, the origins, goals, assumptions, methodologies, and "program content" of these two radical pedagogies not only inform one another, but also inform contemporary social-epistemic practice, which is similarly crafted from the nexus of the social, the political, and the rhetorical.

RADICAL PEDAGOGY IN POST FLASH-CRASH AMERICA

In contradistinction to a radical pedagogy narrowly concerned with teaching resistance to ideologically inscribed discourse, I want to posit this humanist neo-pragmatism in an effort to realize Hardin's call for a "radical revisioning and historicizing of the emancipatory project of critical literacy" (105). The radical praxis I envision not only moves beyond "neo-Marxist theories of reproduction and resistance," but also moves beyond "postmodern, poststructuralist, and postcolonial thought" into a humanist neo-pragmatism, bringing dialogic knowledge to bear on problematic aspects of reality in order to mitigate, eliminate, or transform those realities and their violent effects, in the interest of—not of the privileged few but of the common good.

In this chapter, I envision the possibilities of neo-pragmatism that situate critical inquiry at the intersection of the personal, the political, and the rhetorical. I want to open a new space for Freirean praxis by shifting the focus from teaching "resistance to dominant ideology" to analyzing and engaging the problematic realities of society, which may include the problematic of ideology. I want to open a space that moves beyond the narrow critique of "the way academic culture constructs textual authority" to a more broadly conceived "problem-posing praxis" that poses to students not merely the problem of colonial domination or the problematic of dominant ideology, but also the problematics of the environment, race, class, gender; of capitalism, history, and mass media. I want to wed the radical pedagogies of Socratic inquiry, Freirean praxis, and postmodern pragmatism toward a reconfigured radical praxis that is also enriched by Hawk's pedagogy of "vitalism" and that seeks its "program content" in the problematic realities of post "flash-crash" America—including the problematic of radical capitalism.

Hardin calls for a radical pedagogy that is feasible, in which "scholars and teachers of critical pedagogy ... develop instructional practices" that reinforce the process and outcomes of critical literacy (5). This challenge is made somewhat easier by the fact that Freire has already developed a set of instructional practices associated with dialogic learning, problem-posing analysis, and civic engagement, which if modified and tailored to "read local contexts critically," to read the problematic realities of the American social-political landscape, can form an effective critical methodology. West similarly underscores the efficacy of American pragmatism to the historical struggle for freedom and justice, observing that "pragmatism is, in fact, distinctive in the modern world because it is preoccupied with the prospect of democracy" (*Prophetic*, 31).

Freirean praxis answers Hardin's call for "instructional practices" that reinforce the process and outcomes of critical literacy, as evidenced by its emphasis on dialogic learning, which governs every phase of the process. For example, Freire doesn't posit the "decoding" of a problematic reality as occurring outside the dialogic process, but as always and already dialogic. Analysis of problematic realities occurs concomitantly with discussion of those realities in collaborative groups, by which the investigation is further shaped and informed. As Freire observes, these discussions "initiate decoding dialogues in the 'thematic investigation circles'" (110). Freire's method is significant insofar as it underscores the centrality of dialogue not only for every phase of the investigation, but also for the collaborative group.

This is tantamount to taking Elbow's feedback group and making not just personal edification but civic engagement its raison d'être. It is a dialogic methodology that not only seeks to enact social change, but that is always and already social, emphasizing not only the social ends of knowledge but also the social means of knowledge-making. As Freire asserts, it is reality alone that authenticates knowledge; divorced from reality, and particularly from application to its most problematic aspects, knowledge devolves into an academic exercise.

Education, to be meaningful and ethical, must have consequences—that benefit not just the individual but the citizenry. This is not an either-or but a both-and pedagogic paradigm, insofar as personal edification occurs within the framework of an edifying process that transcends the narrow interests of the self: that leads the self out of itself into dialogic communion with the Other and through their mutual engagement with the World. Dialogic inquiry into the world involves an Othering-of-the-Self, which is the means by which it extends, asserts, and affirms its Self in the world, by which it extends the domain of its agency relative to reality, through a language that edifies self and other, and by altering their relationship to reality, alters that reality. A subject is only a subject insofar as it has agency relative to reality. Thus, genuine subject status implies engagement with problematic realities that tend toward the negation of the self. Further, this engagement commences with the act of signification, of "naming the World." Signifying the world is the first act of self-affirmation relative to it: the means by which the self affirms itself through "symbolic action" upon the world. Sans this dialectic engagement between self and world through language, knowledge cannot exist. As Hawk observes, language "can only construct knowledge through a dialectical development in the world. In this dialectical model, there is no language/world split" (101).

Thus, authentic personal edification cannot occur sans engagement with the real, and the most problematic aspects of it, which work to negate the self. Through language, the self mitigates the signs of violence and the violence of signs, as if fighting fire-with-fire, reclaiming from reality lost realms of the self, which it can now occupy in a "more fully human" existence. This, as West observes relative to postmodern pragmatism, is the value of a consequential education: of an education that has consequences—and whose consequences authenticate the process of edification.

What form do these dialogic "decodings" of reality assume within and beyond the writing workshop? This formal dissemination to peers serves as an intermediate "dress rehearsal" for a broader public dissemination and application of the knowledge to the community, through the various channels best suited to that dissemination. These might range from the construction of a web-site to presentations at local schools, from membership in a local advocacy group to participation in its activities, or a host of other disseminating applications.

Once this "decoding" process is completed, the contents of the analysis must be "codified" according to "the best channel of communication for each theme and its representation" (114). In this dissemination/application phase, the investigator selects from the "channels of communication" available, the one that best codifies the analysis for its broader dissemination to the public: "the visual (pictorial or graphic), the tactile [hand-outs, flyers], or the auditive [presentations/lectures/speeches]" (114). Once codified in the "best channel of communication," the "didactic materials" for the dissemination of the decoding are prepared: "photographs, slides, film strips, posters, reading texts, and so forth" (115)—a list easily supplemented with PowerPoint, over-head projectors, or whatever "didactic materials" facilitate the broader dissemination of the knowledge ("decodings").

The feasibility of a reconfigured Freirean praxis is enhanced by its compatibility with expressivist methodologies (free-writing, journaling, collaborative learning) on the one hand and with Hawk's pedagogy of inventive complexity on the other, insofar as these expressivist activities reinforce writing-as-invention to provide a feasible, critical space for invention within the context of dialogic pragmatism. Invention is thus privileged at both the point of origin and end-point of writing, from free-writing that commences the inquiry to digital applications of the analysis that consummate its intervention at the point of contact with the community realities—through the construction of web-sites, blogs, and so forth that distribute consciousness and, in so doing, turn it into meaningful action, into influence.

I further contend that a reconfigured Freirean praxis does not necessitate an either-or choice between teaching "the skills necessary to 'speak the language of the academy' and to succeed in [a] chosen profession" and teaching the program content of "critical literacy, democratic and economic justice for society, and the liberated consciousness of the individual" (Hardin, 59). Rather, this reconfigured radical pedagogy privileges a both-and continuum, in which the skills associated with academic and professional literacy are developed in the pursuit of critical literacy: through an emphasis on dialogic communication, critical analysis, problem-solving, and civic engagement. I reject as inauthentic the pedagogical "Sophie's Choice" between these two literacies. In this reconfigured Freirean praxis, literacies of the personal, the social, the political, the ethical, and the rhetorical are not distinct and incompatible but conjoined and mutually informed. As James Porter succinctly observes,

> The three arts [ethics, rhetoric, and politics] can be seen to have a mutually reinforcing function: *Ethics* is the practical art of determining the *social* (as well as the *personal*) good; *politics* is the practical art of implementing the social good; *rhetoric* is the productive art enabling ethical and political action. (210, qtd. in Hardin 59, my emphasis).

Unfortunately, this dialogic, problem-posing, analysis-driven, civic-oriented methodology is often ignored at the expense of a narrower focus on the political ends Freire's praxis serves, without fully appreciating the relevant implications of his methodology for American classrooms. Even his defenders, who rally to this focus on "resistance," revolution, and "liberatory pedagogy," have backed themselves into a corner and a pedagogical dead-end, not only reducing the buy-in of practitioners but also reducing Freire's praxis to an emphasis on "resistance" and "liberatory praxis." In so doing, these Freirean defenders have largely ignored the pragmatic, methodological implications of his dialogic praxis, problem-posing analysis, and civic-minded literacy for classrooms in America and around the world.

This reconfigured critical pragmatism posits the realms of the contested world and the critical world as a dialogic continuum, not as distinct and incommunicative. The boundaries between them are permeable and protean, as sites of transgression and transformation. In the process, the student is not only introduced into an ethos of civic engagement and active citizenship, but also the student develops dialogic communication and critical thinking skills, as part of a both-and continuum whose edifying effects serve the interests of the social and the personal.

The practice of analyzing, engaging, and intervening in real-world problems as a student may indeed foster the ability to problem-solve within the sphere of the workplace, in contradistinction to Evan Watkins' assertion that such "critical work is not generally practiced in the mainstream culture." Further, the oft-heard lament of employers for workers who can problem-solve, think outside the box, and communicate effectively would seem to contradict the assertion that "little time is available in most jobs for the kind of 'cultural criticism' that is currently practiced and promoted by radical and critical pedagogy" (28, qtd. in Hardin 50). The needs and expectations of the workplace (as repeatedly articulated by its gatekeepers over the decades) underscore not only the relevance of such critical literacy to the workplace, but also the efficacy of emphasizing it in the classroom. Indeed, as opposed to underscoring the disconnect between critical praxis and the workplace, these workplace priorities reinforce the pragmatic relevance of critical literacy, with its emphasis on dialogic communication, problem-posing analysis, and civic engagement. In the final analysis, the imperatives of the workplace and critical literacy are consonant, even as the literacies of the personal, the professional, and the political are mutually informative—when developed under the sign of a humanistic neo-pragmatism, emerging from a reconfigured Freirean praxis.

In opening a space for a reconfigured Freirean praxis, I want to place the emphasis on the pragmatic problem-posing, problem-engaging, problem-solving nature of his radical pedagogy and on the dialogic modes of analysis used to engage those problems. The question thus arises: which problems to engage through critical praxis? What then should constitute the "program content of education" in this neo-pragmatist, neo-humanist pedagogy? Simply stated, any and all problems that impede the practice of the just, the human, and the good should be central to this inquiry. Not only the problematics of race, class, and gender, which have driven the critical conversation and the content of American education for half a century, but also the problematics of the environment, capitalism, history, and the media invite critical inquiry from this neo-humanist, pragmatic perspective.

I posit this space of a reconfigured Freirean praxis, moving toward a humanistic neo-pragmatism, as a response to critics "unsure about the efficacy of critical pedagogy" or reductively dismissive of its continuing relevance (Hardin 98). I want to test the "feasibility" of Hardin's call for a radical praxis that "moves beyond the need to see itself as the emancipator of students" (5), that "de-emphasize[s] the liberatory aspects of critical work" (8). This neo-humanist pragmatism draws additional warrant from Hawk's call for a pedagogy based not on "mastery, but on relationality" (177). The "post-human" moment Hawk envisions is deeply alliterative with the "neo-human" moment I advocate, given their mutual emphasis on the relational, on a connected, webbed, or networked consciousness, moving toward engagement—a networked "conscientization," if you will. Hawk further underscores this pedagogical alliteration, when he asserts that "this shift to a new form of life is also the condition of possibility for a new form of humanity," or neo-humanism. This neo-humanist emphasis is a necessary corrective to the dehumanizing effects of systemic technology on the one hand and of class struggle on the other, which increasingly marginalizes millions of citizens with respect to the material benefits of American life, which calls into question the compatibility of democracy and radical capitalism.

Thus, analysis of texts and local contexts within the classroom can foster digital action beyond it, as a critical intervention at the material sites of power's circulation. Digital literacy, in other words, is the medium by which the critical word might be distributed and translated into action in the material world, across a much broader field of contestation. Digital literacy in the service of counter-hegemonic struggle offers an enabling complexity that eludes the efforts of power to constrain it. It may form the most effective medium yet for an applied, Freirean pragmatism, by virtue of its distributive complexity, and the indirect relational agency it facilitates.

The efficacy of the environment as a category for implementing a neo-humanist pragmatism also finds warrant in Hawk's vision of "post-process" pedagogy that "requires the inclusion of natural and physical environments and issues in ecology, place, location, and habitat in discussions of the social, language, and interpretation" (223). As advocated by eco-compositionists, the problematic realities associated with the environment not only enable inquiry that is broadly dispersed in global contexts, but also analysis that facilitates the ability to "read local contexts critically," lending a real-world, material immediacy to student inquiry. However, Hawk's critique of the disabling limitations of eco-composition is disabled in turn by its own semantic ambiguity and inherent contradictions. For example, Hawk asserts that "in order to enact the . . . shift that ecocomposition hopes to usher in . . . pedagogues will need to put more emphasis on *the material and affective ecologies that exist in and link to their classrooms?*" (224, my emphasis). Hawk posits this corrective critique without ever defining what is meant by the category "material and effective ecologies" of the classroom. The critique is problematic on two counts: instead of adding "complexity" to the category of eco-composition, Hawk's appropriation of it evacuates it of any and all connection to the environment, in effect reducing it to another meta-academic classroom discourse that has more in common with the meta-academic discourse of classroom ethnography than with eco-composition. Sans its orientation toward the environment, eco-composition is reduced to an empty signifier under Hawk's "post-process," "post-human" pedagogy. Hawk's critique of eco-composition is problematic on a more fundamental level, however, insofar as it reifies the reductive, either-or attack rhetoric that characterizes the cognitive-expressivist-social epistemic paradigm that he critiques for its tendency to shut down dialect and subvert "complexity." Ronald and Roskelly's critique of this tendency applies as well to Hawk's critique of eco-composition: "[O]nce these perspectives are named, they tend to evolve into positions that require defending or attacking. . . . taxonomies don't permit argument, aren't designed for dialectics" (3, qtd. in Hawk 87). By virtue of its engagement with the problematic realities of the environment, eco-composition is a pragmatic, humanist extension of the social-epistemic paradigm. Eco-composition represents a pragmatic complication of that social-epistemic paradigm. After acknowledging this, Hawk's appropriation of eco-composition, instead of enriching its complexity, reduces it to a meta-academic discourse that in effect invalidates it. As a critical discourse, Hawk recycles eco-composition from the environment to the classroom, in the process reducing it to a meta-academic discourse under the nebulous sign of "affective ecologies" of the classroom. The Word is returned from the World, to the closely inscribed world of words, reduced to an academic discourse by a pedagogy of "complexity." This reverses the direction of critical pedagogy, severing the dialectic between Word and World, confining analysis to a meta-academic realm of classroom ecologies that reinscribes the reductive pedagogies it purportedly critiques. In an effort to remove the "blinders to ecological complexity," Hawk substitutes a classroom "ecology" that would radically narrow the critical gaze of eco-composition, limiting it to a myopic concern for classroom ecologies, which instead of constituting an enabling complication of eco-composition, comprises a disabling simplification of it, that disables as well the generative relation (one might even say, dialectic) between the Word and the World.

In this instance, Hawk's pedagogy of relational complexity subverts the dialectic between word and world, enabled through eco-composition, substituting for it another meta-academic discourse, while claiming the exact opposite: that eco-composition "still leans heavily on public action through discourse, on discourse determining and changing material contexts," which he characterizes as a "blinder to ecological complexity, which is post-dialectical" (223). Hawk's pedagogy here does not represent a distributed consciousness, but rather a contraction of its distribution from the environment to the ecology of the classroom. Eco-composition, as currently configured, does signify an effort to distribute consciousness across a broader spectrum of realities than a mere classroom discourse. Hawk's pedagogy of complexity deconstructs its own complex distribution.

Yet by virtue of its vision of a digitally networked distribution of consciousness, Hawk's pedagogy opens up a dynamic space for a neo-humanist pragmatism, seeking to engage problematic realities through a consciousness distributed through digital mediums, as well as across material sites of contestation. I would like to conjoin Hawk's pedagogy of webbed consciousness to a neo-humanist pragmatism that engages problematic realities, toward a distributed consciousness that crosses the material/digital divide—that radically expands the field of distribution of Freire's "conscientization," or consciousness-as-action: toward a webbed consciousness with a social conscience.

In the last ten years, a body of scholarship has emerged theorizing this neo-humanist pragmatism. At the cutting edge of this Freirean neo-pragmatism is Cornel West. In contradistinction to those who ineffectually defend Freire under the sign of teaching "resistance," West is one of the few who rallies to Freire's defense under the sign of "pragmatism," mapping a pedagogical genealogy that links Freire to the pioneers of American pragmatism (Peirce, James, and Dewey), bridging the problematic disconnect between revolutionary Brazil and democratic America. This is the "dilatory space" I want to open for Freire's critical praxis moving forward, emphasizing its generative implications under the signs of "neo-pragmatism" and "neo-humanism," while moving beyond an ineffectual, reductive, and futile apology mounted under the sign of "resistance pedagogy" or "liberatory pedagogy." I want to complicate and enrich this neo-humanist pragmatism with Hawk's pedagogy of a distributed webbed consciousness.

In *Prophetic Thought*, Cornel West pays tribute to Freire's influence on American approaches to teaching, and particularly on the turn toward neo-pragmatism, in the process building a bridge between Freire and the American pragmatists (Dewey, James et al.). Thanks to the work of theorists such as West, Hardin, Enoch, Ronald and Roskelly, Hawk, and Peter Brooks (*Reading for Plot*), a "dilatory space" is being opened for the continuing application of Freire's problem-posing praxis across disciplines and national borders, under the category of "neo-pragmatism" and networked consciousness.

Among the first to recognize the broader, enduring, pragmatic implications of Freire for American education and the contributions of Cornel West to theorizing this Freirean turn to American pragmatism are Kate Ronald and Hephzibah Roskelly. In "Untested Feasibility: Imagining the Pragmatic Possibility of Paulo Freire," Ronald and Roskelly theorize the pragmatic "connections" between Freire's pedagogy and our "particular North American contexts," in "contexts of real work and meaningful action" (612). Like West, they situate "Freire's work . . . within a tradition of North American pragmatic philosophy" (613), discovering common pedagogical ground between Freire's "praxis" and American "pragmatism." Ronald and Roskelly move Freirean praxis into a bold, new space by "connecting his concept of praxis" with the "method of pragmatism" to generate a "pragmatic theory and practice in the work of teaching literacy."

I would like to go one step further: putting this fusion of American pragmatism and Freirean praxis to the test, field testing it under the sign of neo-humanist pragmatism. As Ronald and Roskelly aptly observe, "this puts Freire into a new context where he becomes more than an 'import' to North American classrooms" (613) even as it "invites a remaking of pragmatism" by bringing it into generative dialogue with Freirean praxis.

Central to Freirean pragmatism is its engagement with the historical, both distant and recent, which is often put under erasure by the conditioned amnesia of discourses of domination, which willfully turn a blind eye on the historical in order to perpetuate structures of domination. Analysis of the historical thus becomes a springboard to a liberatory critique of domination. This "recovery of history . . . is, as Freire says, a 'creative dimension' of consciousness that allows people to intervene in reality in order to change it" (4, qtd. in Ronald and Roskelly 613).

Thus, the problematic of the historical becomes a further focus of the "program content" of education as the practice of freedom. Analysis of the problematic of history (recent and remote) becomes part of a "language of possibility" (87, qtd. in Ronald and Roskelly 613). Thus, history becomes one of the sites for the analysis of applied pragmatism, which then applies this analysis to inform contemporary realities, situating them within an historical continuum. This emphasis on the historical underscores the significance for composition studies of works such as Jarratt's *Rereading the Sophists* and Glenn's *Rhetoric Retold*, whose critical re-readings of classical rhetoric inform current pedagogical approaches. It underscores as well the critical immediacy of recent histories of capitalism, such as Naomi Klein's analysis of "disaster capitalism" in *Shock Doctrine*, which also merits inclusion in the "program content" of a neo-humanist pragmatism, given the millions of lives in America and around the world impacted by the policies and practices of "disaster capitalism." If such a critique of radical, free-market capitalism was offered in conjunction with appreciative readings by its advocates, including Milton Friedman's *Capitalism and Freedom*, then a "dilatory space" for critical inquiry could be fostered. Analysis of the historical becomes part of the methodology of applied pragmatism, in which analysis is brought to bear on the current manifestations of a historical problem. One of the methodologies of this neo-pragmatism is "to use the past to influence the present . . . to answer the violence of power" (Freire 87).

The future is posited not as an inflexible, unalterable, and inevitable continuation of the present and past, but as an undetermined, malleable construct arising in response to problematic and problematized realities. Ronald and Roskelly note the Freirean implications of Cornel West's "prophetic pragmatism," particularly as they bear on the relevance of historical analysis to liberatory literacy. In *Keeping Faith,* West places a "premium on garnering resources from a vanishing past in a decadent present in order to keep alive a tempered hope for the future" (614). They observe that West's "emphasis on the past as a resource echoes Freire's belief in the past as a way to help develop critical consciousness and initiate changed action. Freire and West both envision and articulate pedagogy as the practice of hope in the face of that which would destroy it. This pedagogy of access and hope is inherently humanist and pragmatic. In *Prophetic Thought*, West characterizes Freire as "the exemplary organic intellectual of our time" who "puts a premium on dialogue, the construction of new subjects of history and the creation of social possibilities in history" (179, qtd. in Ronald and Roskelly 616).

West's own work is defined "in terms that match Freire's definitions of critical consciousness and reflective action. . . . West uses Freire's term for this belief/action connection, all 'grounded in the painful yet empowering process of conscientization.'" This concept emphasizes the analytic, the humanist, and the hopeful aspects of West's and Freire's praxis, insofar as that praxis involves not only a "broad and deep analytical grasp of the present in light of the past," but also it involves a "human empathy" that "never loses sight of the humanity in others," while keeping "alive the notion that the future is open-ended and that what we think and what we do can make a difference" (West 3–7, qtd. in Ronald and Roskelly 617). Conscientization unites the work of analysis and the humanist struggle for access to the material, political, and healthful benefits of citizenship.

Consequently, the "philosophical tradition that West embraces is remarkably akin to Freire's philosophy of education," even as it draws on the tradition of American pragmatism embodied in Peirce, James, and Dewey (617). West notes the relevance of a renascent American pragmatism, informed by Freirean praxis, observing that its "unashamedly moral emphasis and its unequivocally ameliorative impulse" has a "distinctive appeal in our postmodern moment," whose critique of power and domination across disciplines and geographic borders privileges the ethical in the interest of an inclusive agency that transgresses and transforms divisions of race, class, and gender (*American Evasion* 4, qtd. in Ronald and Roskelly 617). For West, pragmatism privileges a "usable past" that collapses the disconnect between theory, method, and practice in a pedagogy of "reflective action that West—and Freire himself—call for" (qtd. in Ronald and Roskelly 617).

West is not the only American scholar to perceive the practical implications of Freirean praxis. As Ronald and Roskelly observe, Anne Berthof "was one of the earliest to recognize the important connection between pragmatism and Freire's ideas, call[ing] Freire 'thoroughly pragmatic, one of the true heirs of William James and C. Peirce" (qtd. in Ronald and Roskelly 617). Ronald and Roskelly see this fusion of American pragmatism and Freirean praxis as "capable of energizing our teaching and remaking our own contexts" (617). Like them, I want to "read Freire within the context of pragmatic thinking," as a (pre)text for testing the "feasibility" of a humanist neo-pragmatism, informed by the theoretical and practical affinities of Peirce, James, and Dewey, on the one hand, and Socrates, Freire, and Burke, on the other, as recently theorized by West, Hardin, Enoch, Ronald, Roskelly et al.

As Ronald and Roskelly conclude, what we would "'import' from Freire exists already in our own cultural contexts, practiced by pragmatists for a century": a pedagogy that enables the struggle for agency through access. This is the enduring lesson of American history, from the struggle of slaves for freedom to the struggle of blacks for civil rights, from the struggle of women for the right to vote to their subsequent struggle for equality under the law, from the struggle of workers for humane conditions (whether factory workers or Hispanic farm laborers) to the struggle for gay Americans for equal treatment under the law, whether in the military or in marriage. The wedding of Freirean praxis to this tradition of American pragmatism is warranted by this mutual interest in literacy for the common good. As Ronald and Roskelly assert,

> Central to both the pragmatic agenda and Freire's praxis is the necessary connection between action and reflection; this connection leads

both Freire and the pragmatists to a sense of hopefulness, a belief in at least a contingent possibility. For both philosophies, belief means a willingness to act and the assurance that reflection on action will lead to better, more hopeful acts. Freire calls this kind of hope "untested feasibility." (614)

The pedagogy of humanist pragmatism I envision puts this feasibility to the test. It does so by problematizing realities through analysis and civic engagement, by using the past to influence the present toward a "future we have yet to create . . . beyond the 'limit situation' we face now, which must be created by us" (153, qtd. in 615). Far from being a form of "wishful thinking," the "untested feasibility" of Freire's educational outcome is something that is pursued through a "systematic method for enacting change by mediating between what is and what might be" (615). It is no mere academic exercise, but an exercise in the application of dialogic knowledge to problematic realities—as was Socrates' "elenchus" 2,500 years ago.

Armed with the critical vision, the dialogic methods, and the reality-based content of Freirean praxis, American pragmatism, and a distributed, networked consciousness, we might more effectively read "local contexts critically" in order to engage their problematic realities. As Ronald and Roskelly aver, "being able to break through limit situations means being able to see them as problems rather than as givens," and thus as subject to intervention and change. A neo-humanist pragmatism privileges experience or problematic realities as the testing ground of "meaning and truth" (618). Human experience is posited by the American pragmatists as "the most important subject of inquiry." In a neo-humanist pragmatism, that experience would be defined by problematic realities that increasingly deny access and agency to millions of citizens.

Moreover, meaning is dialogically and dialectically generated through "a mediated relationship among word, world, and inquirer" (619). This underscores the "communal" and "contingent" nature of the educative process, which is conditioned by the local contexts it critically reads. Actions are informed by analysis and brought to bear on the problematic realities that limit access and agency. Meaning is an a posteriori, retrospectively determined construct, insofar as it is ultimately determined by the effectiveness of the actions that arise from it and to which it is yoked. Action is not only the effect of meaning but also the source of it. As Ronald and Roskelly assert, "meaning resides . . . in resulting actions," which are the "test of knowledge and the definition for belief" (620). To be meaningful, pedagogy must be "grounded in experience and tested by practice" (623).

Knowledge, to be meaningful, must have a practical application: must, in the end, return to the reality it arises from. As Ronald and Roskelly conclude, "[t]his is the first great pragmatic lesson of Friere's work, that experience must count, must be used, and must drive change" (623). The vehicle for change is dialogic language rooted in problematic realities, for it posits a malleable World susceptible to the transformative power of the Word. The eternal return of the Word to the World requires a medium: that medium is radical pedagogy. Social conscious provokes change in a reticent reality. The practices that sustain problematic realities cease when they no longer reflect mass consciousness—in societies where that consciousness is free to express itself or finds the means of expression where suppressed. Slavery. Prohibition. Segregation. Atomic testing. DDT, to name but a few. Reality is mediated by consciousness. As Ronald and Roskelly observe, "one of the central concepts of pragmatism is mediation, the premise that ideas can move beyond their esoteric or oppositional characteristics and into new relationship" (626). It is the work of radical pedagogy to bring problematic realities and consciousness into relationship, transforming consciousness into " conscientization" (awareness-as-action).

Neo-humanist pragmatism fosters a new relationship between reality and knowledge, the material and the lingual, the World and the Word—in which the merely oppositional becomes dialogic, synergistic, generating a third condition that brings things in opposition into liberatory dialogue, turning capture into consciousness and consciousness into change. Sans this generative relationship between the word and the world, knowledge lapses into an academic exercise, into "sophisticated analysis. Ironic reflection" (West 230, qtd. in 630).

Thought, language, and action are each embedded in the other, as part of a triadic progression whose phases lose meaning if divorced from one another. As Ronald and Roskelly observe, "[p]ragmatic philosophy brings this triadic process ... to bear on history, experience, self, and society. This new relationship yields insights, as each element works with and helps remake the other in a spiraling, symbiotic growth toward understanding" (629). Their words give fresh voice to Freire's words: "To exist, humanly, is to name the world, to change it" (77, qtd. in 630). Thought arises from language and tends toward action. Genuine knowledge is conceived from the union of analysis and hope: the hope that it will awaken reality, and reality will awaken to it. Ronald and Roskelly further underscore Freire's relevance to American pragmatism: "Freire's ideas are deeply embedded in practical use" (620). Knowledge, to be ethical must "be of use," as the poet Marge Piercy reminds us. Aside from its deep political roots, Freire's praxis is more broadly congruent with contemporary American pragmatism by virtue of its emphasis on active and interactive learning, in which "students become subjects—meaning makers—in their own education," and in which knowledge is generated dialogically (621).

TOWARD A "SYMBOL-WISE" PRAGMATISM: BURKE, FREIRE, AND FOUCAULT'S WAR

In addition to the problematic realities of race, class, and gender; of the environment, the economy, and education; of history, mass media, and religion, the problematic realities of war also merit inclusion in the "program content" of a neo-humanist pragmatism. Here, as well, Freire's praxis evidences its relevance to American education, not only to the pragmatism of John Dewey but also to the "symbol-wise" pedagogy of Kenneth Burke, as so usefully elucidated by Jessica Enoch in "Becoming Symbol-Wise: Kenneth Burke's Pedagogy of Critical Reflection." Enoch is quick to establish the inter-textual relevance of Burkean and Freirean theory, revealing the ways Burke's "Cold War pedagogy . . . connects (and complicates) Paulo Freire's conception of praxis . . . [adding] a *rhetorical* nuance to critical reflection" before finally demonstrating the usefulness (if indeed not the necessity) of such a praxis "for teachers and scholars today who, like Burke, live in a time 'when war is always threatening'" (qtd. in Enoch 272). In "Power/Knowledge," Foucault illumines the wellsprings of this ideology of permanent war, noting that "power is war continued by other means":

> If it is true that political power puts an end to war, that it installs the reign of peace in civil society, this by no means implies that it suspends the effects of war. . . . The role of political power is to reinscribe this relation through a form of unspoken warfare, to reinscribe it in social institutions (church, academy, factory) as war. None of these phenomena should be interpreted except as a continuation of war. Even when one writes the history of peace and its institutions, it is always the history of war that one is writing. (90–91)

Foucault's observations are significant inasmuch as they shed light on the possible origins of the "culture war" that has been raging in America for a generation, positing it as an extension of the numerous wars America has fought in the last century, as a "form of unspoken warfare," "of war continued by other means." Since the "flash crash" of 2008, this "culture war" has metastasized into what is increasingly being characterized as "class warfare," waged by ruling elites against the middle and lower classes through the society's political, legal, economic, communicative, and educational apparatuses, in what is also tantamount to a "form of unspoken warfare." Perhaps the most violent effect of this "class warfare" is the diminished access to the material benefits of life (jobs, education, health insurance) experienced by millions of middle and lower class citizens. It is not just the effects of this "unspoken war" that merit inclusion in a neo-humanist pragmatism, however.

As evidenced by the tragedy of the Iraq war, the government's ability to "manufacture consent" through signification and the complicity of the mass media, as Noam Chomsky observes in *Necessary Illusions*, poses an ethical imperative to educators: to act as "guardians who protect the State against its internal . . . enemies," by pursuing in the interest of the common good a critical praxis that decodes the symbolic to defuse the political, that "unveils" reality to transform it. Enoch underscores the pedagogical logic of this "symbol-wise" praxis of critical reflection, observing that Burke "had made war a central concern in his 1950 *Rhetoric of Motives* by defining war as 'the ultimate disease, or perversion of cooperation'" (22, qtd. in Enoch 272). Burke's "pedagogy of critical reflection" privileged the "study of the relationship between rhetoric and war": a study with increasing relevance in our own time. In both *A Grammar* and *A Rhetoric of Motives*, Burke "offers a theory and practice of language study that attempts to abate those aggressive and competitive traits in students that could eventually lead to global conflict" (273). His pedagogical project bears striking similarities to Freire's, using analysis of power within the classroom to mitigate its dehumanizing effects on the individual student: in short, for liberatory ends. Enoch continues:

> According to Burke, education could begin to "cancel off" such destructive ambitions by teaching students to become symbol-wise. Rather than being symbol foolish and using language to compete and combat with each other on a daily basis, students guided by Burke's educational theory and method would become symbol-wise by adopting a "technique of preparatory withdrawal." (qtd. in Enoch 272)

Burke's approach underscores the relevance of Freire's concept of "conscientization," or consciousness-as-action. In *Necessary Illusions: Thought Control in Democratic Societies*, Noam Chomsky provides not only a useful analysis of the way partisan power "manufactures consent" through the mass media, but also he sounds an urgent call for citizens to "undertake a course in intellectual self-defense to protect themselves from manipulation and control, and to lay the basis for more meaningful democracy" (viii). Enoch elaborates on the sign-deconstructing nature of Burke's pedagogy, which by getting students to "reflect upon the ways language contributes to such [war] conflicts" prompts them to "disengage from moments of aggressive argumentation," adopting instead a "reflective attitude that curbs those competitive 'tendencies' that could cause 'the kind of war now always threatening'" (273) and that turns the classroom into another theatre of war by positing discourse as a "form of unspoken warfare."

Burke's pedagogical strategy mirrors Freire's, which similarly privileges critical reflection on the problematic realities, not of war but of colonial domination, including the way "language contributes to such conflicts." The praxis of each enables a liberatory "dilatory space" between the subject and the problematic realities by which its happiness, agency, and access is constrained. This space of reflection upon reality signifies the advent of education as "the practice of freedom." Further, the "process-friendly" activities of the expressivist writing workshop also enrich and enliven the "program content" of a neo-humanist pragmatism. Journaling, freewriting, collaborative "feedback" all function as part of a "social-based" inquiry into problematic realities: one that complicates the usual distinctions between expressivist and social-epistemic pedagogies.

Enoch further underscores the relevance of Burke to Freire, "who continually coupled reflection with action in his definition of praxis—'the action and reflection of men and women upon their world in order to change it'" (60, qtd. in Enoch 273). Just as Burke's pedagogy focuses on the "relationship between education and war" (279), so must a contemporary praxis focus on the relationship between education and the aforementioned problematic realities of our historical moment, including the problematic realities associated with contemporary wars on terrorism: unwarranted wiretapping, torture/water-boarding, the manufacture of consent through the media, airport security searches, imprisonment without trial, the privatization of war (for-profit), and so forth.

Language is nothing more (nor less) than symbols in action, or "symbolic action." A symbol-wise pedagogy is a "symbolic action" of resistance to a "symbolic action" of social control—that attempts to "disarm" the manipulative sign through analysis of that sign, much as Socrates' "elenchus" attempted to do. Analysis of the signifying practices of power thus becomes a symbolic act of rhetorical disarmament. As Burke observes, the moment to introduce students to a "course in symbolic wisdom" would be the "preliminary stages of their high school or college years" (282). Critics might claim that this is just substituting one form of social control with another. The difference is that such analysis of signifying practice restores to the subject the agency to choose its course of action, based on its consciousness of signification, instead of having that choice appropriated by the manipulative effects of signification: it is the difference between a consent that is manufactured by deception and one that is an expression of awareness.

Burke early on perceived the dangerous implications of converting the media to what Chomsky describes as a "propaganda model": "We see democracy being threatened by the rise of the enormous 'policy-making' mass media that exerts great rhetorical pressure upon the readers without at the same time teaching how to discount such devices" (285, qtd. in Enoch 285—or defend ourselves from them. If anything, this consolidation of the political and communicative apparatuses of the democratic State has accelerated since Burke's original critique.

The inherently political and liberatory nature of Burke's pedagogy of critical reflection is further evidenced by its twofold goal of first making "'citizenry truly free' by providing students with 'very thorough training in the discounting of rhetorical persuasiveness'" (285, qtd. in Enoch 286) and second by getting students to systematically "question the many symbolically-stimulated goads that are now too often accepted without question." A pedagogy of critical reflection would restore agency to the self by liberating it from the appropriating and subjugating effects of the sign. Each individual would again be "free" to draw his or her own conclusions, as opposed to having those "conclusions" pre-fabricated for them for mass consumption and driven home by relentless repetition across media (television, print, electronic) and by the shrill volume of its ideological noise. It is essential in this "signifying wise" praxis that the teacher pose the problem under analysis to students in all its complexities, from its diverse ideological viewpoints. It is equally imperative that the teacher not conduct the analysis for the students, but merely equip them with the tools for conducting their own analysis, empowering them with the agency to "name their own world."

This pedagogy of critical reflection would invite students to "take a moment" upon encountering the "sign" to question its claims, assumptions, supporting evidence, and unstated motives, to "read between the signs" as it were to assess the credibility of the source making the claim. As Enoch observes, Burke's pedagogy of critical reflection "invites students to develop an attitude and approach to the world through patient and methodical analysis of language use" (290), even as it "prompts students to hesitate before making assessments, judgments, or moves to action" (287). Burke's pedagogy is an example of how "critical reflection in and of itself can be a kind of action upon the world" (290). In other words, analysis unacted upon is as unproductive as action unreflected upon. Enoch continues: "in Freirean terms, it seems clear that for transformation to occur, reflection must lead to action and/or action must be reflected upon" (291). Enoch underscores the compelling relevance of Burke's "symbol-wise" pedagogy relative to war, arguing that "Burke's theory and practices should become a pedagogical priority":

> [W]hat Burke argued for then is what we must argue for and implement now. Like the students Burke wrote about in LAPE, students today should learn to reflect on the language used to move them to action and war.... Burke's 1955 pedagogy of critical reflection calls educators today to reconsider the active, world-altering potential of reflection, especially in our own war-ready and war-torn world. (291)

No less than Freire's liberatory praxis, Burke's pedagogy of critical reflection "speaks directly and profoundly to the pedagogical and political concerns of teachers and scholars today" (Enoch 288). The inter-textuality of Burke and Freire, as Enoch rightly observes, is due to a common pedagogical genealogy that reinscribes the educational pragmatism of John Dewey: Freire, "like both Dewey and Burke, linked the 'word with the world'" (35, qtd. in Enoch 288). Enoch continues:

> This linkage of Burke, Dewey, and Freire gains importance once we consider how Burke's ideas concerning rhetoric and education inflect Freire's conception of praxis. As Freire argues time and again, praxis is the 'action and reflection of men and women upon their world in order to transform it.' (61, qtd. in Enoch 289)

The seeming pedagogical differences between Freire's colonial situation and the typical American classroom are easily outweighed by the usefulness of his praxis as a model for "reading local contexts critically" (Enoch 289), and as a model for using education to engage the problems of society and the world. As Enoch affirms, "Burke's work in LAPE helps today's teachers and scholars consider how praxis could be *recovered* (instead of imported) inside the local context of the twenty-first century composition classroom" (289)—not to mention the political science, history, communication, biology, sociology, environmental studies, philosophy, or anthropology classroom, to name just a few sites where such analysis could be undertaken with immediate relevance to the "program content." In such a course, rhetorical analysis would be "taught as a tool for critical investigation" (292). Enoch continues: "Before students even begin to formulate thesis statements and argumentative tactics, they would learn to inspect carefully and precisely those texts that linguistically create certain positions and arguments."

Such a critical praxis falls well within the focus of social-epistemic approaches to education. As James Berlin affirms, "social epistemic rhetoric is the study and critique of signifying practices in their relation to subject formation within the framework of economic, social, and political conditions" (77). As Freire similarly asserts,

> It is to the reality which mediates [people], and to the perception of that reality held by educators and people, that we must go to find the program content of education. The investigation of what I have termed the people's "thematic universe"—that complex of their "generative themes"—inaugurates the dialogue of education as the practice of freedom. (86)

The goal of this "symbol-wise" praxis is the same as in the Freirean classroom: to return to students the right to "name their world" in order to transform their relation to its problematic realities, as a precondition for transforming those realities (76). As Giroux asserts, "the ultimate purpose of critique should be critical thinking for social change. . . . critical thought becomes the precondition for human freedom" (18–19). Similarly, knowledge, to be meaningful, must be useful—must serve some broader purpose than the individual's edification. This is the abiding lesson of Socrates and Freire's radical pedagogy: it must somehow serve the interest, the well-being of the common good. Sans such use, it risks devolving into a mere academic exercise. The social construction of knowledge through dialogic analysis fosters the social transformation of reality through the application of knowledge—in the eternal return of the critical Word to a problematic World.

Social-epistemic praxis draws its ethical imperative from its sustained application of dialogic knowledge to problematic realities, as a re-humanizing discourse of the common good. Its collaborative "unveiling" of problematic realities, its exposure of the World with the dialogic Word, is itself a vital action that necessarily transforms reality, by transforming citizens' consciousness of those realities and their relation to them: not as passive objects of immutable realities, but as active agents of transformable realities. However, realities that are unseen cannot be transformed until they are first unveiled. The world seen engenders the world foreseen. The path to the reality that is foreseen leads to and through the reality that is unseen until unveiled. The wondrous progression that defines radical pedagogy is its engagement with the unseen, the seen, and the foreseen. It is indeed to reality that serves the few that pedagogy must go if it is to serve the many—and create reality anew. Teaching is co-creation: of an authentic self, who then recreates reality in the image of itself.

This "symbol-wise," networked, neo-humanist pragmatism breathes fresh life into Socrates' philosophy of the educator-as-public intellectual, whose responsibility it is to "unveil" problematic realities that threaten the common good, with a public discourse as protective as it is corrective, as critical as it is liberatory. In *Theory and Resistance in Education*, Henry Giroux provides a description of social-epistemic praxis as concise as it is compelling, arising from his vision of "schools as democratic public spheres" (xvii). To the extent the work of the intellectual is grounded in analysis and critique and in a critique of power, it functions as a "check and balance" against the excesses and abuses of power. To the extent this critique of power draws its breath from the constitution, it reinvigorates the system of checks and balances that safeguard the practice of democracy. As these systematic checks and balances on power are systematically eliminated by those in power through the politicization of the supreme court, the corporatization of the media, the erosion of the regulatory capacity of government, and the consolidation of power in the political-industrial-military-religious-media complex, it becomes increasingly imperative that education remains a redoubt of free-thinking, of analysis, of knowledge-making, as perhaps the last check and balance on power, circulating through the power of persuasion.

Social-epistemic praxis, and a neo-humanist pragmatism in particular, sustains the democratic critique of power enshrined by the Founding Fathers in the Constitution, whose system of "checks and balances" codifies that critique, by systematically dispersing and distributing power as a safeguard against its dangerous accretion. Our historical moment is not only dangerously reminiscent of the material conditions at the time of the American Revolution, but also during the time of Socrates' Athens, as Field observes:

> Instead of a constitution in which everyone has an equal part in the government of the city, we find in practice that it tends more and more to a form in which the population falls into two social classes, and the larger class of the two ... uses its power in its own interests, and disregards the interests of the others as completely as if its members were disenfranchised ... And if the democracy is overthrown and succeeded by an

oligarchy of wealth, whose members in their turn consult only their own interests, the division of classes becomes more acute still. (85)

Concern for the catastrophic consequences for the common good when power is wielded in interest of the few is voiced by Xenophon's Socrates: "On these accounts . . . I am constantly in the greatest fear lest some evil should happen to the state too great for it to bear" (qtd. in Durant 372). When truth can no longer speak to power, power is no longer constrained to speak the truth—is free to manufacture its own truths. As Bourdieu asserts, "there is no genuine democracy without genuine opposing critical powers. The intellectual is one of those, of the first magnitude. This is why I think the work of demolishing the intellectual . . . is as dangerous as the demolition of the public interest . . ." (*Acts of Resistance*, 8, qtd. in Giroux xix).

What is urgently needed is meaningful inquiry in public spheres, functioning indeed as a "gadfly" to rouse citizens from a complacency born of misplaced trust, from an apathy bred of cynicism, from an indifference fed by insularity, and from an indolence bloated by consumerism. As "democratic public spheres," classrooms can become sites for reconnecting individuals and the citizen to the civic sphere, through the medium of collective inquiry into problematic realities—as a corrective civic discourse and liberatory critique of power and the power of persuasion upon which it depends. Social-epistemic praxis, as Giroux observes, recognizes "the fundamental political nature of teaching and the importance of linking pedagogy to social change . . . and engaging the space of schooling as a site of contestation, resistance, and possibility" (xx).

Giroux, like Enoch, underscores the centrality of Freire's liberatory praxis to social-epistemic pedagogy, asserting that it is "foundational" and "crucial to any radical theory of education" that privileges, not assimilation or accommodation to the problematic logic of the marketplace but "social change," through intervention upon those realities: that educates, not to conform but to transform. It doesn't shape the student to fit reality but rather empowers the student to shape reality to fit his or her own becoming humanity.

Freire's liberatory pedagogy is "foundational" to social-epistemic praxis because it gives material form to the hopes, possibilities, and resistance upon which all meaningful change feeds, and without which it remains in the realm of pure desire, of wishful thinking, of "sophisticated analysis. Ironic reflection." As Giroux observes, Freire provided "an important theoretic premise for overcoming a number of debilitating pessimisms that plagued educational discourses," including the assumption that "schools were . . . locked into a future that could only repeat the present," whose realities and possibilities were defined and determined by the logic of the marketplace—and increasingly by the aberrant logic of radical capitalism. Freire's praxis demonstrated that a problematic reality is not a given that can never be altered, but a composite of conditions as material as they are mutable. Thus, he presents the "reality of oppression not as a closed world from which there is no exit, but as a limiting situation which [people] can transform" (34). A "foundational" assumption of Freirean praxis is that "human life is conditioned rather than determined," and it can change if the conditions are changed (xx). Realities that are made by a few can be unmade by the many, in favor of realities that serve the interests of the many. Freirean praxis assumes human agency with respect to the material conditions of reality. It posits a reality that is mutable, not fixed, that can be acted upon instead of always and already acting upon the subject.

The long struggle to fulfill the promise of American freedom made in the colonial dawn of democracy repeatedly demonstrates that problematic realities are not immutable but subject to transformation—of, by, and for the people. As Giroux observes, the hope that Freire offered for social change "was a crucial precondition . . . in which the strategic gap between the promise and reality of democracy could be taken seriously as an object of critical learning and practical struggle" (xxi). Consequently, "schooling can be addressed as a crucial site of [this] struggle" to keep the promise of democracy made more than two hundred years ago. Such a praxis arises from the recognition that every classroom is "already a space of politics, power, and authority" (xxx). Giroux continues:

> [A]t the very least, radical pedagogical work proposes that education is a form of political intervention in the world and is capable of creating the possibilities for social transformation. . . . as part of a more expansive struggle for individual rights and social justice. . . . the motivation for scholarly work cannot be narrowly academic; such work must connect with 'real life social and political issues in the wider society'. . . . [S]chools should function to serve the public good and not be seen merely as a source of private advantage removed from the dynamics of power and equity. (Bennett, qtd. in Giroux xxvii–xxviii)

Education, thus, must participate in a broader historical and political struggle, in a "politics of resistance that extends beyond the classroom," to unveil realities through critical reflection in order to transform them through the application of that reflection. Central to the "program content" of this pedagogy is an inquiry into the signifying practice of domination, into the relation between power and the power of persuasion, "interrogating how power works through dominant discourses and social relations" (xxxi). This focus on the signifying practices of domination is necessary for the simple reason that "domination has assumed a new form" (23). As Giroux observes,

> Instead of being exercised primarily through the use of physical force (the army and police), the power of the ruling classes [is] now reproduced through a form of ideological hegemony . . . established primarily

> through the *rule of consent,* and mediated via cultural institutions such as schools, *mass media,* churches, etc. . . . (23, my emphasis)

Giroux underscores the immediacy of the peril posed to American democracy by the consolidation of power—as well as the ethical imperative this poses to American education:

> The time for radical democratic change has never been so urgent since the fate of an entire generation of young people, if not democracy itself, is at stake. This challenge gives new meaning, if not new impetus, to the importance of resistance, the relevance of pedagogy, and the significance of political agency. (xxxi)

The question is not merely whether such a neo-humanist pragmatism is feasible, but whether democracy itself is feasible without the kind of civic engagement such an education fosters. Such an inquiry (and the participation in problematic realities it enables) operates like a "check and balance" on un-signified realities, mitigating the signs of violence and the violence of signs upon the self. To the extent such a dialogic pragmatism situates inquiry at the intersection of the personal, social, political, ethical, and rhetorical, it privileges not merely the eternal return of the Word to the World but of education as the "practice of freedom."

Conclusion
Ancient Rhetoric/Radical Praxis: The Personal, the Political, and the Rhetorical

Plato's *Phaedrus* is a cautionary tale about the "dangers of rhetoric," especially the dangers it poses to those to whom its dangers are "not apparent" (Griswold 229). The *Phaedrus* is a cautionary tale not only about the "dangers of rhetoric," but about the dangerous conjunction of power and persuasion, insofar as it dramatizes the extent to which power is dependent upon the power of persuasion. Yet, as a polemic, the *Phaedrus* is significant not only because it exposes a problem as dangerous for democracy today as it was in Plato's time, but because it models a solution to the problem as efficacious today as in Plato's own conflicted and partisan times: a dialogic education that foregrounds critical analysis of reality, and analysis of dominant signifying practices in particular, as a means of mitigating and transforming that reality, in the interests of the common good and social justice.

This critique of prevailing signifying practices, and the problematic effects of the power that circulates through them, establishes Socratic dialectics as an ancient precursor of the postmodern polemic of the relationship between language and power, signification and ideology. Plato's critique of discourse, like that of postmodernism, privileges the ethical, insofar as it is a treatise "on the Beautiful, Ethical." Yet, it is not merely as a critique of power and the signifying practices through which power circulates that the *Phaedrus* demonstrates its abiding relevance to our own historical circumstances, but also as a model of critical pedagogy. Its emphasis on dialectic learning, problem-posing analysis, and civic engagement mark it as an ancient precursor to Freirean praxis and social-epistemic pedagogy. As a pedagogy that situates inquiry at the intersection of the personal, social, political, rhetorical, and ethical, it prefigures by 2,500 years the focus of postmodern pedagogies of civic engagement. Its dialectic methodology similarly informs the contemporary pedagogic emphasis on dialogic learning: on active, interactive, and student-centered methodologies. As pedagogies that model how knowledge is made and what constitutes authenticate knowledge, the radical praxis of Socrates and Freire deeply informs the ontological and epistemological concerns of postmodern pedagogy. Each is nothing if not a demonstration of a meaning-making process that it social, political, and ethical. To the extent each grounds problematic material realities as the site of inquiry, they reinforce the focus of American pragmatism, commencing with Peirce, James, and Dewey, and moving through and beyond Burke, to the "prophetic pragmatism" of Cornel West.

What I have endeavored to do in this book is unveil a pedagogical landscape, open a space for radical pedagogy that moves beyond the critical traditions of Socratic inquiry, Freirean praxis, and American pragmatism by merging them into a reconfigured radical pedagogy, under the signs of "dialogic learning, "problem-posing analysis," and "civic engagement": a neo-humanist, dialogic pragmatism informed by digital pedagogies of webbed, networked communities that distribute "conscientization" across broader sites of contestation, in which material realities are also engaged in virtual mediums. A body of recent scholarship argues the merits, if not the urgent necessity, of privileging just this kind of critical inquiry in the classroom. Susan Jarratt advocates the redefinition of the classroom as a site of "collective inquiry into the function of discourse in democracy," as a "form of action informed by reflection," which positions students as "public intellectuals" (95). Not just the "function of discourse in a democracy," but its actual practices and its affective power upon its subjects, should be the focus of such critical inquiry. Clearly, the excesses of radical capitalism, the ubiquity of environmental degradation, and the signifying practices that perpetuate them warrant inquiry in such a problem-posing pedagogy of civic engagement. This ancient focus on the relationship between language and power is central to social-epistemic approaches to literacy, as theorized by Dewey, Burke, and Freire, which place the "project of human emancipation . . . at the center of the educational process."

Such an ancient praxis is Freirean insofar as it encourages citizen/students to "come to an awareness of the causes of their oppression," and the rhetorical means by which that marginalization is perpetuated, by honing their ability "to engage in analysis." Such a critical praxis is central to the tenets of social-epistemic theory insofar as it sees "language teaching as the key strategy for developing critical consciousness," (108), reinscribing the Freirean praxis of "naming the world as an act of empowerment" (108). Such a praxis draws on the theories of American Freireans, like Aronwitz and Giroux, who "see language learning as a means of distancing oneself from the process of social reproduction" (108). Jarratt continues: "For Freire, knowledge is always knowledge of the world of the student, developed out of the students' own experience and only 're-presented' to them in the form of problems posed by the teacher" (109): in this case, the problematic of concentrated wealth and power in a democracy and its reliance on language to perpetuate itself.

As the career of Socrates and the writings of Plato evidence, the pursuit of knowledge must serve some greater purpose than the individual's edification. Knowledge, to be ethical, must "be of use" to the greater good, as the poet Marge Piercy reminds us. This is what consecrates Socrates' life-long

Conclusion 211

examination of the relationship between power and language. It is the dialectic between knowledge and reality that authenticates knowledge and mitigates the violence of reality. As Freire observes, "knowledge emerges only through . . . the restless, impatient, continuing, hopeful inquiry men pursue in the world, with the world, and with each other" (58). I can think of no more fitting epithet for Plato's Socrates. Jarratt continues: "the aim is not revolution, but rather an awareness of the way culture, structuring thought and action, contains contradictory messages"—including the contradictory message that public "assent" for State policy is all too often manufactured through language that veils, as opposed to unveiling, the truth.

Theorists such as Shor, Giroux, and Aronwitz rightly see the classroom not just "as one of the most significant sites for the practice of democracy," but as one that is deeply informed by the classical educative paradigm (112). Jarratt continues:

> offer[ing] a range of techniques for reintroducing the practice of speaking and writing to students silenced by their experience of United States democracy, [configuring the classroom as] a democratic public sphere [foregrounding] possibilities for democratic mediation in government action in many arenas of social life . . . Aronwitz and Giroux envision a form of "citizenship" like the arête Protagoras taught, a form of political and ethical scrutiny that defines citizenship not as a function of the state, but as a quality that permeates all of social life . . . aimed at developing democratic and just communities. (Jarratt 112)

These and other theorists envision the classroom as a place "where students and teachers can challenge, oppose, and resist those forces" that undermine the freedom of choice relative to government policies and actions, by manipulating that "choice" through the unethical use of the power of persuasion. This is tantamount indeed to "giving arms to madmen."

Thus, I envision, as do these theorists, a classroom "in which students argue about the ethical implications of discourse" (116), where education is indeed configured and consecrated as "the practice of freedom." The educative paradigm of the ancient Greeks, for sophist and philosopher alike, is indeed a "model for emulation" to the extent it foregrounds "the relation of school to politics" (116). Any educational theory or praxis, is, as Jarratt observes,

> an eminently political discourse that emerges from and characterizes an expression of struggle over what forms of authority, orders of representation, forms of moral regulation, and versions of the past and future should be legitimated, passed on, and debated within specific pedagogical sites. (Aronwitz and Giroux, qtd. in 117)

Jarratt's observation regarding the "voice of sophistic rhetoric" applies as well to the humanitarian voice of philosophic discourse, which similarly "speaks out in playful, persuasive, and promising tones," particularly "for those composition teachers who wish to participate in the revitalization of our own democracy . . ." (117). It is not an either-or choice of practicing a pedagogy that serves the interests of the student or the society, but a both-and praxis in which the edification of the individual occurs concomitantly (as it did in the radical pedagogies of Socrates and Freire) with an ethical inquiry into problematic realities that affect not just the Self but the Other. Radical capitalism. Environmental degradation. The social injustice of race, gender, or class discrimination. These are problematic realities by which all are affected. Edification that grounds the dialectic between self and reality to mitigate the violence of reality, grounds as well education as "the practice of freedom."

By virtue of its dialogic methods, pragmatic focus, and edifying outcomes, Socrates' radical praxis has much to offer contemporary educators similarly interested in using dialogic methods to heighten critical thought and to foster participatory citizenship—not merely as ends in themselves, or as a means of personal edification, but on behalf of the common good. How and what we teach has profound implications for democracy. As Ira Shor observes, "since critical thinking is the fundamental precondition for an autonomous and self-motivated public or citizenry, its decline would threaten the future of democratic, social, cultural, and political forms" (47). Education as the "practice of freedom" enshrines the fundamental assumption that language breeds thought and that the offspring of this critical intercourse is freedom, insofar as implicit in the ability to name the world is the possibility of transforming it.

Works Cited

Ashcrofts, Bill, Gareth Griffiths, and Helen, Tiffin. *The Post-Colonial Studies Reader*. New York: Routledge, 1995.
Bakhtin, Mikhail M. "Discourse in the Novel." *The Dialogic Imagination: Four Essays by M. Bakhtin*. Trans. Caryl Emerson and Michael Holquist. Ed. Michael Holquist. Austin: University of Texas P, 1981.
Berlin, James A. "Rhetoric and Ideology in the Writing Class." *College English* 50 (1988): 477–494.
———. *Rhetorics, Poetics, and Cultures: Refiguring College English Studies*. Urbana, Illinois: NCTE, 1996.
Beversluis, John. *Cross-Examining Socrates*. Cambridge: Cambridge University P, 2000.
Bhabha, Homi K. "Sly Civility." *October* 34 (1985): 71–80.
———. "Signs Taken for Wonders: Questions of Ambivalence and Authority Under a Tree Outside Delhi, May 1817." *Critical Inquiry* 12.1 (1985): 144–165.
Bizzell, Patricia and Bruce Herzberg. *The Rhetorical Tradition: Readings From Classical Times to the Present*. New York: Bedford/St. Martin's, 2001.
Blondell, Ruby. *The Play of Character in Plato's Dialogues*. Cambridge: Cambridge University P, 2002.
Brickhouse, Thomas and Nicholas Smith. *Socrates on Trial*. Princeton, NJ: Princeton University P, 1989.
Brooks, Peter. *Reading for Plot. Design and Intention in Narrative*. Cambridge, MA: Harvard University P, 1984.
Brown, Stephen Gilbert. *The Gardens of Desire: Marcel Proust and the Fugitive Sublime*. New York: State University of New York P, 2004.
Cairns, Huntington. "Introduction." *The Collected Dialogues of Plato*. Trans. R. Hackforth. New York: Pantheon Books, 1961.
Covino, William A. *The Art of Wondering. A Revisionist Return to the History of Rhetoric*. Portsmouth, NH: Boynton/Cook, 1988.
Deleuze, Gilles. *Proust and Signs*. Trans. Richard Howard. New York: George Braziller, 1972.
Derrida, Jacques. *Dissemination*. Trans. Barbara Johnson. Chicago: University of Chicago P, 1981.
Doubrovsky, Serge. *Writing and Fantasy in Proust: La Place de la Madeleine*. Lincoln: University of Nebraska P, 1986.
Durant, Will. *The Story of Civilization: The Life of Greece*. Part II. New York: Simon and Schuster, 1961.
Elbow, Peter. *Writing Without Teachers*. New York: Oxford University P, 1973.
Enoch, Jessica. "Becoming Symbol-Wise: Kenneth Burke's Pedagogy of Critical Reflection." *College Composition and Communication* 56.2 (Dec 2004): 272–296.

Ferrari, G.R.F. *Listening to the Cicadas: A Study of Plato's* Phaedrus. New York: Cambridge University P, 1987.
Field, G.C. *Plato and His Contemporaries*. London: Methuen, 1930.
Firor, Ruth. *Folkways in Thomas Hardy*. New York: University of Pennsylvania P, 1931.
Fish, Stanley E. *Self-Consuming Artifacts: The Experience of Seventeenth Century Literature*. Berkeley: University of California P, 1972.
Foucault, Michael. "Two Lectures." *Power/Knowledge: Selected Interviews and Other Writings, 1972-77*. New York: Pantheon, 1980: 78–108.
Freire, Paulo. *Pedagogy of the Oppressed*. Trans. Myra Berman Ramos. New York: Continuum, 1989.
Giroux, Henry A. *Theory and Resistance in Education. Toward a Pedagogy of Opposition*. Fwd. Paulo Freire. Westport, CT: Begin and Garvey, 2001.
Glenn, Cheryl. *Rhetoric Retold: Regendering the Tradition From Antiquity Through the Renaissance*. Carbondale: Southern Illinois University P, 1997.
Goethe, Johann Wolfgang von. "Prelude in the Theatre." *Faust*. Trans. Walter Kaufmann. New York: Doubleday, 1961.
Griswold, Charles L., Jr. *Self-Knowledge in Plato's* Phaedrus. University Park: Pennsylvania State University P, 1986.
Hardin, Joe Marshall. *Opening Spaces: Critical Pedagogy and Resistance Theory in Composition*. New York: State University of New York, 2001.
Hawk, Byron. *A Counter-History of Composition: Toward Methodologies of Complexity*. Pittsburgh, PA: University of Pittsburgh P, 2007.
Jarratt, Susan C. *Rereading the Sophists: Classical Rhetoric Refigured*. Carbondale: Southern Illinois University P, 1991.
Klein, Naomi. *Shock Doctrine: The Rise of Disaster Capitalism*. New York: Picador, 2007.
Knoblauch, C.H. and Lil Brannon. *Rhetorical Traditions and the Teaching of Writing*. Portsmouth, NH: Boynton/Cook.
Kohut, Heinz. *The Restoration of the Self*. New York: International Universities P, 1977.
———. *The Search for the Self: Selected Writings of Heinz Kohut (1950–1978) Vol. 1. (1978–1981). Vol. 3*. Ed. and Intro. Paul H. Ornstein. Madison, CT: International Universities P, 1981.
Landow, George P. *The Aesthetic and Critical Theories of John Ruskin*. Princeton, NJ: Princeton University P, 1971.
Lefevre, Karen Burke. *Invention as a Social Act*. Carbondale: Southern Illinois University P, 1987.
Merriam-Webster's Collegiate Dictionary. New York: Penguin, 2001.
Miller, Richard E. "The Arts of Complicity: Pragmatism and the Culture of Schooling." *College English* 61 (1998): 10–28.
Miller, Susan. *Rescuing the Subject: A Critical Introduction to Rhetoric and the Writer*. Carbondale: Southern Illinois University P, 1989.
Minardi, Cara. "Re-Membering Ancient Women. Hypatia of Alexandria and her Communities." Diss. Georgia State University, 2011.
Neel, Jasper. *Plato, Derrida, and Writing*. Carbondale: Southern Illinois University P, 1988.
Plato. *Phaedrus: or On the Beautiful, Ethical*. Trans. H.N. Fowler. Loeb Classical Library. Cambridge, MA: Harvard University P, 1914.
———. *The Apology*. In *Five Dialogues*. Trans. and Intro. G.M.A. Grube. 2nd ed. Cambridge, MA: Hackett Publishing, 2002.
———. *The Symposium*. Trans. W.R.M. Lamb. Cambridge: Loeb Classical Library, 1925.

Porter, James E. "Developing a Postmodern Ethics of Rhetoric and Composition." *Defining the New Rhetorics*. Ed. Theresa Enos and Stuart G. Brown. Newbury Park, CA: Sage, 1993: 207–226.
Proust, Marcel. *A la recherche du temps perdu: Le temps retrouvé*. (WBG) Trans. C.K. Scott Moncrieff and Fredrick A. Blossom. 2 vols. New York: Random House, 1934.
Rank, Otto. *Art and Artist: Creative Urge and Personality Development*. Trans. Charles Francis Atkinson. New York: W.W. Norton, 1932.
———. *Beyond Psychology*. Camden, NJ: Hadden Craftsmen, 1958.
Roget's II: The New Thesaurus, 3rd ed. Boston: Houghton Miffin, 1995.
Ronald, Kate and Hephzibah Roskelly. "Untested Feasibility: Imagining the Pragmatic Possibility of Paulo Freire." *College English* 63.5 (2001): 612–632.
Rose, Mike. *Lives on the Boundary: A Moving Account of the Struggles and Achievements of America's Educationally Underprepared*. New York: Penguin, 1989.
Sallis, John. *Being and Logos: The Way of Platonic Dialogue*. Pittsburgh: Duquesne University P, 1975.
Santas, Gerasimos. *Plato and Freud: Two Theories of Love*. New York: Basil Blackwell, 1988.
Scott, Gary. *Does Socrates Have a Method?* University Park: Pennsylvania State University P, 2002.
Shakespeare, William. *Hamlet*. In *The Complete Works of Shakespeare*. 5th ed. Ed. David Bevington. New York: Pearson, 2004.
Shor, Ira. *Empowering Education: Critical Teaching for Social Change*. Chicago: Chicago University P, 1992.
Shorey, Paul. *What Plato Said*. Chicago: University of Chicago P, 1933.
Stone, I.F. *The Trial of Socrates*. Boston: Little, Brown, 1988.
Taft, Jessie. *Otto Rank: A Biographic Study Based on Notebooks, Letters, Collected Writings, Therapeutic Achievements and Personal Associations*. New York: The Julien P, 1958.
Vygotsky, Lev. *Thought and Language*. Trans. and Fwd. Alex Kozulin. Cambridge, MA: MIT P, 1986.
West, Cornel. *The American Evasion of Philosophy: A Genealogy of Pragmatism*. Madison: University of Wisconsin P, 1989.
———. "Pragmatism and the Sense of the Tragic" in *Keeping Faith: Philosophy and Race in America*. New York: Routledge, 1993: 107–119.
———. *Prophetic Thought in Postmodern Times*. Vol. 1 of *Beyond Eurocentrism and Multiculturalism*. Monroe, ME: Common Courage P, 1993.

Index

A
Achilles, 37, 75, 100
agora, 21
Alcibiades, 18, 23, 25, 41, 45, 55, 57–59, 75, 142, 150
Anaxagorus, 18, 21, 25–26, 35, 42, 57, 75
aporea, 136
a priori, 5, 27–28, 145, 153
Aristophanes, 37, 182
artiste manqué, 35
Aspasia, 18, 21, 36, 42, 51, 57, 59, 75, 150
Aristotle, 36, 48–49, 117, 183

B
banking model, 10, 168
Berlin, James, 17–18, 204
Beversluis, John, 154, 169–171
Bhabha, Homi, 4, 80, 118
Bizzell, Patrica, 165, 178–179
Brannon, Liz, 7, 15
Brickhouse, Thomas, 69–71, 73
Brooks, Peter, 3, 20, 26–29, 34, 62, 112, 121, 123–125, 127–128, 137, 152, 179, 183–184, 195
Burke, Kenneth, 2–3, 197, 199–200, 202–204

C
Cairns, Huntington, 44, 46, 187
Charmides, 18, 21, 23, 25–26, 41, 45, 51, 55, 57–58, 60, 75, 142, 150
Chomsky, Noam, 200–202
Cicero, 187
conscientization, 3, 50, 194, 197
counter-hegemonic 3, 22, 26, 32, 34
Covino, William, 3, 95
Critias, 18, 21, 23, 25–26, 41, 45, 51, 55, 57–58, 60, 75, 142, 150

D
daemon, 23, 25, 108, 161–162
decode, 19, 87–88, 189–190
Deleuze, Gilles, 123
Delphi, Oracle of, 23, 25, 38, 175
Derrida, Jacques, 3, 5, 7, 45, 98, 104, 117, 139–142, 147, 151–152, 157–158, 169
Dewey, John, 2–3, 180, 187, 194–195, 197, 203, 210
digital literacy, 193
dilatory space, 52, 90, 93, 95, 105, 121, 122–123, 127–128, 140, 147, 153, 195, 201
Dionysus II, 41
Dion, 41
Diotima, 150
disaster capitalism, 196
Doubrovsky, Serge, 95
Durant, Will, 47, 187

E
Enoch, Jessica, 3, 195, 197, 201–204, 206
eco-composition, 193
Elbow, Peter, 145, 189
epideictic, 100, 104
epistemology, 138, 209
expressivist pedagogy, 17

F
feasibility, 51, 187–188, 195, 197–198
Field, G.C., 48, 52, 205
Ferrari, G.R.F., 58, 80–82, 137, 165–166, 172, 174–177, 179, 185
figuration, 113, 130

218 *Index*

Firor, Ruth, 67
Fish, Stanley, 11, 134
Foucault, Michael, 19, 21, 199–200
Frankfurt School, 87
Freud, Sigmund, 4, 20, 35, 42, 127, 156
Friedman, Milton, 196

G
gadfly, 22, 25, 46, 47, 58
Giroux, Henry, 1, 19, 87, 163–164, 204–208, 210–211
Glenn, Cheryl 3, 7, 21, 48, 150, 196
Goethe, JWV, 93
Gorgias, 35, 100
graft, theory of, 92
Gray, Thomas, 72, 114
Griffiths, Garreth, 80
Griswold, Charles L., 55, 56, 57, 58–59, 81, 84, 95, 97–99, 101–102, 109–111, 117–120, 137, 143, 148–149, 153, 163, 165, 171–175, 177, 180, 185, 209
gyre, 133

H
Hamlet, 25, 27, 73, 142
Hand of Glory, 67
Hardin, Joe, 3, 8, 10–11, 14, 15, 16, 188–189, 191–192, 195, 197
Hawk, Byron, 2–4, 11, 13–14, 34, 38, 83, 93, 100, 117, 143, 188, 190, 192–195
Helen, 103
Hesiod, 182
Homer, 103–104
husbandman, 135

I
ideal hunger, 28, 35
inculcate, 10, 16, 166
Isocrates, 35, 41, 80

J
Jameson, Frederick, 70
James, William, 2–3, 187, 194–195, 197, 210
Jarratt, Susan, 3, 7, 150, 196, 210–211
Joyce, James, 114–115

K
kairos, 68, 72, 109, 136, 175
Klein, Naomi, 32, 55, 196
Knoblauch, Cy, 7, 15
Kohut, Heinz, 35, 174

L
Lacan, Jacques, 11, 152
Landow, George, 114
love, hymm to, 130; philosophic, 65, 105, 113, 116, 147

M
Marcuse, Herbert, 87
master-slave, 138, 176
master-pupil dyad, 146
McLaren, Peter, 12
megelagoria, 68–72, 75–76, 109, 160–162
merger hunger, 35
meta-drama, 90, 91, 93–96, 99, 107, 151
metonym, 28, 64
Michelangelo, 40–41
Miller, Richard, 8, 10–11
Miller, Susan, 10
mimicry, 90–91
Minardi, Cara, 150
mirror hunger, 35
Mt. Olympus, 39

N
Neel Jasper, 3, 7, 140–142, 147, 152, 158
Neo-Platonist, 150

O
Oedipal, 34
oligarchic, 24
ontology, 138, 209
Oreithyia, 97, 100, 122

P
palinode, 96, 130
Peirce, 2–3, 180, 187, 193, 197, 210
Peitho, 23
Pericles, 23, 35, 58–59
Perictione, 150
Phidias, 39
pharmakos, 67, 104, 162
Piaget, 130
Piercy, Marge, 199, 210
pleasure principle, 127
Porter, James, 191
post-humanist; process, 193
pragmatism, 198; American, 164, 189, 194, 199, 210; neo-humanist, 1–2, 4, 5, 8, 16, 187–188, 192–194; 197–198, 200, 205; prophetic 2, 3, 31

Praxiteles, 37, 39
prosopropea, 152
protrepticus, 92, 96, 99
Proust, Marcel, 27–28, 72, 112, 114–115, 118, 122–123, 128, 143–144, 161
psychoanalytic, 26, 34
Pythagorus, 150

R

Rank, Otto, 3–4, 20, 24, 34–35, 37, 39–42, 52, 111, 129–130, 136, 143, 155–156, 181
resemblance, theory of, 78, 94
Rilke, Maria, 32
role-playing, 94
Ronald, Kate, 3, 193, 195–199
Rose, Mike, 136
Roskelly, Hephzibah, 3, 193, 195–199
Ruskin, John, 72, 114

S

Sallis, John, 134–135
Santas, Gerasimos, 35, 182–183
Sappho, 100
scapegoat, 22
Shakespeare, William, 40, 41, 122
Shor, Ira, 211–212
Shorey, Paul, 63, 83
Smith, Nicholas, 69–71
social epistemic pedagogy, 1, 5, 7, 19, 44, 52, 78, 139, 164, 179, 188, 193, 201, 205
Stesichorus, 100, 103, 108, 162
Stone, I.F., 69
sublime, theory of, 72, 114
symbolic action, 189

symbol-wisdom, theory of, 199–200, 203–205
Symposium, 39, 111, 183

T

ta, 40
talking cure, 30–31, 127
Thamus, 139, 143, 151–152
Themistocles, 150
Theuth, 100, 143, 152
Timatheus, 35, 41
transcendent, tyranny of, 139–140
Trojan horse, 149, 152
Troy, 103
two-in-one, 41

V

vitalism, theory of, 2, 4, 38, 91, 93, 101, 116–117, 120, 122, 130, 143, 146, 148, 159, 188
Vygotsky, Lev, 3, 84, 125, 130, 133–134, 135–137

W

Watkins, Evan, 191
West, Cornel, 2–3, 31, 40, 130, 134, 145, 164, 180, 190, 193, 195–197, 199, 210
winged chariot, 60, 102
Wordsworth, William, 72, 114

X

Xenophon, 206

Z

zone of proximal development, 133, 136

For Product Safety Concerns and Information please contact our EU representative GPSR@taylorandfrancis.com
Taylor & Francis Verlag GmbH, Kaufingerstraße 24, 80331 München, Germany

www.ingramcontent.com/pod-product-compliance
Lightning Source LLC
Chambersburg PA
CBHW071354290426
44108CB00014B/1541